India and Iran in
Contemporary Relations

India and Iran in Contemporary Relations

Editors

R Sidda Goud
Manisha Mookherjee

ALLIED PUBLISHERS PVT. LTD.

New Delhi • Mumbai • Kolkata • Lucknow • Chennai
Nagpur • Bangalore • Hyderabad • Ahmedabad

ALLIED PUBLISHERS PRIVATE LIMITED

1/13-14 Asaf Ali Road, **New Delhi**–110002
Ph.: 011-23239001 • E-mail: delhi.books@alliedpublishers.com

47/9 Prag Narain Road, Near Kalyan Bhawan, **Lucknow**–226001
Ph.: 0522-2209942 • E-mail: lko.books@alliedpublishers.com

17 Chittaranjan Avenue, **Kolkata**–700072
Ph.: 033-22129618 • E-mail: cal.books@alliedpublishers.com

15 J.N. Heredia Marg, Ballard Estate, **Mumbai**–400001
Ph.: 022-42126969 • E-mail: mumbai.books@alliedpublishers.com

60 Shiv Sunder Apartments (Ground Floor), Central Bazar Road,
Bajaj Nagar, **Nagpur**–440010
Ph.: 0712-2234210 • E-mail: ngp.books@alliedpublishers.com

F-1 Sun House (First Floor), C.G. Road, Navrangpura,
Ellisbridge P.O., **Ahmedabad**–380006
Ph.: 079-26465916 • E-mail: ahmbd.books@alliedpublishers.com

751 Anna Salai, **Chennai**–600002
Ph.: 044-28523938 • E-mail: chennai.books@alliedpublishers.com

5th Main Road, Gandhinagar, **Bangalore**–560009
Ph.: 080-22262081 • E-mail: bngl.books@alliedpublishers.com

3-2-844/6 & 7 Kachiguda Station Road, **Hyderabad**–500027
Ph.: 040-24619079 • E-mail: hyd.books@alliedpublishers.com

Website: www.alliedpublishers.com

© 2014, Centre for Indian Ocean Studies, Osmania University, Hyderabad

ISBN: 978-81-8424-909-5

Published by Sunil Sachdev and printed by Ravi Sachdev at Allied Publishers Pvt. Ltd. (Printing Division), A-104 Mayapuri Phase II, New Delhi-110064

Foreword

India and Iran are the two oldest countries in Asia with distinct cultures. There has been constant interaction between the cultures of these countries since ancient times due to migration of people, which in turn influenced the evolution of Indo-Iranian relations and cultures. As a result people of both the countries share many cultural characteristics and common experiences. There is a small Indian community in Iran. There are also Hindu temples in Bandar Abbas and Zahidas and a Gurudwara in Teharan built in the nineteenth century by the soldiers of the British Indian Army. There are also a few small communities in India whose ancestry is traced to Iran, presence of common experiences, shared values, cultures not only strengthened the bonds between the people of the two countries but also resulted in cultural fusion.

In the post-world war period both India and Iran maintained fairly good relations in diverse fields. With the emergence of Iran as a major power in West Asia, the Indian leaders emphasized on the strategic importance of Indo-Iranian ties. From time to time leaders of both the countries paid official visits to each other to exchange views on global and regional developments. However India's non-aligned policy and her closer relationship with the former Soviet Union and Iran's membership in the CENTO and her alliance with the US pulled both the countries in different directions during the Cold War affecting their political interests during Shah's regime. The bilateral relationship has undergone change with the 1979 Revolution. India could see the revolution in positive terms and viewed it as a reflection of Iran's quest for independence and self assertion and an effort to take to an independent course without major power influence. Iran championing the Islamic cause and her war with Iraq strained relations between India and Iran.

Despite political differences economic relations went on continuing, and strengthened from time to time. Both the countries attached importance to economic ties. Iran is one of the largest exporter of oil to India. Similarly India is one of the largest foreign investors in Iran's oil and gas industry. Both sides are making efforts to expand trade by including other commodities like tea, pharmaceuticals, automobiles, electronics, agricultural products and spare parts.

India is also playing a major role in building the infrastructure in Iran. A highway is being built between Zarang and Delarm with Indian financial assistance. Chabahar Port is jointly financed by India and Iran which is going to connect Central Asia, West Asia and South Asia. Completion of these projects will give impetus to economic relations between Iran and its neighbouring countries. It can also play a role in the delivery of natural gas to India from Central Asia.

India and Iran differed on a few foreign policy issues in spite of shared and common strategic interests. These include Iran's nuclear programme and its likely move towards developing necessary facilities to acquire weapon graded enriched material and sanctions imposed by the West against Teheran's future policy. A positive scenario is emerging in the form of beginning of a dialogue between the new regime in Iran and the West. These aspects can be narrowed down by using diplomacy and having engagement through dialogue. Even a slight change in the West's policy towards Teheran is likely to have a major impact on Indo-Iranian relations.

Both the nations are also likely to cooperate with each other in coming years as the 21st century unfolds itself politically in the form of post-2014 NATO withdrawal from Afghanistan and the impact of Arab Spring on West Asia. The complex scenario is likely to emerge in the region which may demand new ways and means of cooperation between India and Iran.

A great future awaits for India and Iran to move further in strengthening their bilateral relationship. A growing number of students from Iran are coming to India to study in the Indian universities. Their number is increasing year after year and likely to increase further. Similarly the number of Iranians coming to India for medical treatment is also increasing. The city of Hyderabad is an example in meeting the increasing demand for these services. These people are the goodwill ambassadors on both the sides. This aspect would increase people—to people contacts which are likely to improve relations between these two nations. As Track II and Track III diplomacy is assuming importance, this would improve bi-lateral relation-ship between Iran and India, in spite of temporary setbacks and deviations that occur now and then.

The volume contains thought provoking papers written by scholars in the areas examining the relations between India and Iran. They tried to analyze various issues covering political and strategic issues, role of major powers in influencing the bi-lateral relations, economic and trade relations, energy and cultural cooperation between the two countries. Osmania University particularly, the Centre for Indian Ocean Studies must feel proud in organizing a seminar on India and Iran Relations and in bringing out this volume. I hope the effort will continue in promoting greater understanding and peace among the nations.

T. Tirupati Rao (Retd.)
Professor of Political Science and
Former Vice-Chancellor, Osmania University

Contributors

New Areas of Cooperation and Conflict

1. **Prof. Aftab Kamal Pasha**, Former Chairperson, Center for West Asian and African Studies, Jawaharlal Nehru University, New Delhi–110025. Prof. A.K. Pasha teaches at the Gulf Studies, Centre for West Asian Studies, School of International Studies, Jawaharlal Nehru University, New Delhi, where he has served as Chairperson and is now Director, Gulf Studies Program. He has also been Director, Maulana Azad Centre for Indian Culture, Cairo, Egypt. He has been Visiting Professor at the St Cloud State University, Minnesota, USA under Fulbright Visiting Specialist Scheme.

2. **Dr. Sujata Ashwarya Cheema**, Assistant Professor, Centre for West Asian Studies, Jamia Millia Islamia, New Delhi–110025. Her research interests include conflicts in West Asia, India's West Asia policy, politics and foreign policy of Iran, Iraq and Israel, and issues relating to democratization in the region. She has published West Asia: Civil Society, Democracy and State (New Delhi, 2010), several research papers, book and articles.

3. **Dr. Hadi Soleimanpour**, PhD in Development and International Environment from Durham University, England, Senior Executive Jobs: 2011 Present, The head of the Center for International Research and Education affiliated to the Ministry of Foreign Affairs; 2009–2011, Deputy of Africa, Ministry of Foreign Affairs; 2006–2009, Director General of International Economic Cooperation, Ministry of Foreign Affairs; 2003–2005, Deputy of 'Natural Environment and Biodiversity, Environmental Protection Agency; 2003–2003, Director of the study group Sustainable Development Studies, Ministry of Foreign Affairs; 2000–2001, Deputy Director General of Specialized International Economic Organization, Ministry of Foreign Affairs; 1996–2000, Ambassador and deputy of the permanent representative of Iran to "International Specialized Organizations", Geneva; 1994–1996, Director of the office of the "United Nations" (the first international political office), Ministry of Foreign Affairs; 1990–1994 Ambassador and the plenipotentiary representative of the Islamic Republic of Iran to the southern regions of Latin America including Argentina, Paraguay anc Chili; 1988–1990, Director of South America Region, Ministry of Foreign Affairs; 1984–1988 Ambassador and the plenipotentiary

representative of the Islamic Republic of Iran to Spain and the representative of the Islamic Republic of Iran to the 'World Tourism Organization".

4. **H.E. Hassan Nourian**, Consul General of the Islamic Republic of Iran-Hyderabad, Hassan Nourian is Master in international law, Countries visited: Sudan, Italy, Germany, England, France, Tajikistan, KSA, Syria, Pakistan, India, Stockholm, etc. Designations: 2012—consul General of the Islamic Republic of Iran-Hyderabad, 2010–11—Director of MFA branch office in Isfahan province. 2009–10—Secretary of consular commissions between I. r. Iran and Tajikistan, Kuwait, Iraq, Turkey, Kazakhstan, 2004–08—Head of consular affairs, Iranian consulate in Karachi, Pakistan, 2001–03—expert of law in parliamentary and legal department, MFA, 2000–01—Expert in Middle East and North African department, 1996–2000—joined to Ministry of Foreign Affairs School of international relations.

5. **Dr. Prasanta Kumar Pradhan**, Associate Fellow Institute for Defence Studies and Analyses No. 1, Development Enclave, Rao Tula Ram Marg, Delhi Cantt, New Delhi–110010, Conflict and Human rights, Politics and Foreign Policy of Saudi Arabia, PhD in West Asian Studies, School of International Studies, Jawaharlal Nehru University, New Delhi, He completed his doctoral thesis on Human Rights in Islam: The Case of Saudi Arabia in 2007. Before joining the Institute, he worked as a Research Associate at the Institute for Conflict Management, New Delhi, from December 2006 till.

6. **Dr. Mohammed Khalid**, Associate Professor in Political Science, Department of Evening Studies, Punjab University, Chandigarh, India. His primary interest is geopolitics of Indian Ocean. He has worked as Senior Research Fellow in project funded by Department of Ocean Development, government of India. He has been a member of Panjab University Senate, syndicate, Academic Council and Board of Finance.

7. **Ashok Alex Luke**, Doctoral Candidate, Centre for West Asian Studies, School of International Studies, Jawaharlal Nehru University, New Delhi–110025. Area of Specialisation West Asian Politics, India's Foreign Policy and Non Traditional Security.

8. **Anns George**, M.A. Student, Central University of Kerala, Kasaragod, Kerala–671328. Area of Specialisation and Interest is on Defence and Security Studies.

9. **Sukalpa Chakrabarti**, Assistant Professor (IR and Public Policy), Symbiosis School of Economics, constituent of Symbiosis International University 3rd floor SCHC Building, Senapati Bapat Road, Pune 411004 Maharashtra, specializations in politics, international relations

and international business and economy at UG to PG levels for over 10 years now. She is a regular columnist for The Diplomatist, Her areas of interest are International Relations, Politics and Public Policy, International Business Management, Corporate Social Responsibility and Organizational Behavior, Current research interest lies in the broad area of international political economy and international relations (IPE and IR) and centres on debates related to international diplomacy. Policy analysis and issues related to the urban and the environment are also of interest. From an area studies perspective, India's role in Asia has been her major focus.

Energy and Nuclear Security

1. **Col. Rajeev Agarwal**, Research Fellow, Institute for Defence Studies and Analyses (IDSA), New Delhi–110010, Colonel Rajeev Agarwal was commissioned into the Regiment of Artillery in June 1990 and has had varied operational and service experience for over 22 years. He has commanded his Battalion on the Line of Control in Jammu and Kashmir. He has also been a military observer with the United Nations in DRC for a year. He holds a Masters degree in Defense and Strategic Studies from Madras University. Prior to joining IDSA, he was a Director in the Army Head Quarters at New Delhi. He has special interest in International affairs and been following events and trends in West Asia, Central Asia and Afghanistan over past three years.

2. **Abhimanyu Behera**, Doctoral Scholar, Centre for Russian and Central Asian Studies, School of International Studies, Jawaharlal Nehru University, New Delhi–110067. Area of Specialization: Energy, Geopolitics in Central Asia especially in Kazakhstan, India-China engagement in Kazakhstan and also in Eurasia region.

Economic and Trade Cooperation

1. **M. Mahtab Alam Rizvi**, Ph.D., Associate Fellow, Institute for Defence Studies and Analyses, 1 Development Enclave, Off Rao Tularam Marg, Delhi Cantt., New Delhi–110010, PhD in Political Science, Aligarh Muslim University, Aligarh, MA in Political Science from Aligarh Muslim University. Received Jawaharlal Nehru Fellowship for Doctoral Studies from NMML, New Delhi (2005). Recipient of Nehru Scholarship, Centre for Nehru Studies, Department of Political Science, AMU (2002). Research Assistant, Centre for Nehru Studies, Department of Political Science, AMU (January 2006 to January 2007). Visiting

Scholar, Centre for Distance Education, AMU. Research Interests, Political Developments in Iran, Energy Security.

2. **Seyed Hossein Hosseini**, Ph.D Student, Department of History and Culture, Jamia Millia Islamia, New Delhi–110025. Area of Specializations are Economic History, Documents on Contemporary History and Geographical History of Iran.

3. **Dr. Radha Raghuramapatruni**, Associate Professor in International Business and Economics, GITAM School of International Business GITAM University, Visakhapatnam–45. Area of Specialization is Economics, International Trade and WTO Issues and International Banking.

4. **Ramakrishna G.**, Professor of Economics, Department of Economics, Osmania University, Hyderabad–500 007.

5. **Dahiphale Vithal**, Assistant Professor in PG Department of Political Science, Peoples College, Nanded, Maharashtra.

Culture and Civilization

1. **Upamanyu Sengupta**, PhD Scholar, The English and Foreign Languages University, Hyderabad–500007, Area of Specialization: Narrative Studies with Special Focus on the Relation between Literature and Geography.

2. **M. Vishnu Prakash**, Asst. Prof. of Political Science, SVA Govt. College (M), Srikalahasti, Chittoor–517644. Area of Interests are International Relations, Peace Studies, Gandhian Studies, Women and Tribal Empowerment, Political Theory, Good Governance and Civil Society.

3. **Azar Eskandari Charati** is a faculty member, Department of Sociology, Islamic Azad University Azadshar, Iran and PhD Scholar of Sociology, Osmania University, Hyderabad, India.

Preface

India and Iran relations date back to the beginning of the Indo-Aryan civilization in the 7th century B.C. Both the countries shared borders until India's independence in 1947 and shared several common features in their Language, Culture, Traditions, Cuisine, Literature, Monuments, Architecture, Trade, Commerce, Political, Historical and People to People Contact. It is true that civilizational relationship between India and Iran is unique in the world, to quote the first Prime Minister of India, Pandit Jawaharlal Nehru speaking in Teheran in 1958 said "that he doubted if there are any two countries in the world which have had such close and long historical context as India and Iran". India has been very aptly been described as the "Closest Asian Country to Iran" foregoing strong ties between South Asia and Persian Gulf.

Since the end of the Cold War India has been pursuing an active policy to develop a presence and pursue its interest in Western Asia, officially described by the Prime Minister of India, Dr. Manmohan Singh as India's "Look West Policy" to its extended neighbourhood of Middle East, Israel and the Arab States and forge a strategic partnership with Iran based on common economic, energy and security interests.

The Iranian Revolution in 1979 introduced a new phase of engagement between India and Iran, marked by high level visits and meaningful interactions by Prime Ministers of India and the Presidents of Iran and subsequent several high level visits by diplomats from both the countries, giving a new thrust to bilateral relations. In this context the recent visit to Teheran of the Indian External Affairs, Minister Salman Khurshid draws importance towards the strengthening of the existing partnership between the two important regional actors. Earlier, the visit of the Prime Minister of India, Dr. Manmohan Singh to participate in the NAM summit in August 2012 is a clear indication of India's desire to give new implications for strengthening bilateral relations between the two countries. To further highlight this new phase of enhancing their strong contemporary relations, consultative mechanisms through various meetings took place regularly. In addition, the Institute of Defense Studies and Analysis (IDSA) New Delhi and the Institute of Political and International Studies (IPIS), Tehran holds regular round table talks to exchange views and ideas on bilateral and multi-lateral relations.

India-Iran bilateral relations are clouded by the current global controversy over the Iranian nuclear programme. Western countries led by the US subjected Tehran to great pressure by imposing severe sanctions. India obviously is troubled by the sanctions imposed on buying oil and gas from Iran. India voted twice against Iran on the western sponsored resolutions at the International Atomic Energy Agency (IAEA). Iran was disappointed and hurt by the Indian actions, and has moved closer to China. China has become the largest importer of Iranian oil and has been investing hugely in Iran's infrastructural projects. Only bold Indian diplomatic initiatives can ensure Iranian oil supplies to India, which is heavily dependent on these supplies as a fast growing economy. The Iran-Pakistan-India (IPI) gas pipeline project, in which Iran is very keen that India should join, was stalled on the grounds of security and (under) western (American) pressure. Reportedly China is also showing keen interest in this IPI gas pipeline project which will be around 2700 km in length. After 35 years of hostility between Iran and US, India is placed to review the renewing of direct diplomatic contact between US and Iran.

The shift in the Iran's attitude on nuclear programmes and US sanctions, under the new regime of Hassan Rouhani, a moderate President of Iran, exhibits a very positive sign in the international relations in the contemporary context. Diplomats of US and EU hailed it as a 'very significant shift' in Iran's attitude and tone in its first talks on the nuclear standoff since April 2013. At the two days of nuclear talks with six world power (P5+1)—US, France, Britain, China, Russia plus Germany that ended on 16th October 2013 at Geneva, Iran described the dialogue as 'Fruitful' and it is ready to give the UN Atomic Watchdog wider inspection powers to resolve the decade long nuclear dispute with the West. India is happy, if anything which contributes to enhance peace, stability and security within the West Asian Countries in particular and in enhancing the global economy in general. India is also hopeful that the IPI gas Pipeline project would move forward in the near future in the interest of India-Iran bilateral relations and in the interest of South Asia region as a whole.

India-Iran's trade ties are also strong and growing rapidly. Presently bilateral trade stands at US$ 15,968.03 millions in 2011–2012 as compared to 12,887.52 millions in 2007–2008. Iran was India's 2nd largest supplier of crude oil for a long period, but slipped to 6th place due to the US sanctions, and now Iraq stands in the 2nd place. Both the countries hold regular bilateral discussions on economic and trade issues within the framework of India-Iran Joint Commission Meeting (JCM) and several Bilateral Agreements/MOUs were signed in various sectors like Air Services,

Cooperation in New Renewable Energy, Cooperation in Small Scale Industry, Science and Technology, Agricultural Science and Natural Resources, the IPI gas pipeline project, Chabahar Port—a container terminal project, and the Zeraing Railway project. Both the countries are in the process of finalizing a bilateral Investment Promotion and Protection Agreement (BIPPA) and a Double Taxation Avoidance Agreement (DTTA).

Besides economic and commercial ties, the two countries have strong cultural relations. India continues to be a major centre of Shia culture and Persian study in South Asia. Iran has a strong cultural link with Hyderabad with its cuisine, architectural monuments, culture and tradition, which was established during the regime of the last Nizam of Hyderabad, in the erstwhile Hyderabad province. Both the countries maintain regular cultural and educational exchange programmes. A MOU was signed in January 2008 between Indian Council for Cultural Relations (ICCR), New Delhi and the Iranian Cultural Heritage, Handicrafts and Tourism Organization on holding Days of Culture in the two countries. A growing number of students are enrolled in different Indian universities for Higher Education. There are more than 10,000 Iranian students in India spread across Bangalore, Pune, New Delhi and Hyderabad. Osmania University has more than 3,600 Iranian students in different disciplines.

These significant bilateral relations and developments indicate that India and Iran are both significant actors, whose role cannot be overlooked in terms of their political, economic, and cultural involvement in the region. Iran plays an important role in the changing global regional security environment; likewise India is also an emerging power with important role to play not only in West Asian region but also in the Indian Ocean region as well. Today, the regional complexities demand new ways and means of cooperation between India and Iran. In the light of this context and background—on the emerging importance of Iran, this International Conference on India-Iran Contemporary Relation's was envisaged, which will hopefully become significant in the annals of India-Iran relationship. The conference focused on the following five major themes.

1. New Areas of Cooperation and Conflict
2. Extra Regional Powers—India Iran Relations
3. Energy and Nuclear Security
4. Economic and Trade Cooperation
5. Culture and Civilization.

Hope this proceedings of the conference volume would provide an opportunity for interaction and exchange of ideas at a time when Iran has struck a historical agreement with the US and five other world powers, accepting strict constraints on its nuclear programme for the first time in a decade in exchange for partial relief from sanctions. The agreement will boost New Delhi's energy ties with Tehran. The papers in this volume address these concerns of India-Iran relations. We would like to take this opportunity to thank all the contributors for their cooperation in bringing out this volume successfully. All the scholars, academicians researchers and general readers alike should find this edited volume useful and interesting.

Editors
R. Sidda Goud
Manisha Mookherjee

Acknowledgements

This book is the outcome of the International Conference on 'India and Iran in Contemporary Relations', held on 7th–8th November 2013, organized by Centre for Indian Ocean Studies, Osmania University, Hyderabad.

While we would like to thank a number of people who have encouraged and supported us in bringing out this volume, a few deserve special mention. First and foremost our deepest gratitude to Prof S. Satyanarayana, Honourable Vice-Chancellor, Osmania University, Hyderabad for promptly accepting our invitation to inaugurate the International Conference. Despite his busy and hectic schedule, he was extremely generous with his time and his remarks on the bilateral relations between the two countries. A special mention must be made of H.E. Hassan Nourian, Consul General of Islamic Republic of Iran at Hyderabad for envisaging a keen interest in organizing this International Conference and in the publication of the proceedings of the conference.

We express our sincere thanks and gratitude to a host of dignitaries who graced the occasion. We are grateful to Prof. Aftab Kamal Pasha, Director, Gulf Studies Programme, Centre for West Asian Studies, SIS, JNU, New Delhi, who has graciously accepted our invitation to deliver the Keynote Address of the conference, Dr. Hadi Solaiman Pour, Director, Centre for International Research and Education, Ministry of Foreign Affairs, Iran, Chief Guest of the Inaugural function, our thanks to Prof. T. Tirupati Rao, Former Vice-Chancellor, Osmania University, Hyderabad, for accepting as Guest of Honour for Inaugural Session. Mir Mahmood Moosavi, Former Ambassador of Iran in India, Chief Guest of the Valedictory Function; We also express our gratitude to Prof. P.V. Rao Visiting Professor of NALSAR Law University, Hyderabad and former Director of CIOS, for his insightful Valedictory Address, Prof. MSN. Reddy, Registrar of the Osmania University, and Prof. Ravindernath, Dean UGC, Osmania University and all the distinguished delegates from home and abroad.

We deeply appreciate the contributors for their sincere academic support by participating in the International Conference and subsequently submitting the revised papers for publication. The freedom of expression of the contributors have been taken care of and not subdued in the process of editing their papers; thereby the views expressed in these papers are essentially of those of the authors and not of the editors.

We would also like to place on record our acknowledgements to UGC, Osmania University, Consulate General of Islamic Republic of Iran at Hyderabad, Indian Council of Social Science Research (Southern Regional Centre) (ICSSR, SRC), Osmania University. We also express our thanks to Osmania University authorities, faculty members and the non-teaching staff of Centre for Indian Ocean Studies, Osmania University, Hyderabad.

R. Sidda Goud
Manisha Mookherjee

Contents

Section–II: Energy and Nuclear Security

Section–III: Economic and Trade Cooperation

Section–IV: Culture and Civilization

New Areas of Cooperation and Conflict

Key Note Address

A.K. Pasha

In his *Discovery of India*, Jawaharlal Nehru observes: "Few people have been more closely related in origin and throughout history than the people of India and the people of Persia". Many books have been written about the historical, political, religious and cultural contacts between India and Iran since at least 6th century when the Persian ruler Darius conquered Punjab and Sind in 516 BC. Other Kings of the Achaemenid Dynasty who followed Darius maintained extensive relations with Indian rulers. After the demise of the Achaemenid dynasty, Persia was ruled by the Seleucid [Greek], Parthian and Sassanid dynasties. The Indian dynasties which had relations with the Persian rulers were the Mauryas, the Guptas, the Mukharis and the Chalukyas. It is mentioned that Chandragupta won the throne with the help of the Persian army. Persian influence on Mauryan administration is said to have been considerable. Ashoka's fondness for columns and recording of royal orders on rocks and pillars is said to be Achaminian. Kanishka, the greatest Kushan ruler was supposed to have originated from Persian nomads. Many coins have been found in Malwa and Gujarat dating the Indo-Sassanian period. Prince Raghu is identified with Chandra Gupta-II who is reputed with the conquest of Balkh or Vahlika. Many historians confirm that the Allahabad inscription of Samudragupta tells us about his diplomatic relations with Devaputra Shahanusshahi. Persian influence on the Ajanta caves is also considerable. The ancestors of Harshavardhana [7th C AD] are reported to have been influenced by the Sun worshippers of Persia. Harsha himself had close ties with Persia. Persian writers and poets like Tabari [830-923]; Firdous [420–440 AD]; Abul Fazal and others have left their accounts of the numerous interactions between Indian and Persian rulers and people. Not only both had extensive political but trade and other commercial exchanges also flourished. Baluchistan was an important link for the overland route. At the same time extensive sea trade also existed from Hormouz, Bushire and other Persian ports to the West Coast of India from Gujarat to Calicut. It is said that the Sassanid's controlled much of the sea trade between India and China as also in the Gulf Region. It was common for Indian rulers to have Persian soldiers in those periods. Many contend that the Persians and most people in north India are members of the same stock i.e. Indo-European family [Aryans]. Hence relations between India and Persia up to the Arab conquest of Persia in 642 AD had been extensive. Both learnt and exchanged from each other in the fields of religion, culture, politics, and administration including military. It must be mentioned that the Persians ruled over much of West Asia up to Egypt and Central Asia just before the Arabs defeated the Persians. Soon Persia accepted Islam but strongly opposed Arabization. Persian influence over the Abbasids at Baghdad was substantial. The Barmakids [Afghan Brahmins] facilitated the links with India- known as the golden age in Indo-Arab ties. Mongol invasion not only affected Persia but it brought to an end the Abbasid Empire in 1258 AD. Later the Persians regained the initiative and Shah Abbas established the Persian rule when he established the Saffavid Empire in 1501 and made Persia a Shia country. Soon the Saffavids had to face European colonialism from Portuguese, Dutch and the British. Persian influence on India continued through several means reaching its zenith during the Mughal period. The second Mughul ruler was defeated by Afghan ruler Sher Shah Suri but Humayun was able to regain his throne with the help of the Persians. Nader Shah invaded India and looted Delhi's Mughals. The Deccan rulers at Bidar, Bijapur—known as the Bahmani Sultans were largely Persian Shias. Other Indian Shia rulers also had close ties with Persia. The Saffavids were overthrown by the Qajar dynasty. Qajar rulers resisted British-Russian attempts to dominate Persia from South and North. The tobacco movement showed Persian spirit of defiance and desire for independence, nationalism, and pride in them. The constitutional revolution against the Qajar ruler in 1905–06 restricted the autocratic powers of the rulers and gave clergy-ulema certain powers. The British played an important role in the downfall of the Qajar dynasty during the First World War. With full British support Reza Khan established the Pahlavi dynasty. He was head of the Cossack Brigade and wanted to establish a republic and modernize Persia on the lines of Ataturk of Turkey, but the British prevailed on him to establish the Pahlavi dynasty. The Shah modernized Persia and called it Iran. Soon he curbed the powers of the clergy and ruled as a dictator. During the Second World War he was overthrown by the Allied powers for his sympathy for the Axis powers. His son Mohammed Reza became King at a young age.

Jawaharlal Nehru's abiding conviction that India's freedom struggle is closely linked with the struggle of other colonies made him maintain close contacts with other nationalist movements in Asia. As Nehru put it: "India today is a part of a world movement. Not only China, Turkey, Persia and Egypt, but also Russia and other countries of the West are taking part in this movement and India cannot isolate itself from it. We have our own problems, difficult and intricate and we cannot run away from them and take shelter in the wider problems that affect the world. But if we ignore the world we do so at our peril… And if India has a message to give to the world, she has also to receive and learn much from the messages of other people". In this connection the Indian National Congress (INC) passed a resolution in 1927 demanding the withdrawal of Indian troops with the British army from Persia and other British colonies. Even before India's independence, during the Soviet invasion of northern Iran in 1941 to support the Kurds and secure Iranian oil fields, Nehru was supportive of the withdrawal of Soviet forces from Iran. His approach against colonialism rested on two cardinal tenets: support for freedom and strict adherence to a peaceful method. Nehru was the first major Asian leader who identified the implications of European imperialism and set about to work for Asian identity, development and cooperation. It is in this context one should see Nehru's initiative to organize the first Asian Relations Conference in New Delhi which Iran also attended at the Indian Council of World Affairs (ICWA), Sapru House in March–April 1947. The gathering of such large number of Asian leaders in Delhi and the conference call for Asian unity "announced the arrival of Asia on the world stage". Later Nehru declared: "…the world is something bigger than Europe…Asia counts in world affairs. Tomorrow it will count much more than today".

In this backdrop, Nehru began to view Iran as one of the most important countries in the West Asian region with which India should maintain fairly extensive relations in diverse fields. This was especially after New Delhi signed a treaty of friendship with Tehran on 15 March 1950 which called for 'perpetual peace and friendship' between the two countries. Despite differing perceptions on a number of issues, since 1947 most Prime Ministers and other prominent leaders have underlined the strategic importance of Indo-Iranian ties. Notwithstanding Nehru's close ties with Egypt's Nasser, Nehru worked hard to establish cordial ties with Iran. This despite Iran having maintained close ties with the USA and Israel and made Iran a member of CENTO of which Pakistan was also a key member. Perceptions of threats to it seem to have induced Iran to join the western military alliance while India advocated and pursued a non-aligned policy. The cold war, western hostility and more particularly the Iran-China-Pakistan alliance propelled India to have closer ties with Moscow.

It is in this backdrop one should see Nehru's opposition to western backed military alliances as also bilateral military pacts. He was critical of US military assistance to Pakistan, Turkey, Iran and its strategy of collective security through military alliances. The Bandung conference in 1955 was a reaffirmation of the concept of area of peace articulated by Nehru. His approach to secure peace through regional cooperation, Panchshilla, non-aligned policy received a rude shock when the US-UK intervened in Iran in 1952–53 to overthrow Dr Mohammed Mossadeq over the issue of oil company nationalization. Despite US/UK role in the internal affairs of Iran, Nehru being a realist understood the importance of Iran to India and worked hard to normalize bilateral relations. But India should have come out in support of Dr Mossadeq and the Iranian people which Nehru did in the case of Egypt when UK, France and Israel invaded Egypt in 1956 over the Suez issue. But cold war politics ultimately prevailed in the case of Iran. If we had sided with the Iran perhaps things would have been different as far as Indo-Iranian relations are concerned. However he received the Shah of Iran in New Delhi in February 1956 and in turn Nehru made a return visit to Tehran in Sept 1959. Thereafter, a number of high level visits took place but Indo-Iranian relations never matured and in fact remained cool and at times strained. The Shah's close ties with Israel and other pro-US Arab monarchs and his largely authoritarian style of functioning also were other factors which kept the bilateral ties from growing as India took a pro-Arab stand [largely on the Arab-Israeli issues] and was suspicious of Arab monarchs due to their close ties with Pakistan. Iran had openly supported Pakistan in the 1965 and the 1971 Indo-Pak wars. The Shah gave military-financial support to Generals Ayub and Yahya Khan of Pakistan much to the annoyance of India. Tehran and Riyadh's position on the crisis at the UN was that the developments in East Pakistan were Islamabad's internal affair and that no other country had any right to interfere in the same. The Shah of Iran saw India's ties with Moscow with deep suspicion as also pro-Soviet Iraqi interference in Baluchistan. In the event of West Pakistan's disintegration, the Shah was reported to have threatened to occupy Baluchistan so as to deny the Soviets access to warm waters. However, India managed to convince the Saudi-Iranian rulers of New Delhi's sincere desire to live in peace with Pakistan and respect its territorial integrity. The Shimla Pact and the release of Pakistani POWs by India helped the atmosphere, as Saudi-Iranian concerns for Pakistan's territorial integrity had become an issue in India's bilateral ties. The 1971 Indo-Pak war conclusively established Indian predominance in South Asia whereas the defeat of Pakistan pushed the US to look at Iran as the main pillar of its Gulf policy, which resulted in the supply of huge quantities of sophisticated arms to Iran. The Shah used some weapons against his own people to suppress them. The US also, in turn, encouraged the Shah to play an active role in the Gulf and Indian Ocean areas. The division of Pakistan, the emergence of Bangladesh, increase in Iran's income from oil, Arab unity during the 1973 Arab-Israeli Conflict, the OAPEC oil embargo against USA and Israel's supporters, Pakistan's tilt towards the Arab states and India's desire to have close ties with Iran—all of these factors persuaded the Shah to reassess the significance of strengthening ties with India. Soon Indo-Iranian ties developed as reflected in several high level visits including PM Indira Gandhi, and Shah's visits to India, expanding bilateral trade and investments.

India saw the overthrow of the Shah and the emergence of the Islamic Republic of Iran in early 1979 under the leadership of Ayatollah Khomeini as 'positive developments'. Khomeini who mobilized the Iranians on the basis of Islam was described as the 'father figure of the Iranian revolution' by AB Vajpayee, then India's minister for external affairs who also said: "We are waiting for the day when we can welcome Iran in the Non-aligned Movement". More significantly, 'India viewed the revolution in Iran as a reflection of Iran's quest for identity and national self-assertion and a desire to charter an independent course without outside big power influence". Soon Iran's preoccupation with Iraq in the disastrous eight-year war [1980–88] affected its outlook on world affairs. As Head of Non-Aligned Movement, India should have appreciated the Iranian predicament but our fondness for Saddam Hussein blinded us for the second time after the Second World War. But Iran's penchant for taking up Islamic 'causes' also led to strain in India's ties with Iran. Also, Iran's stand on the Kashmir issue, the Babri Masjid and general condition of Muslims especially communal riots introduced new factors in Indo-Iranian relations. Indian response to Iran's attitude was largely muted because of the importance New Delhi attached to economic ties and also due to Iran's role in the Gulf, Central Asia and Afghanistan and also due to India's conviction that the realists ruling Iran wanted to do business with New Delhi. The overthrow of the Shah by Khomeini in a popular revolution was a great blow or setback to the US. Islam was used to mobilize the Iranians against the US and its allies like Israel. Since then especially after US diplomats were taken hostages in Tehran, the US has been trying hard to undermine the Islamic Republic. US-Iran conflictual relations were to impact Indo-Iranian relations gradually. There were growing fears that if the US tries to bring down the Islamic regime it may try to block the narrow waterway of the Straits of Hormouz thereby affecting global oil supplies which may push oil prices still higher. The House of Saud was also shaken by the Iranian revolution as Saudi opponents took over Mecca mosque in Nov 1979. The 1990–91 Kuwait crisis, Soviet withdrawal from Afghanistan, the disintegration of the USSR together with the end of the cold war and the emergence of Pax Americana in the WANA region and identical security threat perceptions brought India and Iran closer. US attempts to isolate Iran under its dual containment policy, economic sanctions on Iran and US influence over GCC states and Iran's bitter experience with Iraq compelled Tehran to strengthen relations with India and China. These common political and strategic concerns also led to improvement in Indo-Iranian relations.

Meanwhile a new chapter was opened in Indo-Iranian ties with the visit of the Indian Prime Minister, P.V. Narasimha Rao after the Babri Masjid issue and Tehran soon extended full support to India's Kashmir issue and made it clear that Jammu and Kashmir (J&K) was an integral part of India. Iran's assurance to India that it had no desire to interfere in India's internal affairs, including Kashmir, was received by Kashmiri Muslims and Hurriyat leaders with "shock and disbelief" because Iran was considered second only to Pakistan in extending support to the Kashmiris in their "struggle for freedom". Iran along with China helped India tide over the Saudi-Pak resolution at UN Human Rights Commission over violation of human rights in Kashmir by India. Soon after becoming President, Hashmei Rafsanjani expressed his desire to visit India but was postponed and some called it a 'transparent ploy' ascribing it to the power struggle between President Rafsanjani and Ayatollah Ali Khamenei's so-called 'politics within Tehran's Byzantine power structure'. As one Indian newspaper noted: "As long as Iran remains a regimented society under an Islamic fundamentalist leadership with only the mere trappings of democracy, relations between New Delhi and Tehran will never be free of tension". Even before he visited India, Rafsanjani had emphasized the need for strategic cooperation between India and Iran to ward off outside interference and domination in the region. He also underlined the significance of cooperation among Iran, Pakistan, India and China. This would give India the much sought after Iran's friendship in view of the importance of the Central Asian Republics, especially the transit facilities offered by Iran for India's trade with the new republics where Iran was equally keen on increasing its influence. The Afghan civil war and Pakistan's support to the Talibans [Jihadist/fundamentalist forces] in Kabul and Iran's desire to involve India in finding a solution to Afghan crisis brought India and Iran closer.

The mutual desire for friendship and cooperation seemed to have lessened misunderstandings that had developed between the two countries in the wake of the turmoil in Kashmir. However, many in India were concerned about the implications of Iran's support to Islamic causes worldwide and especially for Indian Muslims. The cold war between Iran and Saudi Arabia especially the massacre of Iranian hajjes and its impact on Indian Muslim population were seen as likely impediment to mutual cooperation between India and Saudi Arabia. Under the circumstances Mrs. Indira Gandhi visited Riyadh in 1982 and the visit underlined the growing importance of Riyadh, Tehran's isolation in the region and India's concern for peace, security and stability in South Asia and its linkage with the Gulf Region. The GCC States took a number of steps in order to contain Iran. Saudi overtures to India should be seen in this context in view of New Delhi's close ties with both Iran and Iraq. After Iran accepted ceasefire with Iraq in July 1988, Khomeini talked about the need to keep away from the "adventures and the creation of adventures". Also, Rafsanjani made it clear that Iran did not intend to export the Islamic revolution through direct intervention or force. All the new initiatives taken by Iran at the regional and global level gradually led to normalization of ties in the region and beyond. In fact, some GCC States [Qatar] wanted the inclusion of Iran in the security structure for the Gulf. Iran which was initially alarmed at the large presence of the western forces in the Gulf region soon became reconciled to this fact but it also could not prevent the GCC States from concluding security agreements with the US/West.

Despite efforts to normalize Iran's ties with the US under Rafsanjani, the conflictual ties between Iran and the US continued. Even the vigorous efforts of President Mohammed Khatami in this regard and his emphasis on the 'dialogue of civilizations' made little headway. Iran's cooperation with the US after 9/11 bombings in Afghanistan and terrorism related issues with the US did not lessen tension between the two. In fact the US identified Iran as part of the 'Axis of Evil'. Iran's nuclear program further added complications. When the issue came before IAEA, India voted at least thrice against Iran and openly said India opposed the emergence of another nuclear power in the neighborhood although it supported Iran's right to nuclear technology under NPT. Due to lack of transparency in its nuclear program, the UNSC imposed economic sanctions which were tightened many times. The EU also imposed sanctions along with more stringent sanctions from the US. India had an option to abstain at the IAEA and should not have joined the West to punish Iran. We must understand that Iran has not invaded any country whereas it has been a victim of armed aggression. Moreover, continued threats to Iran on regime change issue from US, Israel and others since 1979 should have been more vigorously opposed by India at international foras.

Iran perhaps was keen to develop nuclear technology mainly due to its terrible experience with the eight years of war with Iraq. The entire world merely watched the death and destruction inflicted upon Iran including the use of chemical weapons. Not only the GCC states supported Iraq but the entire West and others were behind Saddam Hussein. Iranians seemed to have learned from the Indian experience as far as self-reliance is concerned. India was also subjected to Western sanctions due to its nuclear program. Despite severe international sanctions Iran [it is proud of its civilization and long history] is willing to talk with its opponents. It has continued to develop its economy and military capability and provided much needed political stability. Despite all possible efforts by the West, Israel, some Arab regimes and others to bring about regime change in Iran, they did not succeed as majority of the Iranian people are behind the Islamic government.

India's desire to have closer ties with US for nuclear energy and other issues led to US pressure on India to cut down ties with Iran. US-Israeli threats to bomb Iran on the nuclear issue put strain on Indo-Iranian ties. Despite India's determination to maintain the historical ties with Iran, US factor continued to impact Indo-Iranian ties. The IPI gas pipeline also became a victim of these conflicting pulls and pressures. All this led to growing misunderstandings and political ties suffered as also trade and other ties as well. Due to international sanctions India is gradually replacing Iranian oil with oil from Nigeria and Angola. But India is unwilling to completely stop importing oil from Iran as it is not willing to damage ties with a long-standing political, economic and cultural partner. To secure a waiver from new US sanctions it has reduced the volume of imports. It imported about 11% of its crude oil from Iran in 2010 but has now cut this down to below 8%. The issue of insurance and reinsurance, payments through banks, and other financial issues has pushed Iran from being number two oil supplier to India. Iraq has now become India's no. 2 oil exporter after Saudi Arabia.

With India meeting 80% of its oil needs with imports, state-owned oil and gas companies have been scouting overseas for energy assets. Since Iran has the world's second largest oil and gas reserves, several Indian firms have invested in the country's energy assets. In 2009, the ONGC-Videsh, Indian Oil Corporation and Oil India Ltd explored for oil and gas in the Farsi block in the Gulf. They proposed investing 5.5 billion US$ in the development of the Farzad-B asset, which holds an estimated 21.68 trillion cubic feet of gas. In the same year, ONGC-Videsh, Petronet LNG and UK based Ashok Leyland Projects Services signed agreements with Iran to develop one of the 28 phases of the South Pars field by taking up a 40% stake. They also agreed to invest 10 billion US$ in sourcing 6 million tones of gas from the field and converting it into LNG. Undoubtedly US-UN-EU sanctions are impeding India's investments in Iran's energy sector: for instance ONGC-Videsh is experiencing funding problems for the South Pars gas field project as banks are reluctant to fund the project. Also firms are prohibited from investing over 20 million US$ per year in Iran's energy sector, thereby slowing the pace of Indian investments.

After Hassan Rouhani's election as Iran's new President in the summer of 2013 and his early October appearance at the UN and preliminary bilateral talks with top Obama officials, including a short phone conversation between Rouhani and Obama, earnest negotiations were launched with Iran's Foreign Minister Javad Zarif. It is very clear that Iran wants an agreement on its nuclear program. Preliminary prognostications suggest an agreement could be reached by late April of 2014. The expected agreement between the P5+1 and renewed US-Iran ties is already leading analysts to predict substantial changes in the geopolitical configurations of the West Asia North Africa (WANA) States. The world is closely watching the current geopolitical and potential geostrategic changes taking place in the Gulf region and the broader WANA region as it would benefit Iran and India among other states. Not only it may result in the reintegration of Iran in the comity of WANA politics but may impact US-Saudi and US-Israel relations. Although all US Presidents have said US-Israel ties are "enduring, unshakable and sacrosanct" but the rapidly changing geopolitical map in the oil-rich Gulf/West Asian region and the need of the US to pivot its geostrategic interests to Asia-Pacific has to be kept in mind. Also by 2015-17 the US is expected to be the largest oil and gas exporter in the world, out-producing Saudi Arabia and Russia. There will be pressure on Israel to sign NPT and the Additional Protocol. All states except Israel want a WMD free WANA.

CONCLUSION

Indian interests in the Gulf region include the safety and security of over six million Indian migrant workers residing in the GCC states, safeguard trade/investments and continued supply of oil and gas from the region. Besides, political stability is a precondition to ensure mutual cooperation through trade, aid and investment opportunities in the region. From the strategic point of view both India and Iran felt they could work towards reducing the role of non-regional states in the region. Those policies especially of the US and Israel, were undermining peace, security and stability leading to periodic threats of military intervention either against Iran or to safeguard Kurds or to prop up threatened fragile regimes against their own population who are demanding political participation[as in the case of Bahrain]. From the Indian perspective increasing bilateral ties with Iran is not only important due to trade, oil and gas, but also due to the unique proximity of Iran to events in Afghanistan, Pakistan, Central Asia, Iraq and the Gulf region. Peace and stability and prosperity calls for new initiatives, dynamism and recognition of the traditionally close historical relationship with Iran. India must be with the people of Iran and support their just aspirations for greater participation in the decision making process and on the broader issue of democratic reforms and also support their desire to see an end to Israeli-US military threats. US domination of the region is slowly elbowing India out from the strategic region as witnessed by sanctions on Iran which has reduced import of oil, declining trade, winding up of joint ventures, so on. India has vast stakes to maintain security and stability in the Gulf region so very essential to protect its vital interests and also to prevent the spread of violence and terrorism from this volatile region to India in future. Hence India needs to not only enhance but widen and deepen its interaction with Iran and support its legitimate aspirations and seek to work with Tehran in cooperation with other interested major powers to enhance peace, security and stability in the Gulf Region as also in South Asia and for India's energy security as well. Just as India has its dreams and ambitions as a major power, Iran which has borders with 18 countries also aspires to play its regional role.

India-Iran Relations in the Post-Cold War: A Neo-Realist Analysis

Sujata Ashwarya Cheema

INTRODUCTION: INTERNATIONAL RELATIONS AND NEOREALISM

A scientific theory of International Relations (IR) leads to an understanding that states behave in a predictable manner in an international system. Such behaviour of state(s) is interpreted and analysed in several ways. Neorealism is one of the many interpretations, which dominates the contemporary theoretical debates in IR. It is derived from the classical realist theory or Realism, a tradition of analysis that gives weight to the broad assumption that states pursue power to protect their national interests. Neorealists accept the basic realist doctrines but reinterpret them in light of the positivistic models of economics. The neorealist theory emphasizes the importance of the structure of an international system and its role as the primary determinant of state behaviour. Unlike classical Realism, which views states behaviour directed by its self-interested nature, neorealists argue that structure directs states conduct. Actors are less important because structures compel them to act in a certain way. All the power struggles and rivalries are viewed not as a function of the nature of states, but as aspects inherent in the nature of an international system.

In giving precedence to structural constraints over states' strategies and motivations, neorealism shuns the classical realism's use of often essentialist concepts such as 'human nature' to explain international politics. Realism equates the behaviour of nation-states to the behaviour of individuals in the state of nature, as defined by the 17th century philosopher, Thomas Hobbes. In the state of nature—a logical abstraction from society—Hobbes imagined each individual to be motivated by the principle of maximization of self-interest and the instinct of self-preservation. More often than not, the interest of one human being comes into contradiction with the interest of the other. In the absence of a common superior to hold the individuals in check, there is a constant condition of war of all against all in the state of nature. Like the Hobbesian state of nature, the international system is anarchic, lacking an overarching authority capable of regulating interaction of sovereign states, each moved by its own national interest. States must conduct relations with other states on their own, instead of being dictated by any overarching authority.

According to Kenneth Waltz, the foremost advocate of neorealism, unvarying behaviour of states, despite different forms of government and diverse political ideologies, can be explained by constraints on that are imposed by the structure of an international system, the primary determinants of international politics. A system's structure is defined by three major attributes: first, the principle by which it is organized; second, by the functions which states as units perform in the system and; third, by the distribution of capabilities (power) across units. Waltz's discussion of the first attribute draws from classical realism to emphasize that the international system is decentralized and anarchic. Since states want to survive, anarchy presupposes a self-help system in which each state has to take care of itself. Thus every state (as units in the system) has a similar function of working in the ultimate interest of survival, as this is a prerequisite to fulfil other goals. In effect, there is no functional differentiation or division of labour among them. All states exist in a competitive system, which 'produces a tendency towards the sameness of the competitors'.[1] While states are deemed functionally similar, they are nonetheless distinguished by their relative capabilities (the power each of them represents) for performing the same function. In Waltz's own words, the state units of an international system are 'distinguished primarily by their greater or less capabilities for performing similar tasks.'[2]

However, the units' capabilities to pursue their interests are not equally distributed. It varies, with the more capable ones, shaping the realm, posing the problems that the others have to deal with. The unequal distribution of states capabilities creates states' balance of power behaviour that may lead to either multipolarity or bipolarity. In any international system, Waltz concludes, the major actors strive towards a balance of power,[3] which shapes international relations. International changes occur when the great powers rise and fall and the balance of power shifts accordingly. There are two ways in which states balance power: internal balancing and external balancing. Internal balancing occurs as states grow their own capabilities by increasing economic growth and/or increasing military spending. External balancing occurs when states enter into alliances to check the power of more powerful states or alliances and when they enter into other formal or informal agreements. Neorealist contend that there are essentially three possible systems—unipolar, bipolar and multipolar—according to changes in the distribution of capabilities, defined by the number of great powers within the international system.

Waltz also dwells upon the concept of national interest: 'each state plots the course it thinks will best serve its interest.'[4] For classical realists national interest is the guiding light of states' foreign policy. It is an idea that must be defended and promoted by the leaders and policymakers of states in the international arena. For Waltz national interest is an automatic signal generated by the constraints and dictates imposed by the international system.[5] John Mearsheimer in his book, *The Tragedy of Great Power Politics* (2001), builds upon Waltz theory to propose that states seek power not only for security and survival but also to dominate the entire system. Hegemony is the ultimate guarantee for security. Waltz, a defensive realist believes that excessive power beyond which is necessary for security and survival is counterproductive because it destabilizes the system and provokes hostile alliances to develop. However, Mearsheimer argues that states seek hegemony and the ideal situation is to be the hegemon in the system. Like Immanuel Kant's says,' It is the desire of every state, or its ruler, to arrive at a condition of perpetual peace by conquering the whole world, if that were possible.'[6]

National interest of the hegemonic state is in global hegemony, 'because states are almost always better off with more rather than less power.'[7] However, the world is too large a place to be dominated easily. Mearsheimer therefore argues that states can only become the hegemon in their own regions of the world. Regional hegemons also act to prevent the emergence of other regional hegemons in any other part of the world. This is what he refers as 'offensive realism,' which rests on the premise that great powers 'are always searching for opportunities to gain power over their rivals, with hegemony as their final goal.'[8] Mearsheimer, like other realists, believes that his argument as universal applicability, across time and space. As Jackson and Sorensen explain, 'There will always be a struggle between nation-states for power and domination in the international system. There has always been conflict, there is conflict, and there always will be conflict over power.'[9]

The demise of the Cold War ushered major changes in the structure of the international system. The disintegration and fall of the Soviet Union rendered the international system unipolar, affecting fundamentally, how states organized their security. With the end of the Cold War, United States emerged as the sole superpower. In the light of the structural theory, major actors, apprehensive of the unbalanced power of the United States and considering it a potential danger, endeavoured to strengthen their positions by internal and external balancing. The second tier states sought alliances to bring the international distribution of power into balance. States also engaged in internal balancing by engaging in mutually beneficial economic relations. The strengthening of India-Iran ties in the post-Cold War period can be seen in this light. This paper argues that Indo-Iranian relationship gained traction as a result of the constraints imposed on the two countries by the structural changes in the international system. By underpinning their relationship in strategic and economic issues, both India and Iran tried to maintain internal and external balance in the unipolar international system.

INDO-IRANIAN RELATIONS: AN ANALYSIS FROM NEOREALIST PERSPECTIVE

The end of the Cold War provided India and Iran with an opportunity to upgrade their bilateral ties. Despite long-standing cultural and historical ties, India and Iran could not develop robust relations during the Cold War years. The Iranian ruler, Mohammed Reza Shah Pahlavi, harboured a deep sense of suspicion toward the Soviet Union, having witnessed the reluctance of the Red Army to vacate Iranian territory after the end of hostilities in the World War II.[10] Consequently, he entered into the US-sponsored Baghdad Pact or Central Treaty Organisation (CENTO) in 1955—with Pakistan, Iraq, Turkey and United Kingdom—that was aimed at containing the Soviet Union by lining up strong states on its southwestern frontier. Throughout the Shah's rule, Iran remained in close strategic relations with the United States.

In contrast, after its independence in 1947, India followed a nonaligned foreign policy that rejected bloc politics of the superpowers in favour of independent decision-making, with multilateralism as its basic underpinnings.[11] Nehru believed alliances sponsored by the superpowers militarised the global community and endangered international peace and security, describing the formation of CENTO as 'a wrong approach, a dangerous approach, and a harmful approach,' to international relations.[12] Thus, 'the bipolar structure of the international system became the ultimate arbiter of bilateral relations between India and Iran.[13] These contrasting approaches to the Cold War situation determined the contours of India-Iran relations for many succeeding years during which their ties remained low-keyed, suspicious, and even hostile at times.[14]

In the early 1990s, both countries started reordering their foreign policy priorities in the context of the changed international milieu. With the disintegration of the Soviet Union, the balance of power of the Cold War era was disrupted in favour of the United States, the surviving superpower. In view of America's long history of intervention in weak states, power concentration at its end generated distrust among the second-tier states like Russia, China, Iran and India. Although they were in no position to challenge US dominance in any significant measure, they made attempts at balancing power accumulation at one pole by upgrading bilateral relations amongst themselves. This imperative brought Indo-Iranian interests to converge on a number of issues impacting their strategic environment.

The emergent unipolar nature of the international system was a frightening prospect for both India and Iran. Despite being one of the pioneers and founding members of the Non-Aligned Movement of 1961, India developed closer ties with the Soviet Union during the period of the Cold War. India's cooperative strategic and military relations with Moscow and strong socialistic policies had a markedly adverse impact on its relations with the United States, to the extent that until the end of the Cold War Indo-US relationship was cold and often prickly. After the dissolution of the Soviet Union, India began to assess its foreign policy direction in a unipolar world, and took steps to develop better ties with the United States.

The post-Cold War situation was equally challenging for Iran. The Islamic Revolution and the subsequent seize of American Embassy by the revolutionaries for 444 days ended diplomatic relations between the states. Since the late 1970s Iran had been the subject of American diplomatic isolation and economic sanctions. Under the 'dual containment' strategy (meant for both Iran and Iraq but was mostly directed towards Iran), the first Clinton Administration 'imposed comprehensive unilateral sanctions on Iran, threatened secondary sanctions on non-American companies doing significant business with Iran's oil industry, and rejuvenated the moribund covert action campaign against Iran.'[15] This was done despite the fact that Hashemi Rafsanjani, the first president of the post-Khomeini period, embraced a moderate position internationally and especially adopting a conciliatory approach towards the US and the West.[16]

Significantly, both India and Iran, in separate ways, intensified the pace of their nuclear programmes, in order to feel more secure in the unipolar international system. India was already a nuclear weapons power, facing American sanctions on any transfer of nuclear technology and material from the nuclear club. India refused to sign the CTBT in 1996, went ahead with the second round of nuclear tests in 1998, and declared its intent to build a 'credible minimum nuclear deterrent.' Nonetheless, desirous of rapprochement with the hegemonic power, India showed sensitivity for US non-proliferation concerns by declaring a moratorium on further tests and by committing itself to no-first-use of nuclear weapons.[17]

In contrast to India's open and decisive nuclear policy, Iran followed a partially open, partially concealed nuclear strategy. Even as the Islamic Republic sought Russia and China's assistance to build nuclear reactors, it went on to challenge America's containment policy and non-proliferation regime, by secretly constructing nuclear facilities. This act on Iran's part invited even more sanctions and political isolation. Despite different trajectories to greater nuclear security, both India and Iran were in part responding to the hegemonic tendencies of the superpower, evidenced in the decisive way in which the US asserted itself in the Persian Gulf, by expelling Iraq from Kuwait in the Gulf War of 1990.[18] America's hegemonic designs were also manifest in the fervour with which the Clinton Administration picked up the issue of nuclear proliferation issue in South Asia, especially targeting India in its goal 'to cap, roll back, and eliminate' nuclear capabilities in the region.

To balance the disproportionate concentration of power at one pole of the international system, India and Iran sought to align on issues of mutual concern, so as to prevent the superpower from interfering in their strategic environment. While cooperation in trade and economic areas was directed towards internal balancing (strengthening of self), strategic cooperation signified the resolve of the two states to achieve external balance. Two major bilateral agreements constitute the framework for India-Iran relations in recent years. The *Tehran Declaration* (2001) signed by former Prime Minister of India Atal Bihari Vajpayee and Iran's then-President Muhammad Khatami laid the foundation for cooperation on a wide range of issues. It focussed heavily on energy and commercial concerns, reaffirmed a commitment to develop the North-South transport corridor (for the movement of goods via Iran into Central Asia, Russia and Northern Europe), and enshrined agreements to promote scientific and technical cooperation. This meeting resulted in the establishment of India-Iran Strategic Dialogue to address regional and international security issues. Two years later, both leaders signed the *Delhi Declaration* (2003) along with seven additional Memoranda of Understanding and agreements, which constituted the most substantial set of frameworks guiding Indo-Iranian relationship. The Delhi Declaration focussed on international terrorism (in the wake of 9/11) and shared concerns about US unilateralism in Iraq. Both countries also articulated a mutual interest in pursuing enhanced cooperation in areas of science and technology and most significantly, underlined a commitment to forge defence linkages and develop strategic relations.[19]

ENERGY TIES

India's energy relations with Iran are hamstrung by US containment policy towards containing Iran and through imposition of punitive economic and trade sanctions. As a hegemonic power, the United States is structurally constrained to limit Iran, another hegemonic power in the West Asian region, especially as the Islamic Republic refuses to toe the US line on the nuclear issue. The United States wants that Iran should stop nuclear enrichment for its nuclear reactors, which the superpower and the major western powers believe is being carried out to produce nuclear weapons. Iran contends that its nuclear programme is for civilian nuclear purposes and that it has the right to enrich uranium under the NPT. Iran's refusal to give up uranium enrichment is considered as questioning the US-led order in the region and a security threat to its position and assets as well as that of its regional allies.

Iran's energy sector has been the target of American sanction because the nation earns 80 percent of its revenue from trade in energy. Since 1996, sanctions imposed by United States have introduced measures to force foreign energy firms to choose either between operating in the US market or continuing to conduct energy-related transactions with Iran. Under this broad direction of sanctions related to energy issues, the Iran and Libya Sanctions Act (ILSA, later renamed the Iran Sanctions Act, ISA) of 1996 is the core of the energy-related US sanctions in the sanctions regime. It is intended to block Iran's energy market by sanctioning entities (companies, persons) that invest more than $20 million an year in Iranian energy projects.

The Comprehensive Iran Sanctions, Accountability, and Divestment Act (CISADA), 2010, bolstered ILSA as it restricted Iran's access to bank transactions and insurance, extending the extra-territorial reach of the extant sanctions. It also amended the definition of 'investment' to include pipelines to or through Iran, as well as contracts to lead the construction, upgrading, or expansions of energy projects to gasoline and gasoline production equipment. Another set of sanctions introduced by the *National Defence Authorization Act* (NDAA, 2012)[20] contained sanctions that impacted on the monetization of Iranian oil trade. It contained the first-ever sanctions against Bank Markazi, the central bank of Iran. The Act required the US President to deny foreign banks or financial institutions that process payments through Iran's central bank access to US financial markets. These new measures were aimed at reducing foreign demand for Iranian oil by punishing dealings with Bank Markazi, clearinghouse for crude oil transactions. But, recognizing the need to avoid upending global financial health, the sanctions allowed the US administration to make exemptions to countries that 'significantly' reduced their volume of purchases of Iranian oil, determined on a case-to-case basis. These sanctions came into full effect in July 2012.

More US restrictions on trade in Iranian crude came into effect vide the NDDA 2013,[21] which included provisions that force countries buying Iranian crude to only use banks within their own borders to make payments for that crude. With this regulations, the consumers' banks have been debarred from transferring that money to Iran or any other bank overseas, in effect, compelling Tehran to buy local products with the local currency from its crude sales. Further, the US Act restricts the kind of goods Iran can buy with its oil proceeds, including prohibition on precious metals.

Sanctions have had a detrimental impact on India's energy trade with Iran. With high rates of economic growth and over 17 percent of the world's population, India has become a significant consumer of energy resources. As the world's fourth largest energy consumer in the world, India imports about 80 percent of its crude oil and 25 percent of its natural gas requirements. In this scenario, India's policymakers are well aware of the need to diversify sources of energy supply. In 2010, around 11 percent of India's total oil import came from Iran, the second largest from a West Asian source. Before the US-led sanctions on monetisation of Tehran's crude oil export took effect in January 2012, Iran was India's second largest crude supplier from West Asia and New Delhi was Tehran's second largest purchaser after China. From that figure, Iran has fallen to the seventh position, constituting a much less, but significant 6 percent of the total oil import by source (See Tables 1 and 2).[22]

Any disruption in energy supply has the potential to upend India's energy security. It is, therefore, not difficult to understand India's well-publicized initial reluctance to announce immediate cuts in Iranian crude imports in the wake of 2012 US sanction on Iran's oil sector.[23] Although it gave the impression that India would defy US sanctions, this was not borne out by facts. Even as it publicly condemned US sanctions, India substantially reduced its purchase of Iranian crude in order to get the sanctions waiver.[24] This has led to Iran slipping to the seventh position from second among oil suppliers to India in 2010, still constituting a much less, but significant 6 percent of the total oil import by source.[25]

Table 1: India's Crude oil Import by Source (2010)

Country of Import	Percentage of total Import
Saudi Arabia	18
Iran	11
Other West Asian Countries (Iraq, Kuwait, UAE and Others)	34
Western Hemisphere	10
Africa	22
Other	5

Table 2: India's Crude oil Import by Source (2012)

Country of Import	Percentage of Total Import
Saudi Arabia	19
Iraq	13
Kuwait	10
UAE	9
Iran	6
Other West Asian Countries	6
Western Hemisphere	18
Africa	17
Other	4

Source: Energy Information Administration (EIA), Country Analysis Brief, November 21, 2011 and March 18, 2013, www.eia.gov

Fear of sanctions under ILSA and CISADA compelled India to shelve the much-touted Iran-Pakistan-India (IPI) project for transporting gas from Iran to India via Pakistan because of open American opposition to it. Also known as the peace pipeline project for its potential to foster economic cooperation between India and Pakistan, it envisaged the transportation of natural gas from Iran through a 2,600-kilometres pipeline from its South Pars fields via Pakistan to Gujarat in India. The Bush Administration opposed the project because of the crucial revenue it would give to Iran, which is facing punitive economic sanctions for its controversial nuclear programme. US laws such as the ILSA and CISADA have further complicated India's ability to obtain natural gas from Iran.[26] Several other India's natural gas deals with Iran remain unimplemented due to sanctions. A $22 billion, 25-year LNG deal signed by India's GAIL (Gas Authority of India Limited) and NIGEC (National Iranian Gas Export Company) in 2005 remains unrealized. It commits GAIL to construct a LNG liquefaction port in Iran involving high investment that could run afoul of the CISADA. Another impediment is the restriction on the use of components and processes designed by American companies, which are restricted for circulation in Iran. Similarly, natural gas exploration and production projects of Indian companies in Iran are also on hold due to sanctions.

Nonetheless, in the light of extant energy ties and potential for greater cooperation in this sector, India is wary of severing its energy relations with Iran. It is, therefore, not difficult to understand India's well-publicized initial reluctance to announce immediate cuts in Iranian crude imports in the wake of 2012 US sanction on Iran's oil sector and its gradual but eventual compliance to them.[27] This apparent contradiction between India's public defiance of the US diktats and its reluctant adaption to them reflects a complex structural dilemma that impacts on New Delhi's foreign policy. India's continued engagement with Iran in the energy sector reflects the importance India as a lesser power attaches to internal balancing in face of the superpower's unbalanced power, which is discernible in the slew of sanctions imposed on Iran. In the face of continued US pressure and in the backdrop of benefits[28] that have accrued to India as a consequence of the Indo-US nuclear deal, it would be an easier option for India to 'band-wagon' with the superpower. However, structural theory tells us that in an anarchical order bandwagoning strengthens someone who may later turn on you. As Burchill says, 'the power of others—especially great powers—is always a threat when there is no government to turn to for protection. "Balancers" attempt to reduce their risk by opposing the stronger party.'[29] India is structurally constrained to maintain its oil trade with Iran in order to balance the United States.

ACCESS TO CENTRAL ASIA AND AFGHANISTAN

With the disintegration of the Soviet Union in the early 1990s, Central Asia emerged as a well-demarcated region with five independent republics. The region immediately became the target of US hegemonic designs. American companies were eager to exploit the oil and gas resources in the region. Other powers such as Turkey, Western Europe, Russia and China competed for economic opportunities in the Central Asian republics (CARs) in an expected balancing act. Within a decade of its emergence, the region also became strategically important for the US, as it invaded Afghanistan after September 2001 attacks. Kazakhstan, Kirgizstan and Tajikistan provided bases for American forces operating in Afghanistan. India and Iran sought to balance and improve their relative power position vis-à-vis the US and other powers in the region through building trade routes to the CARs. Iran emerged as India's gateway for access to these locations, given Pakistan's refusal to allow India to have overland access to Central Asia and Afghanistan.

India and Iran have agreed to build an extensive multi-modal trade corridor, called the International North-South Transport Corridor (INSTC), which would facilitate the transfer of goods from India to northern Europe and Central Asia via Iran. The two countries along with Russia signed an agreement to this effect in St. Petersburg in September 2000. As this corridor is part of an Indo-Iranian initiative to expand trade into Central Asia, both India and Iran entered into an earlier trilateral trade agreement with Turkmenistan in 1997. The corridor, when fully operational, would permit facile transport of goods from the western ports of India to the southern Iranian port of Bandar Abbas and Chabahar. They would then transit Iran via rail to Iran's Caspian Sea ports of Bandar Anzali and Bandar Amirabad. A further onward route would see goods being transferred to the Russian and Central Asian sectors of the Caspian Sea. From Russia, the route extends along the Volga River via Moscow into northern Europe. While the route through the Suez Canal and the Mediterranean takes 45–60 days, the North-South Corridor will take 25–30 days. From India's point of view, the North-South Corridor will enable India bypass Pakistan and yet reach Central Asia. It would also cut the costs involved in transporting goods to Central Asia by 30 percent.[30]

The massive American presence in Afghanistan in the wake of the war placed structural compulsions on regional players to balance the United States. This was obvious in the rivalry among several regional players competing for a stake in the war torn country. Commercial stakes related to reconstruction and development, were the most sought after. India and Iran agreed that their long-term commercial stakes in Afghanistan depended upon better accessibility for their goods and services. Enhanced trade and commerce with regional states was understood to harbinger prosperity and peace in Afghanistan. In pursuance of this idea, India, Iran and Afghanistan held a trilateral meeting in Tehran in the first week of January 2003, to discuss the development of transit and transport corridors, elimination of barriers and constraints, and providing safe, smooth, rapid and low-cost transportation for goods moving from one country to another. A Memorandum of Understanding on the Development and Construction of Transit and Transport Infrastructures that would connect Chabahar to Afghanistan ring road system at Delaram was signed between the three countries and was aimed at improving access to Afghanistan and Central Asia.[31] India agreed to expand the port of Chabahar and lay railway track that would connect Chabahar to the Afghan city of Zaranj on the Iran-Afghan border. As part of the development of this route jointly with Iran and Afghanistan, India, unfazed by the Taliban attacks, completed a 213-kilometre strategic highway in 2009 linking Zaranj to Delaram. While Iran has built the road connectivity from Chabahar to the Afghan border, India is helping Iran to upgrade the Chabahar-Milak railroad. The aim is to build a hassle-free Chabahar-Milak-Zaranj-Dilaram route from Iran to Afghanistan, which would boost tripartite trade.

India is keen to upgrade the capacity of the Chabahar port so that it becomes equipped to handle large cargoes. Under the trilateral agreement, Iran has completed 70 percent of work with India's assistance in the first phase, with an investment of about $340 million in the venture. In the second phase, India is considering several options for the port's expansion with a total investment of $300–400 million.[32] Under the terms of the trilateral agreement, Indian goods, heading for Central Asia and Afghanistan, would receive preferential treatment and tariff reductions at Chabahar. In March 2012, ships from India docked at Chabahar and unloaded 100,000 tonnes of wheat headed for Afghanistan. Since this was a humanitarian aid shipment, the US found it difficult to oppose the move. It was, nonetheless, a test run for future commercial use of the port.[33] Though the United States objects to India's use of Chabahar for commercial purposes, India considers it as a gateway to Afghanistan and Central Asia bypassing Pakistan, which blocks the country's mainland routes to these areas. The Indian government is also putting in resources toward the construction of a 900-km railway line to connect Chabahar to Afghanistan's iron ore regions of Hajigak and its copper mines of Zabul Province.[34] The Chabahar port will also provide Afghanistan with supplementary access to the warm waters of the Gulf, eventually reducing its dependence on Pakistan's Karachi port and ultimately augmenting trade with India.[35]

COOPERATION ON TERRORISM AND SECURITY

In a self-help system, states organize their own security through alignments and agreements with other states. India and Iran are geographically located in a dangerous neighbourhood. A shared threat from Sunni radicalism emanating from Pakistan and Afghanistan has then emerged as one of the most significant areas of cooperation between the two countries. As far back as the early 1990s, the consolidation of power by the Taliban in Afghanistan emerged as a major source of anxiety for both the countries. India and Iran with large Shia Muslim populations were wary of Sunni-Wahhabi extremists in their proximate neighbourhood. India was, moreover, deeply apprehensive of Taliban's 'jihadist' ideology and its potential for fomenting trouble in Kashmir and other parts of the country. As opposed to Pakistan that quickly recognised the Taliban regime, India and Iran backed Afghanistan's anti-Taliban Northern Alliance. India coordinated extensively with Iran and Russia to contain Pakistan's involvement in Afghanistan and its support to the Taliban. When the Taliban was routed by the Northern Alliance in November 2001, both India and Iran welcomed its fall and made Afghanistan's reconstruction and development a common critical goal.[36]

Currently, both countries share similar concerns about the role of Pakistan in fostering a host of terror outfits on its soil and providing safe haven to Taliban on its western and southern frontiers. The Pakistani military considers them as counterweights to India's developmental efforts in Afghanistan and as a means to deepen its own strategic depth in the war-torn country. In a similar vein, Pakistan also dislikes Iran's alliance with the Tajik and cultural ties with Shia Hazara, who together constitute 36 percent of the Afghan population, a significant number that can undercut Islamabad's influence inside Afghanistan.[37] Iran is also feeling the heat from increasing Sunni militancy within its territory, mainly in Zahedan— a predominantly Sunni city along Iran's frontier with Pakistan—which has been attributed to Pakistan-based Jundullah (with possible links to Taliban or al-Qaida or elements within the Pakistani government).[38] Therefore, both India and Iran have strong stakes in a stable Afghanistan.

A rapidly expanding Taliban insurgency against the US-led NATO forces made Washington realize during 2009–10 that there can be no easy victory in the Afghan war. When President Obama announced his plan in June 2011 to begin the drawdown of US troops from Afghanistan, the US administration opened the door to a reconciliation process in which the American military would reach out to moderate elements of the Taliban, much as it did with Sunni militias in Iraq.[39] India and Iran have expressed strong reservations on the United States' policy of negotiating with the Taliban. The policy of integrating Taliban into the government would redouble Islamabad's leverage in Kabul to India and Iran's detriment. India and Iran are informal allies here, as they both fear a resurgent Pakistan-backed extremist government in Afghanistan when NATO forces withdraw from the region.[40] Both India and Iran have been isolated in the American search for an Afghan settlement, even as they face an uneasy scenario of a Taliban dispensation in Kabul. It is, therefore, in the interests of the two countries, to intensify coordination with each other and with other regional players such as Russia and Central Asian Republics, to stabilize Afghanistan. Indo-Iranian Joint Working Group on Terrorism is a ready instrument to begin renewed cooperation on combating the Taliban insurgency and the narcotics trade that sustains it.

STRATEGIC AND DEFENCE COOPERATION

Indo-Iranian cooperation in defence and security areas has two pronged structural directions: balancing the superpower in their common neighbourhood and balancing other emerging powers that undermine their security. One of the key instruments of the New Delhi Declaration is the 'Road Map for Strategic Cooperation', which envisages robust defence cooperation between the two countries, including training and exchange of visits. Though, defence ties between India and Iran have been clouded in secrecy, a number of reports from secondary sources seem to suggest that India was willing to upgrade Iran's Russian-supplied weapon's system, supply conventional military equipment and spare parts, provide expertise in development of military hardware, and train Iran's armed forces.[41] Several reports indicate that Iran has allowed India to have access to its military bases in the event of war with Pakistan. If true, this could fundamentally alter regional balance of power in India's favour.[42]

An 'open' display of military cooperation between India and Iran has involved their navies. The first joint naval exercise in the Arabian Sea in March 2003, reflected Indo-Iranian disquiet over mounting presence of American military in the Persian Gulf and Arabian Sea. It was significant, more so, because the military exercises involving the armies, navies and air forces of India and the US had been burgeoning since the mid-1995.[43] The second Indo-Iranian naval exercise took place on March 3–8, 2006, coinciding with President Bush's visit to India and weeks before Congressional hearing of the proposed US-India civilian nuclear deal. The conduct of the exercise signalled to both Washington and Tehran that

New Delhi's bilateral relations would be independent of pulls and pressures of a third party.

Some also speak of close security ties between India and Iran, inferring from the presence of an unusually large number of Indian consulates at strategic locations on the Iranian territory. The establishment of Indian consulate in Iranian port city of Bandar Abbas in 2002, which evoked protests from Pakistan, permits New Delhi to monitor movement of ships in the Persian Gulf and the straits of Hormuz. Observers in Pakistan note that the Indian engineers working to upgrade and develop the Iranian port of Chabahar can easily monitor their country's activities at the Gwadar port, currently being developed as a naval base with Chinese assistance.[44]

In addition to the commercial advantages that would accrue to India with the development of Chabahar, the port also appears to have immense strategic significance for the country. Chabahar is about 100 miles east of Gwadar port, where China is developing a large new naval base for Pakistan. India perceives this as a two-pronged threat. India is wary of the growing capability of Chinese navy and Beijing's emergent maritime presence in the seas around its landmass. It is believed that Gwadar will provide China with a 'listening post' from where it can 'monitor US and Indian naval activity in the Persian Gulf and Arabian Sea, respectively, as well as any future maritime cooperation between India and the US.'[45]

Some apprehension has also been expressed "on the future vulnerability of energy imports through the Strait of Hormuz due to China's strategic "foothold" in Pakistan's Gwadar port, as part of its overall 'String of Pearls' strategy."[46] The dual-use civilian-military facilities at Gwadar, providing a base for Chinese ships and submarines, could pose a direct security threat to India. Equally, Gwadar's closeness to the Straits of Hormuz would enable Pakistan to exercise control over energy routes and as implications for energy traffic to India.[47] India's response to Gwadar was to help Iran develop Chabahar, from where India can in turn observe the activities of Pakistan and China in the Arabian Sea.

THE NUCLEAR ISSUE

In September 2005, India voted for the IAEA resolution finding Iran to be in 'non-compliance' of the safeguard obligation under the Nuclear Non-Proliferation Treaty (NPT) and then it voted to refer Iran to the UN Security Council in February 2006. The votes stirred fierce controversy in India but went a long way in placating those policymakers, who questioned India's engagement with Iran in the backdrop of the Congressional debates on the US-India civilian nuclear deal.[48] Even though at the time the government defended its vote as an independent decision by saying it worked actively to help Iran during stand-offs in the negotiation process and ensured that the issue remained with the IAEA instead of immediate referral to the UN Security Council, New Delhi understood that the failure to take a clear stand on the Iranian imbroglio would thwart the much sought after nuclear deal with the United States.[49] Even as India voted with the United States on the IAEA resolutions, it asserted that Iran had a right to peaceful use of nuclear energy under the NPT.

India's position has been to hold Iran accountable to its obligations under the NPT, IAEA and UNSC guidelines and insist that Iran address questions related to its nuclear programme to the satisfaction of the international community. On November 27, 2009, India once again joined the United States in voting against Iran in a resolution at the IAEA, which demanded that the Islamic Republic immediately suspend construction of its newly-revealed uranium enrichment plant at Qom—a site kept secret until recently. This unambiguously demonstrated that New Delhi does not view any further proliferation in its neighbourhood as conducive to its security environment. Manmohan Singh said as much in a question and answer session during his visit to Washington, a week before the vote.[50]

India's stand on the Iranian nuclear issue reflects its traditional balance of power exercise of geopolitics. A middle power, trying to move up the ladder in the hierarchy of powers, and faced with the strategy of containment on the part of the great power, may opt for short-term policy of alliance to preserve its foreign policy independence and cope with pressures of containment. However power transition in the post-World War II has become aberrant as the possibility of large-scale, system-changing war, that caused the rise and fall of great powers, has become redundant with the advent of nuclear weapons. The escalation of conflict to a nuclear war would mean the destruction of all belligerents; in effect the nuclear weapons have rendered war unthinkable among the great powers. In order to fortify their ranks and preserve their status in the international system, the great powers have created the non-proliferation regime to prevent any rising power from acquiring nuclear weapons. India rejected the non-proliferation regime and practiced its nuclear option on the normative argument,[51] to circumvent the barrier to its rise in the international system. This hurt India in the form of economic sanctions, political condemnation and exclusion from nuclear and high technology trade.

After India conducted the nuclear tests in 1998 and weathered the economic sanctions on the strength of its economy, it was engaged in strategic dialogue with all major powers. It became hard for major powers to ignore the country, especially when they could derive economic benefits from engaging India. A major outcome of this development was the Indo-US nuclear deal, which lifted the nuclear embargo on India and also made high technology available with the great powers, accessible. In fact, Indo-US space technology and defence agreements have been called the 'other nuclear deals', for their scope and expanse. Thus, India's votes against Iran underlines the necessity of a rising power, in face of containment by the great power, to adopt a short-term policy of alliance in single-mined pursuit of national interest.

It is important to note that even though the option of a full-fledged alliance with the United Sates is available to India, it has chosen to build long-term economic and military capability to assure the autonomy of its foreign policy. In the same vein, and side-stepping the US line, India has asserted Iran's right to peaceful nuclear energy, including mastery over the entire fuel cycle. India's reluctance to censure or isolate Iran internationally in the context of the continuing Iranian nuclear imbroglio marks the end of New Delhi's short-term alliance with the US. The decline in the United States' regional influence in the wake of withdrawal from Iraq, repeated setbacks in Afghanistan, and the advent of the Arab Spring, has made India less beholden to a strategic-security partnership with Washington. India's refusal to severe trade and economic ties with Iran in the wake of US sanctions reveals that New Delhi wants to see the international affairs of its proximate neighbourhood as an arena where it is the 'system-builder'. As a rising power, India is concerned about the nuclear ambitions of Iran, an anti-status quo and revolutionary power. While it does not endorse the military component of Iran's nuclear programme, India also does not believe that Iran can acquire nuclear weapons capability anytime soon. Even if it does, which would be at best rudimentary, given Tehran's lack of access to sophisticated technical know-how of the West, New Delhi does not feel threatened by such a possibility. India remains deeply sceptical that the United States can (or should) roll back Tehran's nuclear programme. What is needed here, in India's view, is the understanding and management of Iran's nuclear scenario.

From its own experience of having resisted attempts by the nuclear-weapons powers from being drafted into an unequal regime of the NPT without any security guarantees, Indian political elites believe that the

Iranian quest for nuclear weapons, if any, is defensive rather than offensive.[52] Therefore, Indian policymakers remain unconvinced of the Western argument that the threat of military action can force Iran to abandon its nuclear programme. On the contrary, India contends that these would only reinforce Iran's desire for some kind of a deterrent capability. New Delhi's position is to hold Iran accountable to its obligations under the NPT through consistent diplomatic engagement, so that it feels confident enough to address questions about its nuclear matters. Simultaneously addressing the larger issue of Iranian security within the context of a comprehensive regional security framework would go a long way in addressing Iran's fears.[53] For the moment, however, India considers Iran an effective balancer in the region, capable of putting a break on the superpower's reach. This also agrees with Tehran's image of its own self. It is, therefore, not surprising that India is aiming to expand its trade ties with Iran despite US sanctions and political pressure.[54]

CONCLUSION

Theories of neo-realism argue that behaviour of states is defined not only by self-interest but also by structural constraints imposed by changing international environment. The unipolar nature of the post-Cold War international system, the United States' attempt to isolate Iran globally, the increasing strategic importance of Central Asian republics, the threat of Sunni Islamic extremism, the imperative to protect the sea lanes and integrity of energy supplies and the prospect of mutual benefit from economic cooperation in a broad range of areas—all created conditions for convergence of strategic and economic interests between India and Iran and led them to refurbish their ties in the context of changed international situation. India's relationship with Iran is likely to grow in the future as New Delhi expects real and substantive gains from this partnership both in terms of material benefits and strategic advantage. At the same time, India like all states, would take measures to strengthen internal balancing. This explain India's vote against Iran in the IAEA. Given its vast developmental needs, India's vote was to secure the India-US nuclear deal that would facilitate building of economic and technological capabilities of the country. Systemic constraints also dictate that India-Iran ties will endure. Both the states complement each other on a number of issues, enabling them to realise internal and external balance in an anarchic international system.

REFERENCES

[1] Kenneth Waltz, Theory of International Politics (*New York*: *Random House, 1979),* 127.

[2] Ibid, 97.

[3] Ibid, 128.

[4] Ibid, 113.

[5] Robert Jackson and Georg Sorensen, Introduction to International Relations: Theories and Approaches (Oxford: Oxford University Press, 2013) fifth edition, 81.

[6] Quoted in John Mearsheimer, "Anarchy and Struggle for Power," in Karen A Mingst and Jack L Snyder (ed.), Essential Readings in World Politics (New York: WW Norton and Company, 2004) second edition, 56.

[7] Mearsheimer, 2004, 57.

[8] Ibid.

[9] Jackson and Sorensen, 85.

[10] Ali Ansari, Confronting Iran: The Failure of American Foreign Policy and the Roots of Mistrust (New Delhi: Foundation Books, 2006), 24.

[11] In reality, however, India was more sympathetic towards the USSR. When massive reversals in the Indo-Chinese war (1962) revealed India's stark strategic vulnerability, the Soviet Union emerged a formidable ally, fulfilling New Delhi's need for modern defence hardware and weaponry.

[12] Farah Naaz, "Indo-Iranian Relations: Vital factors for the 1990s," Strategic Analysis (New Delhi), Vol. XXIV, No. 10 (January 2001), 1913–14.

[13] Harsh V. Pant, "India and Iran: An 'Axis' in the Making," Asian Survey (University of California Press), Vol. 44, No. 3 (May–Jun, 2004), 370.

[14] See, A.H.H. Abidi, "Relations between India and Iran, 1947–1979", The Iranian Journal of International Affairs (Tehran, Iran), Vol. VII, No. 4 (Winter 1996), 882.

[15] Kenneth, M. Pollack, "Containing Iran," The Iran Primer (United States Institute of Peace), http://iranprimer.usip.org/resource/containing-iran.

[16] See, R.K. Ramazani, Revolutionary Iran: Challenge and Response in the Middle East (Baltimore, Maryland: The Johns Hopkins University Press, 1987).

[17] Baldev, Raj Nayar and Paul, T.V., India and the World Order: Searching for Major Power Status (New Delhi: Foundation Books, 2004), 234.

[18] Bernard Reich and Stephen H. Gotowicki, "The United States and the Persian Gulf in the Bush Administration after the Gulf War," http://fmso.leavenworth.army.mil/documents/aftrgulf.htm.

[19] Fair, C. Christine, "Indo-Iranian Relations: Prospects for Bilateral Cooperation after 9/11", in Robert M. Hathaway, et al., "The 'strategic partnership' between India and Iran," Asia Program Special Report, No.120 (2004), Washington: Woodrow Wilson Centre, 10; Harsh V Pant, "India and Iran: An 'Axis' in the Making?" Asian Survey, Vol. 44, No. 3 (May/June 2003), 371. For the text of the "PM's Opening Statement at Delegation-Level Talks" of April 10, 2001 outlining common areas of cooperation and the "The New Delhi Declaration," 25 January 2003 signed between the Republic of India and the Islamic Republic of Iran, see, www.meaindia.nic.in.

[20] Section 1245. "Imposition of sanctions with respect to the financial sector of Iran," National Defence Authorization Act for Fiscal Year 2012, www.thomas.loc.gov.

[21] See Subtitle D—"Iran Sanctions," National Defence Authorization Act for Fiscal Year 2013, http://www.govtrack.us/congress/bills/112/hr4310/text; "New US sanctions in FY 2013 National Defence Authorization Act expand on trend to apply pressure on third country business with Iran," Lexology, January 16, 2013, www.lexology.com.

[22] "India," Energy Information Administration (EIA) Official Energy Statistics from the US Government, March 18, 2013, www.eia.gov.

[23] "Indian trade delegation to Iran may put Indo-US ties under strain," Economic Times, http://articles.economictimes.indiatimes.com, February 11, 2012.

[24] In the wake of sanctions and in order to on avoid falling afoul to the US reprisal for not following its sanctions' regime, India's oil imports from Iran fell 18 percent in June 2012 from a year earlier, bringing import of Iranian crude to below 9 percent. India is expected to slash import of crude oil from Iran by as much as 27 percent in 2013 because US and European sanctions have made it difficult to ship oil from the Persian Gulf nation. See Kabir Taneja, "Oil imports from Iran to fall further," The Sunday Guardian, www.sunday-guardian.com, July 22, 2012; "India may cut oil import from Iran by 27 percent," The Hindu, www.thehindu.com, March 18, 2013.

[25] "India," Energy Information Administration (EIA) Official Energy Statistics from the US Government, March 18, 2013, www.eia.gov.

[26] CISADA was passed by Congress on June 24, 2010 and signed into law by President Obama on July 1, 2010. The Act expands upon the restrictions of the Iran Sanctions Act of 1996 (the ISA) and the Iranian Transaction Regulations administered by the Department of Treasury's Office of Foreign Assets Control (OFAC). CISADA covers a significantly broader range of areas than the ISA that makes it of particular interest to companies with, or considering business activities related to Iran. For full text of the Act, see "Comprehensive Iran Sanctions, Accountability, and Divestment Act of 2010," The Library of Congress, June 24, 2010, http://thomas.loc.gov/home/gpoxmlc111/h2194_enr.xml.

[27] "Indian trade delegation to Iran may put Indo-US ties under strain," Economic Times, February 11, 2012, www.articles.economictimes.indiatimes.com.

[28] With the Indo-US nuclear deal, 2005, the United States agreed to lift three-decade moratorium on nuclear trade with India. Subsequently, the ties between India and the United States have expanded to include cooperation in areas such as defence, space technology, energy, education exchange and collaboration, maritime partnership, and health among many other areas. There has been a remarkable expansion of the bilateral relationship since the inaugural Strategic Dialogue in 2010, which includes comprehensive consultation on security issues in Asia, the Indian Ocean region and the Pacific region. See, Paul K Kerr, "US Nuclear Cooperation with India: Issues for Congress," CRS Report for Congress, www.fas.org, July 30, 2008; "India-United States of America Relations," Ministry of External Affairs, Government of India, www.mea.gov.in, March 2012; "Joint statement on the Third round of Indo-US strategic dialogue," US Department of State (Washington DC), www.state.gov, June 13, 2012; "Report to Congress on US-India Security Cooperation," US Department of Defence, www.defense.gov, November 2011.

[29] Scott Burchill *et al.,* Theories of International Relations (Basingstoke, Hampshire: Palgrave Macmillan, 2005), 36.

[30] An exposition on the North-South Transport Corridor can be found in C. Christine Fair, "Indo-Iranian Ties: Thicker than Oil," Middle East Review of International Affairs, Vol. 11, No. 1 (March 2007), 48; Donald L Berlin, "India-Iran Relations: A Deepening Entente," Asia Pacific Centre for Security Studies (October 2004), http://www.apcss.org/Publications/SAS/AsiaBilateralRelations/India-Iran RelationsBerlin.pdf (accessed 14 August 2012); Harsh V Pant (May–June, 2004), 377; Regine A Spector, "The North South Transport Corridor," Central Asia-Caucasus Institute Analyst, March 7, 2002, www.cacianalyst.org . On the importance of Central Asian region to India, see, Stephen Blank, "India's Rising Profile in Central Asia," Comparative Strategy, Vol. 22, Issue 2 (2003), 139–157; and Teresita C. Schaffer and Vibhuti Haté, "India's 'Look West' Policy: Why Central Asia Matters," South Asia Monitor, No. 110 (September 5, 2007), 1–3; Elizabeth Roche, "India pitches strongly for SCO membership," livemint.com, June 8, 2012, www.livemint.com.

[31] "New Transit Agreement between India, Iran and Afghanistan," Rajya Sabha Unstarred Question No. *3878, 28 April 2003, http://bj.panda.name/html/quest_orissa_container_archive.asp?id=145;Vijay Prashad, "The India-Iran Tunnel," *Asia Times Online*, May 7, 2012, www.atimes.com.

[32] Iran's work on the Chabahar project has been slow and far beyond schedule, despite India having built the Zaranj-Delaram road from the Afghan side of the Iran-Afghanistan border way back in 2008. Although the post is functional, it has a limited capacity of only 2.5 million tons per year, whereas the target was 12 million tons. However, at a time when its economic health is suffering on account of international sanctions, the necessity to engage India has prodded Iran to move forward and complete its part of the project. India will make investment in the expansion of the port that will come from the rupee payments for oil that it is importing from Iran. One of the three investment options that India is considering is to construct and operate a multi-purpose cargo berth at Chabahar with an investment of about $20 million. The second option is to build a container terminal at an estimated investment of $30 million. And, the third plan is to develop yet another bigger container terminal at a cost of about $65 million. India's interest in the Iranian port has increased beyond direct access to Central Asia and Afghanistan, but also to facilitate import of minerals from Afghanistan via Chabahar. Iran has plans to ramp up the port's capacity from 3–6 million tonnes in the first phase to 10 million tonnes. India is keen to involve Afghanistan in the building of the Chabahar port as it would involve a commitment from the latter to prioritise its trading through this port as opposed to the Karachi port. "Chabahar port: India, Iran, Afghanistan to set up group," The Indian Express, August 27 2012, www.indianexpress.com; Dipak K Dash, "India eyeing Iran's Chabahar port for direct access to Central Asia," The Times of India, 26 August 2012, http://articles.timesofindia.indiatimes.com; "Trilateral meet to discuss Iran's Chabahar port," The Times of India, August 26, 2012, http://articles.timesofindia.indiatimes.com; "India discusses Chabahar port project with Iran, Afghanistan," Indian Defence News, August 27, 2012, http://indiandefencenews.in.

[33] Mullen, Rani D. and Ganguly, Sumit, "The Rise of India's Soft Power," Foreign Policy, May 8, 2012, www.foreignpolicy.com; Prashad, *Asia Times Online*, May 7, 2012.

[34] Hajigak, 130 km west of Kabul in Bamiyan province, holds Afghanistan's largest iron ore deposits. Of the 22 companies shortlisted for the bid for these mines 14 are Indian, including a consortium led by the public sector Steel Authority of India Limited. It is a kind of dream project for India: it helps Afghanistan in industrialization and creation of jobs and it offers India vast amount of resources, while according a chance to showcase Indian engineering skills. Jayanth Jacob and Saubhadra Chatterji, Hindustan "India's Track 3: Afghan-Iran rail link,"Hindustan Times, November 1, 2011, www.hindustantimes.com; Eltaf Najafizada, Afghanistan Awards Indian Group Hajigak Iron-Ore Mining Rights," Bloomberg, November 27, 2011, www.bloomberg.com; MK Bhadrakumar, "India's road to Hajigak passes through Iran," Rediff.com, December 1, 2011.

[35] The Zaranj-Delaram road has encouraged Afghan businessmen to shift their transit of goods from Karachi harbour of Pakistan to Chabahar port in southern Iran. See "Iran and Afghanistan," Institute for the study of War (Washington DC), http://www.understandingwar.org/iran-and-afghanistan.

[36] Iran pledged US$ 560 million at the Tokyo Conference on the Reconstruction of Afghanistan in 2002, and an additional US$ 100 million at the 2006 London Conference. Much of the Iranian aid to Afghanistan has been spent on infrastructure project—mainly transportation links between Iran, Afghanistan, and the Central Asian Republics. See Mohsen Milani, "Iran and Afghanistan," The Iran Primer (United States Institute of Peace), http://iranprimer.usip.org/resource/ iran-and-afghanistan; Maseh Zarif and Ahmad Majidyar, "Iranian Influence in Afghanistan: Recent Developments," Iran Tracker, August 21, 2009, www.iran tracker.org. India is one of the biggest donors in Afghanistan, spending about $2 billion on civilian projects ranging from the construction of highways, dams, Afghan parliament, and projects in the areas of agriculture, telecommunication, education, health and capacity building throughout Afghanistan, making it the 5th largest bilateral donor after the US, UK, Japan and Germany. See "Afghanistan", Background Briefing, Ministry of External Affairs, Government of India, May 2012, http://meaindia.nic.in; Gulshan Sachdeva, "The Delhi Investment Summit on Afghanistan," IDSA Comment, June 26, 2012, www.idsa.in.

[37] "Afghanistan," The CIA World Factbook, August 20, 2012, www.cia.gov.

[38] Michael Slackman, "Iran Blames US and Britain in attack," New York Times, October 19, 2009, www.nytimes.com; Arthur Bright, "Sunni Rebels Claim Deadly Terror Attack in Iran; Car Bombing by Jundullah Insurgents Kills at Least 11 of Iran's Elite Guards," TheChristian Science Monitor, February 14, 2007, www.csmonitor.com.

[39] For Obama administration policy shift on the Afghanistan war and perils involved in separating 'good' and 'bad Taliban' and separating the Taliban from al-Qaeda, see "Good and Bad Taliban? U.S. Tries to Separate," Associated Press, Feb 2, 2010, www.msnbc.msn.com; Indrani Bagchi, "In search of "good" Taliban", Times of India, March 5, 2009, http://timesofindia.indiatimes.com; Brahma Chellaney, "Barack Obama's Taliban itch," Japan Times, Feb 26, 2009 http://search. japantimes. co.jp.

[40] Harsh V. Pant, "India in Afghanistan: The 'Soft Power' Question," Swiss Federal Institute of Technology, October 15, 2009, www.isn.ethz.ch; MK Bhadrakumar, "Pakistan warns India to back off," *Asia Times*, October 10, 2009, www.atimes.com;

Ahmed Rashid, "The End Game," Outlookindia.com, March 12, 2010, http://outlookindia.com; Robert D Kaplan, "Obama Takes Asia by Sea," New York Times, November 11, 2010, www.nytimes.com.

[41] More specifically, Indian aeronautical engineers will help Iran maintain and provide mid-life upgrade for its MiG fighter aircraft. Iran has also sought India's help to refit and maintain tanks, infantry fighting vehicles, and artillery guns. India is also planning to sell Konkurs anti-tank guided weapons and spare parts. In the past, India has helped Iran adapt four Russian-built Kilo-class submarines for warm water conditions in the Persian Gulf. Iran is also seeking combat training for missile boat crews and hopes to purchase simulators for ships and submarines from India. See Rizwan Zeb, "The Emerging Indo-Iranian Strategic Alliance and Pakistan,"Central Asia Caucasus Institute Analyst, February 12, 2003, www.cacianalyst.org; Ehsan Ahrari, "As India and Iran snuggle, Pakistan feels the chill," Asia Times, February 11, 2003, www.atimes.com; John Calabrese, "Indo-Iranian Relations in Transition," Journal of South Asia and Middle Eastern Studies, Vol. 25, No. 3 (Summer 2002), 75–76.

[42] As cited in Berlin, "India-Iran Relations: A Deepening Entente"; Ahrari, "As India and Iran snuggle, Pakistan feels the chill."

[43] Fair, 2007, p. 50.

[44] Berlin, October 2004.

[45] Pant, Harsh V., "China's Naval Expansion in the Indian Ocean and India-China Rivalry," *The Asia-Pacific Journal: Japan Focus*, www.japanfocus.org.

[46] "Navy Chief 'concerned' over new Pak port,"Indian Express, January 23, 2008, quoted in Gurpreet S. Khurana, "Aircraft Carriers and India's Naval Doctrine," Journal of Defence Studies, Vol. 2, Issue 1 (Summer 2008), 99–100.

[47] See Christophe Jaffrelot, "A Tale of Two Ports," YaleGlobal Online, January 7, 2011, http://yaleglobal.yale.edu.

[48] For example, India conducted its second naval exercise with Iran in 2006 at a time when the US Congress was considering a civilian nuclear deal, which invited the ire of the Chairman of the House Foreign Relations Committee, Tom Lantos, who opined that relationship with 'the current terrorist regime in Tehran is unacceptable behaviour by any country seeking to be our strategic ally.' Aziz Haniffa, "India not a Threat to NPT: Lantos," Rediff.com, April 6, 2006.

[49] For a positive assessment of the importance of civilian nuclear agreement with the US and its implications for India's position in the global order and the relationship with Iran, see Sadanand Dhume, "India's Tough Choice on Iran," Washington Post, August 11, 2007, www.washingtonpost.com.

[50] Manal Alafrangi, "No support for Iran's nuclear weapons, Indian minister says," October 19, 2009, Gulf news, http://gulfnews.com; Rajesh Kumar Mishra, "Iran's Nuclear Case and India," IDSA Comment, January 2006, http://www.idsa.in; Pranab Dhal Samanta, "Again, India votes against Iran's nuclear programme," The Indian Express, November 28, 2009, www.indianexpress.com.

[51] See Nayar and Paul, 2004, 7–8.

[52] Ayoob, Mohammed, "India and Iran: Similar experiences, converging interests," CNN World, February 21, 2012, http://globalpublicsquare.blogs.cnn.com.

[53] Sikri, Rajiv, Challenge and Strategy: Rethinking India's Foreign Policy (New Delhi: Sage, 2009), 152.

[54] Mehdudia, Sujay, "Sector-based approach to expand trade with Iran,"The Hindu, June 2, 2012; "India keen to expand exports to Iran: Ranjan Mathai," The Economic Times, August 25, 2012, http://articles.economictimes.indiatimes.com; Rebecca Byerly, "Why India is trying to expand trade with Iran," The Christian Science Monitor, March 29, 2012, www.csmonitor.com; Jim Yardley, "Indians Host Clinton While Also Wooing Iran," The New York Times, May 8, 2012, www.nytimes.com.

Iran and India: The Axis of Consistency and Development in West and South Asia

Hadi Soleimanpour

Iran and India are two oldest civilizations of the Asia and have age old relationship in exchange of thoughts among each other. Late Jawahar Lal Nehru, the first Prime Minister of India in his book "Discovery of India" wrote, "among the many peoples and races who have come in contact with and influenced India's life and culture, the oldest and most persistent have been the Iranians". I believe he was honest in his opinion regarding the influence of Indian civilization on Iran. The Kalilah and Damneh with Hindi material pertaining to the rulers about 1500 years before, on order of Anushirvan were translated into Pahlavi language and were used by Sasani Dynasty to rule. During the various centuries most of the Persian books were translated into Hindi and the Indian writers especially from this region played a vital role in enriching the Persian language and literature. 'Mysticism' from India is one of the most important aspects that have its impact on Iranian writers.

The relationship between Iran and the Indian sub-continent was strongly based on the common values, life style and traditions of our people. The common values of our culture has been created by the efforts of our elites, intellectuals, and scientists and they had vital role to transfer these values to create our two Glorious civilizations. During the last 800 years Hyderabad/ Deccan has been the central part of this important interaction. The relationship between the two civilization did not limit to Literature and Mysticism, and it has its influence in Architecture and Art. The uniqueness in the historical interaction is that this cultural value are not in existence because of the rulers or military efforts, but by the help of scholars, poets, literates in the annuls of civilization.

Thousands of unique Persian manuscripts in the libraries' and the museums of Hyderabad, such as Asafiyyeh Library, Osmania University library, Nizam's library, Emadiyeh library and Salar Jang Museum's library, shows the pivotal existence of the Hyderabad in preserving of shared values of Iran and India. These great treasures not only can play their role in the

Iran and India civilization and discussion on our common values,but also conveys the Asian shared values.

In the latest development, Asian scholars are trying to form the Asian identity, and in this way they have considered Asian connectivity and Asianness. Today the cognition and introducing these shared local values in Asia and make them global values, should be a must. These values can play an important role along with the western values in the formation of the next civilization. High civilization values of Iran and India, hidden in the treasures such as Hyderabad can create an environment for Asian dialogue on Asian values and civilizations.

During the last few years we have been witnessing the increase in visits of high ranking politicians from both the countries. This aspect is the outcome of the common determination of the higher authorities of both the countries Iran and India. It is also noteworthy that the strategic conversation between both the countries has been a continuing phenomenon since last several years. While this dialogue has different political, economical, cultural and military dimensions, the present international and regional situation requires India and Iran to carry forward this traditional and expand their dialogue to the new and emerging issues. In Iran at present the new government which is elected by majority of votes is relying on the democracy. The new government of H.E. Mr. Hassan Rowhani offers new policy approach towards our neighboring countries, the region and the east. This policy is based on common values and mutual respect, peace, prosperity and regional development.

During the last summer, when most of the people in capital of the countries in the middle east were objecting the administration and were protesting against it on the streets, in Tehran especially, people were celebrating the election of the new government and those who were in opposition to this elected government and the supporters of the other presidential candidates also joined them in celebration. This is something unique in our region.

Iran at present enjoys a pivotal anchor in the middle east, same as India being the pivotal anchor and development entity in our Asian continent. Enhancing dialogue based on the principles of cooperation at all levels between the two countries is economical, profitable, socially viable, and regionally reliable. History has witnessed that harming the developmental process and instability in each of the countries, India and Iran will have direct impact on each other.

From the strategic point of view, there are certain necessities between the two countries' relationship and we, are well acquainted with the idea of Transitional Period of International Order. However the bi-polar system has collapsed at the beginning of the last decade of 20th century and till date it is not being replaced with new order. One of the major characteristics of this period is the evaluation on regional order. The western region of Asia and Middle East are among the regions which has been influenced by the old bi-polar order during several years and it has not faced the basic changes for the adoptability of the regional order with the international order.

The Arab Spring or the Islamic Awakening was the answer to this backwardness. At present the regional order in the Middle East is in its transitional period and has its own characteristics. The restricted changes in regional security system has created conditions for the Asian players to have the opportunity to participate in an active debate on new and novel regional security arrangements. Iran and India can jointly upgrade its missions in this respect. Without any doubts the decrease in dependency of America on the energy resources of the Middle East and Persian Gulf and the changes in the energy consumption markets from west to east has created extra ordinary opportunity for the consumers and producers of Asia who can initiate the new arguments related to energy market and energy security. Iran and India have a deciding role in this matter.

With the increase of power of social network and non governmental actors in the transitional period in the regional order and while taking into consideration the tribal nature of the majority of the Middle East countries in the region, we face the danger of disintegration and balkanization. Governments such as India and Iran which have the historical background of democratically transition of power, and empowerment of the people can collaborate with each other to assist the region to overcome this serious turmoil. One of the most important phenomenon related to the transitional period of the regional order is Extremism and Sectarianism. Extremism challenges the basic principles and cultural values in all the civilizations of the region and also diversifies the ethical and moral values of our societies. No doubt that the sectarianism and violence are the product of extremism and hence the civil society and democratic governments should take necessary measures to avoid the side effects of using sectarianism and violence as a political tool by extremism in the region.

Extremism and violence are at the door steps of the democratically elected governments of the region and if this is not solved, it will enter into all the territories and will crop up in all corner of the region. Therefore, no one will be spared from this. The new president of Islamic Republic of Iran has recognized properly the idea of the world against violence and extremism wave, and declared the same in the United Nations General Assembly this year. The dialogue among the intellectuals of Iran and India in this area and other above mentioned areas will enable us to have a better understanding and will create the common fields for the development of both the countries.

From the regional point of view, Iran and India, both the countriesare unstable and also insecure, and are facing security challenges due to terrorism, smuggling of drugs and instability in the regional countries especially Afghanistan is the most important challenge and threat to the region.The Iranian approach in its foreign policy is the regional approach. Iran and India are two important countries in the west and south west of Asia and they can help in facing the challenges. Iran and India need a secure and stable environment for the stable development. Instability and insecurity of the region will prevent them from economic development. The collaboration of two countries in administration, and solving regional dispute will ease the approaching of the development which is the priority in this matter. Experiencing the presence of the foreign forces as an assuring force for security has not been a successful experience but continuation of instability and is a threatening alarm for the countries in the region.

The first and the most important challenge for the future of Afghanistan in 2014 would be the decrease of foreign presence in Afghanistan. The presence of the foreign forces did not help the security and development of Afghanistan. The foreign intervention in Afghanistan and Middle East under the pretext of fight against terrorism and extremism became the cause of strengthening and development of these groups. The danger of the return of these extremist groups to Afghanistan and creating instability and its penetration to the neighboring countries still continues. During the 90's in Afghanistan, there was no winner and the continuation is alarming for the region. As such we should prevent the happenings of the 90's in Afghanistan. The challenges of Afghanistan is due to the intervention of former Soviet Union and America. If these interventions had not taken place, Afghanistan would have approached its natural progress and development today.

An independent Afghanistan as a stable and developed nation is an advantage for all the countries in the region. Afghanistan experience shows that not only intervention is a solution but also its freedom is not an answer to that. A regional mechanism supporting stability according to the development and partnership in Afghanistan create an independent and developed country. According to the last experiences we can count on the support and help of the international powers. Afghanistan is not adventageous to any of the international existing powers and similarly leaving Afghanistan to its own fate will be another security challenge to other countries of the region.

Unfortunately the topic of Afghanistan like other challenges such as extremism or drug trafficking got entangled. The cooperation of Iran and India in fighting against drug abuse and extremism has become a necessity. The financial and human loss due to the drug smugglers and extremist groups which has been imposed on the regional countries is much higher than the expenses caused on America during the 9/11 attack by terrorists. Lastly, the group of drug smugglers have attacked the Iranian border security forces. The regional countries have the right to be anxious about this threat. Co-operation between the regional countries in fighting against these threats has become a necessity.

Both the countries have a common stand in the region including the changes taking place in Syria, and have shown their deep concern regarding violence and requested all the parties in Syria to stop violence and resolve all the issues with the help of negotiation and respecting the tendencies of Syrian people in a peaceful manner. In this regard, Iran and India have supported the Geneva agreement which consists of six articles of Kofi Annan. They also welcome Lakhzer Ebrahimi as a common representative.

Iran and India have opportunities and are not a threat for each other, and they should work together. The existence of a number of Iranian students in India can helping the development of co-operation between Universities and Educational Institutions and help in research projects. The support of the industrial and commercial section of both the countries from these projects will flourish more talents and it will also result in good research. As the future is in their hands they should not return with pessimist views to the country. Therefore, the officials should try their best to provide the best education to them.

Co-operation between the mass media of both the countries, by holding joint meetings with the authors and journalists of Iran and India will help in introducing in the best way of each of these countries, and strengthen the social and intellectual links to its people. The Centre of Education and Research of Ministry of Foreign Affairs of Islamic Republic of Iran is willing to organize the joint meetings among the intellectuals of both the countries to find ways for development of relations and clear any hurdles or limitations.

The relationship between India and Iran is based on the mutual benefits and values of both the countries and not on the requirements of other countries. We don't follow other countries' policies towards India and we expect the same from India. To achieve stable development in all spheres is an important priority for both the countries. Development and security are necessary for both the countries. Development without stable security cannot bring stability and security cannot be without development. Security and development cannot be separated. We cannot survive and live safely in a backward and insecure region.

Those who believe in regional co-operation are seeking more security and welfare and they should not keep themselves away from this. The weakness of friends becomes the strength of the enemies and will result in unwanted consequences for the people of the region.

CONCLUSION

From the Iranian point of view, the security, administration and development of the region should be in their own hands and for this matter they should adopt a mechanism for a regional dialogue with the co-operation of the countries of the region. The sources for this opinion is that, we cannot divide security and development of the region or separate them from each other. In this mechanism, the security challenges and the hurdles to the developments with the presence and co operation of the educational institutions, civil societies, private sector and official authorities of the region will discuss and exchange point of views. Extremism in Asia, with its economical, security and political consequences is one of the issues which should be dealt with seriousness.

India and Iran on the Threshold of Strategic Relations

H.E. Hassan Nourian

INTRODUCTION

Relations between India and Iran date back to the Neolithic period. The existence of several empires spanning both Iran and India ensured the constant migration of people between the two regions and the spread and evolution of the Indo-Iranian language groups. As a consequence, the people of India and Iran share significant cultural, linguistic and ethnic characteristics. It is also a well known fact that there have always been connections, relations, interchanges and borrowings between great civilizations which have enriched each other. Thus, the age long historical relations between the Iranians and the people of the Indian subcontinent date back to a very remote past. Both the two countries shared a common border till 1947. Besides sharing several common features in their language, culture and traditions they have strong commercial, energy, cultural and people-to-people links.

CIVILIZATION AND CULTURE

In the splendid civilization of Mohenjodaro and the Sindh Valleywhich flourished between 2500 and 1500 BC, there are visible signs of relation-ship with the Iranian civilization. The ancient relics, earthenware and the marked resemblance in their designs and patterns are strong evidences in favor of this assertion.[1] India and Iran's common civilization is followed by the arrival of the Aryans in this region. Although the factors which lead to this mass migration are yet not fully known but the various similarities found in the legends and religious texts of the two peoples allude to such connection. Some of the scholars are of the opinion that Sanskrit, Old Persian and Avestan languages are the sisters born of the same mother.[2] During the pre-Islamic Iran and Vedic civilization era in India, the languages of the northern, western, central and eastern regions of India belonging to the Indo-Aryan family have originated from the same source as the Iranian languages, namely the Indo-Iranian language family. Vedic Indian people referred to themselves as Aryas and the word "Iran" means "the Land of the Aryans". In authentic books of history some references have been made to the continuous relations of the two people during the days of the Medes, Pishdadiyan and Kiyanian. In the holy book of Zoroastrians, i.e. Avesta, too, mention has been made of North India.[3]

During the Achaemenid rule, the artisans, craftsmen and traders travelled from Iran to India and from India to Iran and even in some battles between Iran and Greece the Indian soldiers fought as a part of the Iranian army of Achaemenid. The relics of Persepolis too confirm this view. Iranian nobles were also present in the courts of Mauryan kings.[4] After the invasion of Alexander and the subsequent establishment of the Seleucid reign, Sindh and some other parts of the Indian subcontinent, which were till then under the dominance of the Achaemenids, came under the sway of the Seleucid.[5] Following the fall of the Seleucids and foundation of the Parthian rule 228 Common Era/Christian Era (CE) in Iran, the relations between India and Iran was further enhanced. Similarly there are several other examples of very close cultural relations in the pre-Islamic era such as the well-known translation of Panchtantra—the Indian book of fables into Pahlavi during the reign of Anushiravan, better known as Nowsherwan the Just, and the arrival of chess in Iran from India.[6] and sending of back-gammon to India by Nowsherwan which was an invention of Bozorgmehr, Nowsherwan's wise minister. There was also the presence of several Indian translators in the royal courts of the Sassanids[7] and ever-growing commercial and trade relations between the two countries, followed by the constant trail of traders' caravans.[8]

With the advent of Islam and the subsequent gradual conversion of the Iranians to Islam particularly after the end of Yazdgerd III, the last Iranian king in 652 CE which led to the end of the Sassanid rule in Iran, Islam entered the Indian subcontinent via Iran. Keeping in view the historical–intellectual traditions of this region, the migrant mystics and Sufis from Iran played a very important role in the dissemination of Islam in India. After the fall of Yazdgerd III, some Iranian Zoroastrians migrated to India and now the world's largest population of Zoroastrians is the Parsi community in India. In the modern era, the Parsi community have contributed significantly to India in the areas of politics, industry, science, and culture. Prominent Indian Parsis include Dadabhai Naoroji (three times president of Indian National Congress), Field Marshal Sam Manekshaw, nuclear energy scientist HomiBhabha, industrialist JRD Tata and the Tata family. So the Iranian culture was effectively grafted on the Indian soil and consequently the ever existing cordial relations between the two people were further enhanced. It is also considered as the beginning of the influence of the Persian language which developed more and more with the passage of time.

LANGUAGE AND LITERATURE

The rulers of Iranian origin ruled the Indian subcontinent for about 800 years starting from the Ghaznavid period to the British period, i.e., up to the year 1857 CE from when the British rule in undivided India began and lasted upto the year 1947 CE. During these eight centuries, the rulers in India played an important role in the promotion and spread of Persian language and literature and consequently the Iranian culture. During the 11th century, Abu Reyhan al-Biruni, the famous versatile scholar of Iran, visited India during the Ghaznavid period. He wrote his famous Kitab-ul-Hind in Arabic, which involved a detailed study of Indian customs, traditions and the Indian way of life. He studied Sanskrit manuscripts to check earlier Arabic writings on India. Al-Biruni composed about 20 books on India—both originals and translations.

With emergence of Mughal rule in India and the rise of the Safavid Empire in Iran the relations between India and Iran were many faceted, covering politics, diplomacy, culture, literature and trade. The second king of the famous Mughal dynasty was Humayun who after the defeat at the hands of Afghan Sher Shah Suri fled to Iran and as are sult of military help by Shah Tahmasp Safavi, was able to return to India accompanied by a number of Iranian scholars and poets. It was during the reign of Humayun, and due to the acquaintance and long stay of himself and his family in Iran, the number of poets, writers, scholars and Sufi saints who migrated from Iran to the subcontinent increased gradually.

As already mentioned, the sweet language of Persian had been the official language in this region and during this long span of time thousands of books had been written in Persian by the scholars and poets of the Indian subcontinent on different subjects. The history of this period had been written invariably in Persian. In addition of anthologies and Diwans of poetry, Persian dictionaries are among the most important works compiled. There have been more than one hundred Persian dictionaries compiled in India. Many translations had also been done and even religious books of Hindus like Ramayana, and Upanishads were translated into Persian. Even today many books of Persian language are translated into Urdu and other languages and the books written in the subcontinent are rendered in Persian. The process of cultural exchange between the two nations has continued and it is hoped that this dialogue between the two civilizations will further enhance.

DIASPORA

There is a small Indian community in Iran. There are Hindu temples in Bandar Abbas and Zahedan as well as a Sikh Gurudwara in Zahedan and Tehran. There is also small community of Iranian nationals residing in Mumbai, Pune and Hyderabad and the Iranian restaurants in these cities are famous for Irani Chai (tea) and delicious cuisine. A growing number of Iranian students are enrolled at universities in India, most notably in Pune and Bangalore and there are about 8,000 Iranian students studying in India.

STRATEGIC RELATIONS

Independent India and Iran established diplomatic links on 15 March 1950. But with the establishment of Islamic Republic in Iran in 1979 anew phase of engagement between India and Iran was marked by exchange of high level visits of dignitaries to each other's capitals which discussed a whole range of bilateral issues including economic cooperation, energy security, expansion of bilateral trade, surface transport, and regional issues and common concerns about terrorism.

Following the victory of Islamic revolution in Iran in February 1979, relations between Iran and India strengthened momentarily. The two countries share many common strategic interests. Since the victory of Islamic revolution in Iran in 1979 on one pretext or other the United States and its European partners have continued their illegal economic sanctions against the people of Iran. Thus, Iran is replacing the United States and its European partners with the Asian countries in particular India.

Iran is the second largest supplier of crude oil to India, supplying more than half million barrels of oil per day, and consequently India is one of the largest foreign investors in Iran's oil and gas industry. In 2011, annual oil trade between India and Iran was US$ 15.9 billion and via third party countries like UAE this figure touches $30 billion despite the illegally imposed economic sanctions and bilateral trade between India and Iran is even increasing due to the close and cordial relations and deep under-standing existing between two brotherly countries.

India welcomed Iran's inclusion as an observer state in the SAARC regional organization. In June 2009, Indian oil companies announced their plan to invest US$ 5 billion in developing an Iranian gas field in the

Persian Gulf. A highway between Zaranj and Delaram (Zaranj-Delaram Highway) was built with financial support from India. The Chabahar port has also been jointly financed by Iran and India.

The Iranian port of Chabahar located on the Makran coast of the Sistan and Baluchistan province of Iran criss-crosses some of the most important international corridors and is considered as one of the most strategic transit locations. It is often referred to as the 'GoldenGate' to the landlocked Commonwealth of Independent States (CIS) countries and Afghanistan. From India's point of view, the strategic importance of Chabahar is immense. It not only gives access to the oil and gas resources in Iran but also provides access to Central Asian Republics. India and Iran have already taken initiatives to enhance connectivity through bilateral agreements.

In April 2008, an important initiative was taken by both countries when India and Iran signed an agreement to establish a new rail link between Iran and Russia. India offered assistance for technical training of personnel, railroad signalling projects as well as the supply of locomotives and spare parts. The trilateral agreement between the governments of India, Iran and Afghanistan to develop the Chabahar route through Melak, Zaranj and Delaram will also facilitate regional trade and transit and thus contribute to regional economic prosperity. During the current visit of the External Affairs Minister, the proposed North-South corridor linking Russia with Iran was also discussed with the objective of clearing the hurdles. The potential of these corridors are immense. India's recent decision to invest USD100 million in free trade zone in Chabahar can be viewed as a forward movement in terms of enhancing bilateral ties. India sees Iran as a way to reconnect to its longstanding trade routes to Central Asia and onward into Russia and Europe despite US and her allies illegal sanctions against Iran. India with the help of the International North-South Corridor, uses Iranian ports, highways, and railroads to connect to parts of Europe in half the time required by current trade routes through Egypt's Suez Canal.

Given India's geopolitical position with Iran, it sees Iran as a strategic long-term partner in particular beyond 2014 when US forces withdraw from Afghanistan. India and Iran have also been working to build the regional transport networks—International North South Transport Corridor, which will help connect South, Central and West Asia to Europe for regional economic development. Equally important is the regional security dynamics, particularly the developments in Afghanistan in the post-2014 scenario. Both India and Iran have stakes in the stability of Afghanistan. In past, India-Iran and Russia have jointly cooperated on Afghanistan. In the light of the US withdrawal in 2014, India and Iran need to evolve strategies to help Afghanistan in rebuilding their country. These efforts could include building infrastructure connecting Afghanistan with Central Asia via Iran. In addition, regional countries like Russia and China will have to play a far more active role in Afghanistan's economic development.

India and Iran are in discussions for the setting up of a number of projects such as the IPI gas pipeline project, a long term annual supply of 5 million tons of LNG, development of the Farsi oil and gas blocks, South Pars gas field and LNG project, Chahbahar container terminal project and Chahbahar-Zaranj railway project, etc. Both countries have set up joint ventures such as the Madras Fertilizer Company and the Chennai Refinery. Indian companies such as ESSAR, OVL, etc. have a presence in Iran. The State Bank of India (SBI) has a representative office in Tehran. India is also a member of the International North-South Corridor project. The two countries are in the process of finalizing a Bilateral Investment Promotion and Protection Agreement (BIPPA) and a Double Taxation Avoidance Agreement (DTAA). Both the countries hold regular bilateral talks on economic and trade issues at the Indo-Iran Joint Commission Meeting (JCM) and also hold Joint Business Council (JBC) meetings regularly.

The two countries have in place several bilateral consultative mechanisms at various levels whose meetings take place regularly. In addition, the Institute of Defence Studies and Analyses (IDSA) of India and the Institute of Political and International Studies (IPIS) of Iran hold regular round table to exchange views and ideas on bilateral and multilateral issues. Views are exchanged on combating global terrorism, energy security, the North-South Transport Corridor, developments in Afghanistan and regional security and stability. Till now nine sessions of the Strategic Dialogue between Iran and India have been conducted.

India and Iran maintain regular cultural and educational exchanges. AMoU was signed in January 2008 between the Indian Council for Cultural Relations (ICCR), New Delhi and the Iranian Cultural Heritage, Handicrafts and Tourism Organization (ICHHTO) on holding of "Days of Culture" in two countries. To give further push to the cultural ties and increase people to people contact between the two countries, the External Affairs Minister of India, Mr. Salman Khurshid during his recent visit to Iran on May 4, 2013 inaugurated the Cultural Centre of India in Tehran. Iran has two Cultural Centers in Delhi and Mumbai. Therefore, opening up of the Centre is significant from a historical and cultural context. To enhance people-to-people contacts, the two sides felt the need to liberalise the visa regime. India over the years has emerged as one of the favourite tourist destinations for Iranian tourists and every year around 40,000 Iranians visit India for various purposes.

In past few years both India and Iran have been working towards managing its energy and economic cooperation under the shadow of the US and European Union (EU) sanctions. Despite the tightening of sanctions, India did not halt the import of crude oil from Iran. Iran was India's second largest supplier of oil. India is trying to expand trade in other commodities like tea, pharma, automobile, electronics, spare parts and agricultural products. India has already approved USD364 million (20 billion rupees) fund to provide reinsurance to local refineries that process Iranian crude oil and the quantum of the fund can be raised in future.

Iran has been able to manage both these challenges by developing strong political, economic and strategic relations with the states in the region and beyond. Iran and India look towards consolidating their bilateral relations. It is in this context that the recent visit of External Affairs Minister, Salman Khurshid merits some attention. This is yet another diplomatic push towards strengthening the existing partnership between the two regional actors. Earlier, the visit of the Indian Prime Minister, Manmohan Singh to Iran on August 28, 2012 to participate in the NAM summit was a clear indication of New Delhi's desire to give new impetus to bilateral relations and enhance economic cooperation. The Prime Minister said: "there is lot of interest in doing business with India and getting Indian investment in infrastructure. There are of course difficulties imposed by western sanction, but subject to that I think we will explore ways and means of developing our relations with Iran". After the Indian Prime Minister's visit, a new thrust was given to the bilateral relations. Subsequently, several high-level visits have taken place from both sides.

Significant among the various interactions has been the recent 17th India-Iran Joint Economic Commission meeting held in Tehran on May 4, 2013. During this visit many MoUs were signed and four important areas were identified.

1. Regional connectivity
2. Enhancing bilateral trade and economic cooperation
3. Cooperation on regional security issues
4. Enhancing cultural and people-to-people contact.

On regional connectivity, both sides agreed to work on a trilateral transit agreement involving Afghanistan. A draft agreement is expected to start soon. India's participation in Chabahar port project has been under discussion for the last few years but the decision to upgrade the Chabahar port was conveyed during the External Affairs Minister's visit. India and Iran bilateral trade during 2011–2012 was USD 15.9 billion as compared to 12.8 billion in 2007–2008. During the External Affairs Minister's visit, both countries have decided to increase the bilateral trade to USD 25 billion in the next four years.

There are other ways of enhancing energy cooperation between the two countries. Since Iran has a strong petro-chemical base, it would provide investment opportunities to Indian companies and they can export finished products to India. Moreover, the feasibility study of deep sea pipeline project has been carried out and the prospects will soon be discussed.

Regarding Iran's nuclear program for peaceful purposes India's position has been very clearly articulated on this issue. India has always emphasized that Iran has a right for peaceful use of nuclear energy while fulfilling its obligations owing to its membership of Nuclear Non-Proliferation Treaty (NPT). India has urged all sides to resolve the issue diplomatically through discussions and negotiations.

The recent visit of the External Affairs Minister of India to Tehran can be viewed as continuation of new bilateral relations as both sides are attempting to reenergize economic cooperation and enhance regional connectivity. Iran's relationship with India in the last decade has been built on the strong underpinnings of ancient links and goes beyond bilateral ties. India is also continuing pro-active diplomacy to secure its core national interests by maintaining and strengthening further the political, economic and cultural relations with Iran.

Thus, we can conclude that the ancient historical brotherly links between India and Iran are on the threshold of strategic relations.

REFERENCES

[1] Prof. Hehmat, Ali Asghar, Sarzamin-i-Hind, Tehran University, Tehran, 1337, 1958, p. 36.

[2] Shehabi, Khorasani Ali Akbar, Rawabit-i-Iran-o-Hind, Tehran, 13161 1937, p. 58. Also see foreword by Prof. Mohammad Moqaddam on Dr. Hyder Shahryar Naqvi's Farhang Nevisiye Farsi dar Hind-o-Pakistan, Ministry of Education, Tehran, 1341/1962, p. 19.

[3] For example see Farsnameye Ibn Balkhi, edited by R.A. Nicholson, Cambridge, 1921, 25, 28, and 50, Masudi, Muruj-al-Dhahab, Beirut, 1965, II, p. 132.

[4] S.M.R. Jalali Naini, Hind Dar Yek Negah, Shirazeh Publication, Tehran, 1997, p. 7.

[5] Tabari, Mohammad Jarir, Tarikh, al-Umam va al-Muluk, Leiden, 1964, I, p. 66; Ibn-i-Miskawayh, "Tajarib al-Umam," Leiden, 1909, I, p. 153.

[6] Mustaufi, Hamdullah, "Tarikh-i-Guzide", Tehran, 1983.

[7] Ali b. Mohammad b. Bal'ami, "Tarikh-i-Bal'ami," Tehran, 1962, pp. 1098–1099.

[8] Shustary, A.M.A., Outlines of Islamic Culture, Lahore, 1966, I, pp. 30–31.

Impact of Intra-Regional Conflicts in West Asia on India-Iran Relations

Prasanta Kumar Pradhan

India-Iran relations have been affected by a number of factors in the past and the relationship continues to be shaky even today with a number of challenges on the way. Among many other factors the intra-regional conflicts in the region have played a crucial role in affecting the India-Iran relations. It should also be mentioned here that in many of the intra-regional conflicts, Iran itself has been a major party to the conflict. Thus, Iran being a party to the conflict naturally affects India's relationship with Iran as well as other countries of the region. India has adopted a balances policy in West Asia and distanced itself from the regional conflicts. But the conflicts among the countries of the region have affected India's relationship with them. Thereby, this paper intends to examine the impact of the intra-regional conflicts in West Asia on the India-Iran relations.

INDIA'S INTERESTS IN WEST ASIA

India has huge stakes and interests with all the countries of West Asia. India's relationship with the West Asian countries has been moving in an upward direction especially during the last two decades. The region is important for India for its trade, energy supply, the presence of Indian expatriate workers and for security reasons. India's total trade with the region at present is around US$ 250 billion. The Gulf countries are the primary source of energy for India. The presence of around 6.5 million strong Indian community working and living in the region is an important link between India and the region. Their safety and security is an important concern for India as well. The recent growth of terrorist elements has made India and some countries of West Asia to join hands together to fight the menace. Similarly, both India and the West Asian countries have been victims of piracy in the Indian Ocean. Both India and some Gulf countries are mulling over plans to cooperate in dealing with the pirates in the high seas. Besides these, other elements such as criminal elements, arms smuggling, drugs peddling, etc. are some other issues of mutual interests between India and West Asia.

The vastness of the region, its geography, different history, culture and political and economic systems are some of the important factors which determine regional politics and security. At present, there are three major players in the region—Iran, Saudi Arabia and the Gulf Cooperation Council (GCC), and Israel. India has stakes with all of them for various reasons.

India has interests with the GCC in economic, political, security and strategic fields. In recent times both the countries have been looking for new areas of cooperation and are trying to improve their relationship. Economic relations have been the backbone of India-GCC ties, with trade and business growing steadily. The Gulf region has also been a lucrative market for Indian manufactured goods like textiles, spices, food products, and lately, electrical goods and machineries and IT products. At present India's total trade with the GCC countries as US$ 158.4 billion.[1] The GCC countries are a primary source of energy for India. In 2012–13 the GCC countries supplied 83.74 million tonnes of crude oil worth over US$ 63 billion.[2] Nearly 6.5 million expatriate workers from India, constitute the largest workforce in the GCC countries, which prefer Indian workers as they are generally found to be skilled, efficient, low-waged and law-abiding.[3] Protecting the interests of the Indian workers has been an important objective of Indian foreign policy in the region.

For India, Iran is an important country in the region, due to its geopolitical and strategic location, long coastline along the Gulf, and its influence over the Strait of Hormuz, and an important source of energy make it an important country in the region. Cooperation in sectors like investment in upstream and downstream activities in the oil sector, LNG/natural gas tie-ups and secure modes of transport have been mooted by both the countries. Investment in sectors like oil and gas, steel, fertilizer, infrastructure and railways is being considered. Good ties with Iran would provide India an access route to Central Asiaand both could play an active role in Afghanistan. India, Iran and Afghanistan are discussing to develop the Chahbahar route through Melak, Zaranj and Delaram, which would facilitate regional trade and transit, to Afghanistan and Central Asia. India has also constructed the Zaranj–Delaram road in Afghanistan. India and Iran have signed an agreement to give Indian goods heading for Central Asia and Afghanistan, a preferential treatment and tariff reductions at Chahbahar.[4] This will help India transport its goods, including humanitarian supplies, to Afghanistan and Central Asia. India is also helping Iran to develop the Chahbahar port, which would give India access to the oil and gas resources in Iran and the Central Asian states. Maritime security is also another area of mutual concern for India and Iran.

Israel has emerged as another important country for India ever since the diplomatic ties were established between the two countries in 1992. Both the countries are cooperating in the areas of trade, science and technology, agriculture and military technology. In recent times, both the countries have intensified their cooperation over issues such as counter-terrorism and have increased cooperation in military and intelligence fields, and has also emerged as a major defence supplier for India.

INTRA-REGIONAL CONFLICTS IN WEST ASIA

Saudi-Iran Rivalry

Saudi-Iranian relations have witnessed severe bitterness since the Islamic Revolution of 1979. The 1979 takeover of the Grand Mosque in Mecca by Juhayman al Utaibi, and the charges of Iranian involvement in it and the subsequent demonstration by the Iranian pilgrims during the Hajj pilgrimage, the killing of more than 400 Iranian pilgrims in 1987 by the Saudi security forces during a protest, etc. have further depleted the relationship. During the Iran–Iraq war of 1980–1988, Saudi Arabia supported Iraq against Iran; on the other hand Iran called the Al Saud regime un-Islamic and openly called for its overthrow, and criticized the Saudi regime's relationship with the United States.[5]

Saudi Arabia's relations with Iran have been strained for a number of reasons. Firstly, the Ideological rivalry, wherein Saudi's allegation of Iran inciting the Shia population in Saudi Arabia's Eastern Province, and on the other hand the Iranian allegation of Saudi Arabia inciting Iran's Sunni population, secondly, regional power struggle between the two, thirdly, the Iranian nuclear programme, and lastly, the close Saudi-US relations. Saudi Arabia, having the two holiest sites of Islam, Mecca and Medina on its soil, has been claiming to be the world leader of Muslims. It has also used Islam as a tool in its foreign policy to spread its influence among other Muslim countries. The Saudis have spent millions of dollars all over the Muslim world to spread their own influence as well as the Sunni Wahhabi brand of Islam. Iran has challenged the Saudi leadership of the Muslim world and sought to take over that role.[6] In recent times, the Iranian nuclear programme has been a major point of suspicion and contention between the two countries. Saudi Arabia has questioned the "peaceful" nature of the programme and has supported the USA in imposing sanctions against

Iran. Saudi Arabia's apprehension lies in the fact that a nuclear Iran would drastically alter the balance of power in the Gulf. It will increase Iranian strategic influence, at the same time, it would also challenge the Saudi authority in the region. This kind of a rivalry between two important regional players in the Gulf region poses a challenge for India's foreign policy in the region.

GCC-Iran Tensions

The GCC-Iran conflictual relationship has been a major source of instability in the region. The GCC was formed in 1981 in response to the Iranian Revolution of 1979. After the Islamic Revolution, Ayatollah Khomeini openly declared his intention to export his brand of Islam and support the Shias in other countries of the region in order to overthrow the neighbouring Sunni regimes. Khomeini declared that: "Our revolution is not limited to the boundaries of Iran. Economic and political difficulties should not compel our officials to forgo the principal task of exporting our lofty Islamic Revolutionary goals ... The true meaning of export of our revolution is to awaken the Muslims and their governments so that they can change themselves and not allow their precious resources to be plundered by anti-Muslim outsiders."[7] This posed a challenge, both in terms of ideology and national interest, to the Arab Gulf countries, particularly Saudi Arabia, whose claims to be the leader of the Muslim world, as well as to remain the regional super power, were challenged by the new Iranian regime. It also increased the vulnerabilities of other smaller Gulf Sheikhdoms who also use Islam as the legitimising force to continue their regimes and have good numbers of Shias populating their countries.[8] Similarly, the territorial dispute over the three islands, namely Abu Musa, Greater Tunb and Lesser Tunb in the Gulf, which are claimed by the UAE are a major source of tension between GCC and Iran. While Iran claims that historical facts are in its favour and the islands were handed over to Iran by the British, acting on behalf of Sharjah and Ras al Khayma.[9] GCC supports the right of the UAE to "regain sovereignty over her three islands: the Greater and the Lesser Tunbs and Abu Musa, and over the territorial waters, the airspace, the continental shelf, and the economic zone of the three islands, as they are an integral part of the State of the United Arab Emirates."[10] Iran has also opened two administrative offices in Abu Musa which, it claims, are for the purpose of ship registration and maritime rescue. The GCC fears that this will give Iran greater control over shipping traffic through the Strait of Hormuz.[11]

The Iraqi invasion of Kuwait in 1991, created further instability in the region. The war threatened to limit India's access to Iran, particularly, the importing of energy from that country.[12] Saddam Hussain's attack on Kuwait certainly threw up a challenge for India's foreign policy towards the Gulf region, which hampered India's relations with the other countries of the region.[13] Saddam's aggression on Kuwait brought the Western forces to the Gulf region. They were stationed all over the GCC countries to launch attack on Iraq. Even after the end of the war and execution of Saddam Hussain, American forces still maintained their bases in all the GCC countries and provide security to the Gulf monarchies. The presence of the American forces in the neighbouring GCC countries has been a key concern for Iran. Iran feels that it has been surrounded by the American forces in all its neighbouring countries from Pakistan and Afghanistan in east, to Central Asia in north and in the GCC countries to the West. Iran suggests that any security architecture in the Gulf region should include the countries of the region only and the external powers should have no role in Gulf security. On the other hand, the GCC countries, who are close allies of the US, feel threatened by the growing Iranian might and intent. In the present context, they cannot leave the US and believe Iran to build regional security architecture in the Gulf. Thus the conflict between the GCC and Iran over the presence of the US troops in the region will continue in the foreseeable future. It seems the GCC–Iran relationship will remain antagonistic for many years to come as the areas of convergence of interests still remain unexplored or obstructed. India cannot afford to take sides in this conflict for regional dominance.

Iranian Nuclear Controversy

The controversy over the Iranian nuclear programme which started in 2002 has become a passionately debated issue in the region and beyond. The West and the neighbouring Gulf Arab states have alleged that Iran is enriching Uranium with an intention to make nuclear weapons. This has been a major concern for the countries of the region who fear shifting of the balance of power significantly in favour of Iran if it goes nuclear. They also allege that Iran intends to militarily dominate the Gulf region by making strong efforts in enriching Uranium. Iran has claimed that being a signatory of the NPT it has got all the rights to develop its nuclear programme for peaceful uses. Though there are conflicting reports of the Iranian nuclear enrichment capabilities and progress, the issue has gained a lot of international publicity.

The issue was discussed in the IAEA and voted upon. India voted against Iran both the times in 2005 and 2009 which upset Iran, who believes that India's vote has been coerced and India has bowed before the pressure from the US and other Western countries. India has clearly stated that it does not support Iran in making a nuclear bomb. India has also asked Iran to come clean over its nuclear programme so as to avoid any ambiguity in the minds of the West and the neighbouring Arab Gulf states. Such a position of India on the nuclear controversy has come to hamper the India-Iran relations at a time when the relationship was moving upwards after the signing of a defence cooperation agreement in 2001. Though in the explanation of the vote in 2009 India clarified that this decision "cannot be the basis of a renewed punitive approach or new sanctions",[14] this has not helped to remove the strains from the relationship. Despite the IAEA votes, India realises the importance of Iran and is against imposing more sanctions on Iran. India believes that the issue should be resolved peacefully through dialogue and negotiations. Though India is serious on improving its relationship with Iran, the Iranian nuclear controversy stands as a hindrance on the way, as it has created misunderstandings in Iran over the actual Indian intentions.

India-Iran relationship has been affected by the sanctions imposed by the West on Iran. India's trade, especially, import of oil from Iran has been affected by the sanctions, as channel for payments has emerged as a major problem for India. The banks through which India made the payments to Iran have come under the sanctions thus creating problems of payments which hinders the smooth conduct of trade. But despite the sanctions both the countries decided in 2012 to make 45 percent of payment for oil in Indian rupee and the rest of the amount through other modes.[15] Both countries agreed on the percentage after meetings between officials of the Reserve Bank of India and the Central Bank of Iran. But Iran has been reluctant to receive payments in Indian currency beyond 45 percent while India proposes to make the full payment in its own currency. In turn, Iran has turned down India's request for full payment in Indian currency for oil imports.[16] In recent years, India's crude imports from Iran has fallen significantly as a result of the sanctions on Iran. In 2009–10 Iran was the second largest supplier of crude oil to India supplying 22.08 million tonnes only after Saudi Arabia who supplied 26.88 million tonnes of crude.[17] In 2012–13, crude oil supply from Iran has come down to 13.22 million tonnes.[18] As a result of falling imports from Iran, India has relied upon imports from Iraq and other Gulf countries.

Iran-Israel Conflict

At present the relationship between Iran and Israel is at an all-time low. Leaders of both the countries have kept no secret of their bitterness towards each other. The war between the Hezbollah and Israel in 2006 has led to the deterioration of the relationship. Israel accuses Iran of funding and supporting the Lebanon-based Hezbollah which is targeting Israel and is a threat to its national security. Iran is also accused to have been supporting the Palestinian Hamas in its activities against Israel. Thus, when the controversy over the nuclear programme of Iran came out in open, Israel called for more international pressure on Iran. Israel also supported use of economic sanctions against Iran. While the George Bush administration included Iran in the "Axis of Evil" along with Iraq and North Korea in 2002, the Obama administration has adopted policy of rapprochement towards Iran. President Obama has also called for more talks and negotiations with Iran over the nuclear programme. Israel has expressed its displeasure towards such policies of the US towards Iran. Israel has also threatened to launch an attack on Iranian nuclear sites. On the other hand, Iran has accused Israel of assassinating its nuclear scientists and launching cyber attacks on its nuclear programme.

Iran and the Israel-Palestine Conflict

India has from the beginning supported the Palestine cause. Despite India's growing relationship with Israel, its position on Palestine remains undiluted. India was the first Non-Arab country to recognize the Palestine Liberation Organization (PLO) as sole and legitimate representative of the Palestinian people in 1974. India recognised the State of Palestine in 1988 and opened its Representative Office in 1996 in Gaza, which has now been shifted to Ramallah since 2003.[19] India believes that "There can be no durable peace in West Asia without a just and comprehensive settlement, based on the realisation by the Palestinian people of their inalienable right to a state of their own with internationally recognised borders, living side by side and in peace and security with Israel."[20]

But there has been a change in Iranian policy towards the conflict after the Iranian Revolution in 1979, which brought Ayatollah Khomeini to power. Both the countries enjoyed warm relations till 1979 with increasing trade and commerce between them. The overthrow of Shah of Iran led to the deterioration of ties, as the new Islamic regime refused to recognise Israel as a State. It rather funded and supported the organisations like Hezbollah in Lebanon and the Hamas in Palestine to fight against Israel. Though

Iran supports statehood for Palestine, its methods of achieving the same is different from that of India's. Thus, because of the differences in the approach of Iran and India towards the Israel-Palestine conflict, no consensus has been possible for a strong cooperation between the two countries over the issue.

ARAB SPRING AND FURTHER AGGRAVATION OF REGIONAL TENSIONS

The onset of the popular uprising known as the Arab Spring has further complicated the regional politics. It has not only brought about regimes changes in some countries but also changed the relationship among the countries, thus affecting the regional balance of power. While the Arab countries were witnessing protests against their rulers, Iran continued to support the protesters against their rulers. Many in Iran claimed that the Arab uprisings are inspired by their Islamic Revolution of 1979 and claimed that the Arab Spring is the 'second Islamic Awakening' in the region. Iran also tried to internationalise the issue.

The Arab Spring has aggravated the relationship between two important players in the region—Saudi Arabia and Iran. It has led to the appearance of temporary uncertainties over the regional security of the Gulf region. Iran's support for the protesters intended to overthrow the authoritarian Arab rulers, thereby thus changing the Arab world order was against the Saudi interest in the region. Saudi Arabia perceives itself as the custodian of the Arab affairs and wants Iran to stay away from the internal affairs of the Arab countries. Such kind of Saudi thinking aims at continuing its influence over the Arab politics and keeping Iran away from it.[21] Such a tense situation in the relationship between two important countries in the region poses a challenge for India's foreign policy. India has important stakes and interests with both the countries, thus India cannot take sides in this situation. As India tries its best to calibrate its policies carefully, the situation is certainly proving to be more testing. Similarly, the GCC as a whole is also at odds with Iran. Balancing interests between Iran and the GCC will remain a challenge for India.

Iranian response to the protests in Syria was completely different from that of its approach towards the other Arab countries. Bashar Al Assad is an important ally of Iran in the region for several reasons and Iran cannot afford to lose Syria at this juncture. Thus, Iran has put in all its efforts to save the regime of Assad and maintain its strategic influence over the region. The deteriorating situation has proved to be more challenging for

Iran. World opinion has been sharply divided over the developments in Syria. While Iran and Russia do not want regime change or use of force against Assad regime, other countries such as the US, EU, Saudi Arabia and other GCC countries are enthusiastic about a military intervention to remove Assad. Countries like Saudi Arabia and Qatar have been supplying arms to the Syrian opposition forces. This kind of a situation becomes challenging for India's foreign policy in the region. While India favours intervention at the behest of the UN, other countries have their own different views. Clearly, Saudi Arabia and Iran are the two most important regional players in the Syrian conflict, where in both of them are rallying for more support of their views. Saudi Arabia has even gone to the extent of quitting its UNSC seat, alleging that the world body has not done enough to end the violence in Syria.

The Arab Spring has also brought to the fore a sharp sectarian division between the Shias and Sunnis in the politics of West Asia with Iran and Saudi Arabia leading the respective blocks. The regional politics of West Asia has created friends and allies of these two major players. The small Arab Gulf countries such as Bahrain, Oman, UAE, Kuwait and Qatar have remained staunch allies of Saudi Arabia and their bond has been further strengthened with the formation of the GCC. Beyond the Gulf region other countries such as Jordan and Egypt have remained friends of the Saudi Arabia led Sunni block. On the other hand, Syria, Hezbollah in Lebanon and Iraq are the major forces at present representing the Shia block in the region. The Arab Spring has further worsened the sectarian conflict and at present it seems that the sectarian politics would remain in the political landscape of West Asia in the foreseeable future. If the situation continues to remain tense in the region over sectarian issue, it would certainly affect India-Iran relationship.

CONCLUSION

India-Iran relationship has been affected by a number of intra-regional conflicts in West Asia. This has primarily happened because of the deep animosity and clash of interests among the regional powers. Ever since 1979 when the Islamic regime took over power, it wanted to project itself as a completely different entity than the previous Shah regime. The Islamic nature of the regime which was ideologically challenging for the neigh-bouring Sunni-Arab regimes became the main issue of conflict between them. Ayatollah Khomeini's open declarations against the Arab regimes made them feel insecure and they began to feel that Iran is intending to dominate the region both politically and militarily. The revolution was followed by the war against Iraq which continued for eight long years. Only a few years after the end of war against Iraq, the region witnessed Iraqi aggression on Kuwait which brought the external forces to the region which has been another major point of discontent between Iran and the GCC countries. Thus, Iran has been an active and a prominent actor involved in the regional conflicts. India, on the other hand, does not have much leverage to play any proactive role in the conflicts in the region. Iran's involvement in the conflicts has been an important factor in affecting its relationship with India as the later's position over these conflicts has not always been favourable to Iran. The controversy over Iranian nuclear programme, voting against it at the IAEA and sanctions against the country etc. has further aggravated the situation and has not allowed a strong foundation to be built in the India-Iran relationship. It is for these reasons that India always want peace and stability in the West Asian region.

REFERENCES

[1] "Export–Import Data Bank", Department of Commerce, Ministry of Commerce and Industry, Government of India.

[2] "Export–Import Data Bank", Department of Commerce, Ministry of Commerce and Industry, Government of India.

[3] Prakash C. Jain, "An Incipient" Diaspora: Indians in the Gulf region", in Prakash C. Jain, ed., *Indian Diaspora in West Asia: A Reader*, New Delhi, Manohar, 2007, pp. 198–9.

[4] Trade Promotion Organisation of Iran, at http://en.tpo.ir/documents/document/12236/12247/portal.aspx.

[5] Gwenn Okruhlik, 'Saudi Arabian-Iranian Relations: External Rapprochement and Internal Consolidation', *Middle East Policy*, Vol. 10, No. 2, 2003, p. 116.

[6] Al-Mani, Saleh, "The Ideological Dimension in Saudi-Iranian Relations", in Jamal S. al-Suwaidi, ed., *Iran and the Gulf: A Search for Stability*, Abu Dhabi: The Emirates Center for Strategic Studies and Research, 1996, pp. 158–74.

[7] Quoted in M.E. Ahrari, Bribid Starkey, and Nader Entessar, 'Iran, the Persian Gulf and the Post-Cold War Order', in M.E. Ahrari (ed.), *Change and Continuity in the Middle East: Conflict Resolution and Prospects for Peace*, MacMillan, London, 1996, p. 80.

[8] Prasanta Kumar Pradhan, "The GCC–Iran Conflict and its Strategic Implications for the Gulf Region", *Strategic Analysis*, Vol. 35, No. 2, 2011, p. 266.

[9] For an analysis of the Iranian perspective of the conflict over the three islands see Pirouz Mojtahed-Zadeh, 'The Issue of the UAE Claims to Tunbs and Abu Musa vis-à-vis Arab-Iranian Relationships in the Persian Gulf', *Iranian Journal of International Affairs*, Vol. 8, No. 3, Fall 1996, pp. 601–626.

[10] See the "The Closing Statement of the Thirtieth Session of the Supreme Council of the Cooperation Council for the Arab States of the Gulf (GCC) held in Kuwait on 14–15 December 2009, at http://www.gcc-sg.org/eng/indexce7c.html?action=Sec-Show&ID=303.

[11] 'Iran's Island Offices Condemned', *BBC News*, 3 September 2008, at http://news.bbc.co.uk/2/hi/7596339.stm.

[12] Campbell, Kurt M., Patel, Nirav and Weitz, Richard, "The Ripple Effect: India's Responses to the Iraq War", Centre for a New American Society, Working Paper, October 2008, available at http://www.isn.ethz.ch/Digital-Library/Articles/Detail/?ots591=0c54e3b3-1e9c-be1e-2c24-a6a8c7060233&lng=en&id=93646.

[13] Baral, J.K. and Mohanty, J.N., "India and the Gulf Crisis: The Response of a Minority Government", *Pacific Affairs*, Vol. 65, No. 3, Autumn 1992, pp. 368–384.

[14] "Again, India votes against Iran's nuclear programme", *Indian Express*, November 28, 2009, at http://www.indianexpress.com/news/again-india-votes-against-iran-s-nuclear-programme/547319/ .

[15] "India to make 45% of Iran oil payments in rupees", *The Hindu Businessline*, February 7, 2012, at http://www.thehindubusinessline.com/economy/india-to-make-45-of-iran-oil-payments-in-rupees/article2868666.ece.

[16] "Iran rejects India's plea for full rupee payment for oil import", *The Hindu*, October 3, 2013, at http://www.thehindu.com/news/national/iran-rejects-indias-plea-for-full-rupee-payment-for-oil-import/article5182797.ece.

[17] "Export–Import Data Bank", Department of Commerce, Ministry of Commerce and Industry, Government of India.

[18] "Export–Import Data Bank", Department of Commerce, Ministry of Commerce and Industry, Government of India.

[19] Ministry of External Affairs, "India—Palestine Relations", Government of India, New Delhi, January 2013, at http://mea.gov.in/Portal/ForeignRelation/INDIA__PALESTINE_RELATIONS__2013.pdf.

[20] "India raises Palestinian issue", *The Hindu*, September 27, 2012, at http://www.thehindu.com/news/international/india-raises-palestinian-issue/article3942765.ece.

[21] Pradhan, Prasanta Kumar, "Arab Spring: Redefining Regional Security in West Asia", in S.D. Muni and Vivek Chadha (eds.), *Asian Strategic Review*, New Delhi, Pentagon Press, 2013, p. 185.

Indo-Iran Relations: Strands of Cooperation and Potential for Conflicts in the 21ˢᵗ Century

Mohammed Khalid

"Few people have been more closely related in origin and throughout history than the people of India and the people of Iran".

—**Jawaharlal Nehru**
(Discovery of India)

Situated in southwestern Asia, Iran is a mountainous, arid, and ethnically diverse country. Flanking the Persian Gulf on its north, northeast, and east, Iran is located to the north of the Gulf of Oman. Known as Persian Empire in ancient times, the land was conquered by Alexander the Great in about 330 BC and later was invaded by the Romans and Afghans. In late 16ᵗʰ and 17ᵗʰ centuries, the Safavids emerged as native Iranian rulers after a long period of dominance by the outsiders. Nadir Shah captured a large part of Iran in early 18ᵗʰ century. After his death in 1747, Zand rulers, so far dominant in the south, vied for power but were overcome by Qajars in 1794.[1] The Qajars ruled Iran until the rise of Reza Khan who became Minister of war in 1921, Prime Minister in 1923, and took over the state in a coup soon thereafter. In 1925 he proclaimed himself the King Reza Shah, the founder of Pehlavi Dynasty. An ardent nationalist, Reza Shah showed his determination to raise Iran from the depths of decadence, division, corruption and subjugation to foreign (European) powers and build a free, strong and modern Iran.[2]

At the beginning of Second World War, in 1939, Reza Shah declared his country's neutrality in it. The spread and success of Axis (German-Italy-Japan) arms congealed in 1941 the Franco-British-American-Soviet alliance. The allies, to secure Iranian oil fields and in order to provide succor and supplies to Soviet Union through Iran, compelled Reza Shah to abdicate in favour of his son, Mohammed Reza Pehlavi, and leave the country. After the end of the War, there was lot of diplomacy and politicking among the Soviet Union, the US and Britain as the Soviet Union was reluctant to withdraw from Iran citing "threats to Soviet security." However, well after six months of the end of the War, the Soviet and the British forces left Iran in 1946.[3]

Challenged by the other nationalist factions such as Mohammed Mosaddeq (Prime Minister of Iran in 1951–53), who forced the king to leave the country though briefly, Reza Shah ruled the country backed by the United States till January 1979 when, under the circumstances he had to leave Iran and power was handed over to Ayatollah Ruhollah Khomeini who returned to Iran after 14 years of exile, on 11 February 1979. The country was declared as the Islamic Republic of Iran in 1980, based on 1979 constitution and under a Supreme Leader who is the head of state and highest ranking politico-religious authority in the country.

INDO-IRAN RELATIONS

The relations between India and Iran go back to the ancient times. Being geographical neighbours, sharing a common border till 1947, several Persian rulers had maintained close relationship with the rulers of northern India encouraging constant migration of people and helping in the evolution of the Indo-Iranian language and culture. As a consequence, the people of northern India especially Punjab and Iran share significant cultural, linguistic and ethnic characteristics. Such interaction was there in the pre-Islamic period but became a regular feature during the Muslim rule especially with the consolidation of Delhi Sultanate from the 13th century onward. Persian was the official language of the Delhi Sultanate, the Mughal Empire, and their successor states, as well as the language of poetry and literature and the socio-political elite. Persian became the lingua franca of the sub-continent during the reign of Akbar. Even Maharaja Ranjit Singh, the founder of the Sikh Empire in Punjab, made Persian as the language of his court.

During the Qajar rule 1794–1925, the weak rulers of the time were forced to extend many oil concessions to the European powers. Most serious of all was under the Anglo-Russian Agreement of 1907, when Britain and Russia agreed to divide Iran into spheres of influence. The Russians were to enjoy exclusive right to pursue their interests in the northern Iran and the British in the south and east.[4] During this period India and Iran could not maintain the same old-age close relationship. After its independence, India established diplomatic links with Iran in March 1950 and since 1947 both the countries have exchanged high level visits beginning with the visit of Shah of Iran to India in February/March 1956 to the Iranian President Mahmoud Ahmadinejad's visit to New Delhi in April 2008 and Prime Minister Pandit Jawaharlal Nehru's visit to Iran in September 1959 to Prime Minister Manmohan Singh's visit to Tehran in August 2012. Both the countries have exchanged numerous delegations at the ministerial and secretarial level visits. During these visits India and Iran have signed many bilateral agreements such as the Air Services Agreement; Agreement on Transfer of Sentenced Persons; MoU on Cooperation in New and Renewable Energy; MoU on Cooperation in Small Scale Industry between National Small Industries Corporation (NSIC) and Iranian Small Industries and Industrial Parks Organisation (ISIPO); Programme of Cooperation on Science and Technology and MoU on Cooperation between Central Pulp and Paper Research Institute of India (CPPRI) and Gorgan University of Agricultural Science and Natural Resources (GUASNR).[5]

During the last 66 years of independence India's relations with Iran have witnessed many phases. During the Cold War period, relations between the two countries suffered as India, though non-aligned, fostered strong civil and military links with Soviet Union while Iran under Reza Shah enjoyed close ties with the United States. Indo-Iran ties have been reconfigured once again in the changing strategic context of the post-Cold War era. With the end of Cold War, a new thrust was witnessed in Indo-Iranian relations converging around energy security, Central Asia, terrorism emanating from AfPak region, and security concerns etc. India sought to establish closer ties with Iran as the later emerged as a critical oil-partner for India with a potential to provide access to Afghanistan and Central Asia. Converging security interests in war-torn Afghanistan also reinforced this emerging strategic partnership. This closeness reached its peak in 2003 when a Delhi Declaration was signed by the Prime Minister Vajpayee and Iranian President Seyeed Mohammad Khatami on Jan 25, 2003.[6] The Declaration pledged to build a new strategic partnership, urging that the global fight against terrorism should not be based on "double standards". They also discussed Iranian proposal for an overland gas pipeline to India through Pakistan which could ensure a mutually acceptable, secure and stable arrangement for transfer of gas. India's growing engagement with United States and Israel, Iran's continuous close relations with Pakistan, India's Civil Nuclear Deal with United States and its voting against Iranian Nuclear programme at International Atomic Energy Agency (IAEA) in 2005 and 2009 are some of the emerging contentious issues between the two long standing partners in international relations.[7] In the light of emerging contemporary geopolitical realities, there is needed to look at Indo-Iran relations as to what are visible strands of cooperation and potential areas of conflict between the two countries in the times ahead.

Strands of Cooperation

Trade between India and Iran has been the bedrock of their bilateral relations since long. They signed first trade agreement in 1962. Trade has traditionally been buoyed by Indian import of Iranian crude oil resulting in overall trade balance in favour of Iran. India shares 8.1 percent of total Iranian trade. India-Iran trade was US$ 13.4 billion in 2010–11 of which import of Iranian crude oil were US$ 10.9 billion. India's exports to Iran include rice, machinery and instruments, metals, primary and semi finished iron and steel, drugs/pharmaceuticals and chemicals, processed minerals, manmade yarn and fabrics, tea, organic/inorganic/agro chemicals, rubber manufactured products, etc. Indian exports to Iran were worth US$ 2.5 billion in 2010–11.[8] It is believed in India that decisive victory of moderate cleric Hasan Rouhani over conservative hardliners in Iran's recent Presidential elections is promising news and trade may go up in the near future.

In 1994 Iran and Pakistan began discussions to construct a pipeline to deliver natural gas from Iran to Pakistan. Later Iran proposed to extend the pipeline into India and signed a preliminary agreement with India In February 1999. In February 2007, India and Pakistan agreed to pay Iran US$ 4.93 per million British thermal units (US$ 4.67/GJ) but some details relating to price adjustment remained open to further negotiation. In 2009, India withdrew from the project over pricing and security issues. However, in March 2010 India called on Pakistan and Iran for trilateral talks. On 4th September 2012, the project was announced to commence before October 2012 and be completed by December 2014. Given to the usually tense relations between India and Pakistan, India has expressed its apprehensions that Pakistan may pull the plug any time, stopping gas supplies to India. However the newly elected prime minister of Pakistan, Nawaz Sharif has allayed any fears regarding the abandonment of the project and said that the Pakistani government is committed to the fulfillment of the project and targets the first flow of gas from the pipeline in December 2014.[9] If this project materializes, it will be a big boost to Indo-Iran cooperation.

Iran was the second largest supplier of oil to India and lost this position to Iraq due to decreased purchase of oil supplies in the wake of sanctions. India reduced imports by 11 percent, although the government claimed it was part of a long-term strategy to diversify energy resources. There is a chance of increasing Indo-Iran cooperation in the areas of energy. Iranian diplomacy is working to put a liberal and more acceptable face to the US and the West. This reduces the impact of harsh economic sanctions. This will also make India to import more oil from Iran directly. The Mangalore Refinery and Petrochemicals (MRPL) which is Iran's major Indian client to process crude oil, had to halt imports from Iran in April because of the impact of sanctions is now working on plans to resume oil imports from Iran. India is expected to import about 13 million tonnes of crude oil from Iran during 2012–13 and plans to increase crude oil imports from Iran.

India and Iran share common concerns in Afghanistan. As the United States and its NATO allies prepare to withdraw most of their forces from Afghanistan in 2014, Iran and India will have a common objective to help stabilize Afghanistan. This is an important area of cooperation between India and Iran.

India has long and historical relations with Afghanistan and Central Asia. Pakistan more often does not allow transit facility from India to Afghanistan. As there is no land connectivity between the two, India has asked Iran to develop Chabahar Port on the coast of the Gulf of Oman in Sistan and Baluchestan Provinceof Iran. Connectivity through the Chabahar which is a designated free port, could become an important route linking India to Afghanistan and Central Asia. Upgrading the Chabahar Port by investing US$ 100 million in free trade zone will facilitate a transit route for India to the land-locked Afghanistan.[10] India needs to beef up its cooperation with Iran given to the fact that in recent years, China has emerged as major trading partner of Iran and has already offered Euro 60 million credit to Iran to upgrade the Chabahar Port. A key bilateral project is the International North-South Transport Corridor (a ship, rail, and road route for moving freight from South Asia to Europe through Central Asia, the Caucasus, and Russia), which India views as the most strategic project for India's relations with Iran. This corridor will facilitate trade in Eurasia by opening up that enormous market to India.

Bilateral investments between India and Iran have been going on since a long time. Way back in 1965 Chennai Petroleum Corporation Limited (formerly known as Madras Refineries Limited) was established as a joint venture between the Government of India, and National Iranian Oil Company. This is going on since then under different proportions of investments and organizational restructuring. The Irano-Hind Shipping Company was established in 1975 as a Joint Venture between Islamic Republic of Iran Shipping Lines with 51 percent and Shipping Corporation of India with 49 percent share. The company owns 6 oceangoing vessels active in carrying crude oil, bulk and general cargoes. The asset value of the company is approximately US$ 250 million. Madras Fertilizers ltd. was incorporated on December 8, 1966 as a joint venture between GOI and

AMOCO India incorporated of U.S.A in accordance with the Fertilizer Formation Agreement executed on 14.5.1966 with equity contributions of 51 and 49 percent respectively.

Indian Investments in Iran include, US$ 7.34 million investment in Chrome Project in Jogatai near Sabzewar, US$ 4 million investment in Chrome Project in Serbishe near Birjand, Essar Pars Steel, by Essar Group which has investments in Steel and Mining sectors in Iran. Persia Rohit Mines and Industries Company, Tehran. ONGC Videsh Ltd. signed The Exploration Service Contract for Farsi Offshore Exploration Block in December, 2002. In 2005 Tata Steel signed a joint venture agreement with Iranian Mines and Mining Industries Development and Renovation Organisation (Imidro) to set up three plants in Iran.[11]

Having many common cultural traits, India and Iran have maintained regular cultural and educational exchanges. Indian Council for Cultural Relations (ICCR), signed an MoU in January 2008 with Iranian Cultural Heritage, Handicrafts and Tourism Organization to celebrate a cultural week in New Delhi and Mumbai in April–May 2008. India observed its "Days of Culture" at the Niyavaran Palace in Tehran and Hafezia in Shiraz from May 10–17, 2011. Iran Artists Forum and Indian Tourism and Development Corporation (ITDC) too exchange artists and food specialists. In May 2012 Indian Embassy organised an Indian Cultural Week in Tehran. About 8,000 Iranian students study in various universities and institutes in India and approximately 800 Indian students pursue studies in Iran especially theological studies in Qom. India provides 67 scholarships every year to Iranian students under Indian Technical Education Co-operation (ITEC), ICCR, Colombo Plan and IOR-ARC schemes. About 40,000 Iranian tourists visit India every year.[12]

India and Iran are actively involved in other areas of cooperation. For instance both are active in Indian Ocean Rim Association for Regional Cooperation (IOR-ARC) which has been established to promote the sustained growth and balanced development of the region and of the Member States, and to create common ground for regional economic co-operation. Flagship projects of IOR-ARC include Regional Centre for Science and Transfer of Technology (RCSTT), University Student Mobility Program for The Indian Ocean Region (UMIOR), Tourism feasibility study, maritime, cultural promotion, preferential trade agreement, fisheries support unit etc.

India and Iran are two most trading nations in the Indian Ocean. Their Ocean going ships are always at risk due to the presence of Somali pirates in the Gulf of Aden and north-western Indian Ocean. Many of Iranian ships or ships with Iranian crew have been hijacked by these pirates. India too has similar story to tell. To protect its ships in the Indian Ocean, Iran sent its 25th fleet, consisting of Larak logistical warship and the Alborz missile-launching destroyer. Iranian navy has performed many successful rescue operations at the sea and by doing so, Iran's Navy has occasionally flexed its muscles in the fight against piracy. Indian nave also keeps its permanent presence in the Gulf of Aden to protect its Ocean worthy vassals. This is one important area where the two countries can cooperate in the Indian Ocean region.[13]

Potential Areas of Conflict

Iranian nuclear programme and Indian opposition to it is emerging as a major bone of contention between the two countries. As the US and the West feels that it is a weapon oriented and development programme the Arab neighbours of Iran and Israel too feel that Iran's nuclear programme is dangerous for the stability of the region. Supporting the US stance, India voted at the International Atomic Energy Agency (IAEA) in favour of economic sanctions to deter Iran from pursuing a nuclear programme. Many in the circle of international relations argue that the two votes India cast against Iran at the IAEA were coerced votes. This move has forced for a decline in the relationship between the two countries. Due to the signing of civilian nuclear deal with the United States in 2005 which established India as a legitimate nuclear power, bilateral cooperation declined between 2005 and 2008. While India has joined United States and the West to stop Iran from continuing uranium enrichment, Iran argues that it is being discriminated because United States recognizes India's claim as a nuclear power though it has a number of nuclear reactors with some more under construction, and does not allow Iran which has only one reactor.

Another important geopolitical hurdle in normal relations between India and Iran can be anticipated by emerging close equation between India and Israel in the region. Iran is third largest provider of oil to India and simultaneously India heavily relies on Israel for science and technology, defense supplies and fight against terrorism. Some think tanks feel that India could have easily abstained on Iran's nuclear issue. Knowing the risks involved fully well India, aboard its Polar Satellite Launch Vehicle (PSLV), launched the Israeli spy satellite in 2005. This speaks volumes of growing strategic cooperation between Israel and India. For India it is a tricky politics to balance this relationship and manage the situation keeping her own interests in mind.[14]

Similarly, US relations with India have improved dramatically over the recent years, while Iranian relations with US still remain overtly hostile notwithstanding the notable telephonic talks between the US and Iranian President on September 27, 2013, a highest level talk after a gap of 34 years. It is too early to jump to any conclusion on US-Iran relations, but India's relations with United States for sure are bound to be closer further.[15] This was evident from the talks of Indian Prime Minister Manmohan Singh had with the US President Barak Obama in the White House, to address the stalemate in the ties over a civil nuclear deal finalised five years ago. In fact it was after the talks with Manmohan Singh that Obama phoned President Rouhani. Improvement in relations between Iran and United States has a direct bearing on Indo-Iran relations. Again it depends on the outcome in Syria where US tends to support the rebels and Iran is clearly backing Bashar al-Assad regime.

India's relations with Pakistan are normally tense, while Iran always had good working relationship with Pakistan. Since Iran has no diplomatic relations with the United States; the Iranian interest in the United States is represented by the Pakistan Embassy in Washington. Future extension of Iran–Pakistan gas pipeline to India also depends heavily on equations that emerge between Iran and United States, India and Pakistan, and India and Iran. Therefore it can be inferred that contemporary relations and future prospects of Indo-Iran relations cannot be seen in isolation from their equations with Pakistan, Israel and United States.

REFERENCES

[1] Azimi, Fakhreddin (1989). Iran, The Crises of Democracy, I.B. Tauris, London, pp. 1–10.

[2] For the rise of Reza Shah and the condition of Iran before and thereafter, see, Avery, Peter (1965): Modern Iran, Ernest Benn, London, pp. 210–44.

[3] Banani, A. (1961). The Modernisation of Iran, 1921–1941, Stanford University press, pp. 137–43.

[4] Katouzian, Homa (2006). State and Society in Iran: The Eclipse of the Qajars and the Emergence of the Pahlavis, I.B. Tauris, London, pp. 327–40.

[5] "India–Iran Economic Relations", FICCI Publication, available at, http://www. ficci.com/international/75186/Project_docs/India-Iran-Economic—Relations.pdf

[6] For full text of Delhi declaration see, "The Republic of India and the Islamic Republic of Iran "The New Delhi Declaration", available at, http://www. satp.org/satporgtp/countries/india/document/papers/iran_delhidecl.htm

[7] See the interview Ali Ardeshir Larijani, Speaker of the Iranian parliament, to The Indian Express Editor-in-Chief Shekhar Gupta about Israel, India's vote against Iran at IAEA and Iran's right to a "peaceful nuclear programme", published in Indian Express March 12, 2013.

[8] India-Iran Relations, Embassy of India, Tehran, available at, http://www.indianembassy-tehran.ir/india-iran_relations.php

[9] Bhutta, Zafar, "Annual plan 2013–14: Govt. will not scrap Iran gas pipeline project", The Express Tribune, June 13, 2013.

[10] Roy, Meena Singh, "Iran: India's Gateway to Central Asia", Strategic Analysis, Vol. 36, No. 6, November–December 2012, pp. 957–975.

[11] "Tata Steel signs JVs for steel-making, mining in Iran", See more at: http://www.tata.in/company/Media/inside.aspx?artid=PxK2CWUHooY=#sthash.cpe8Cew3.dpuf

[12] "India–Iran Economic Relations", FICCI Publication, *op. cit.*, p. 11.

[13] For a detailed view of Somalia based piracy and its impact on the shipping in the Indian Ocean, see, Khalid, Mohammed, "Somalia and its lawless Coast: India's Growing Security Responsibility in the Indian Ocean", *Journal of Indian Ocean Studies*, Vol. 18, No. 1, April 2010, pp. 67–80.

[14] Beck, Noah, "India, Israel, and Iran", American Thinker, September 20, 2013; also, Khalid, Mohammed, "India and Israel: Strategic Partners on the Indian Ocean Littoral", paper presented at, The Oceanic Conference on International Studies, held from 18–20 July, 2012 at University of Sydney, Australia (unpublished).

[15] Purushothaman, Uma, "American Shadow over India–Iran Relations", Strategic Analysis, Vol. 36, Issue 6, November 2012, pp. 899–910.

[16] Ramana, Siddharth, "The Pakistan Factor in the India–Iran Relationship", Strategic Analysis, Volume 36, Issue 6, November 2012, pp. 837–847.

Engaging with Iran: Contemporary Challenge to India's Foreign Policy

Ashok Alex Luke

INTRODUCTION

As a newly independent nation in 1947 India set out to engage with the rest of the world sharing the vision of a peaceful coexistence. The colonial nightmares together with the devastating events in Hiroshima and Nagasaki shaped some of the principles and objectives of its foreign policy such as world peace, nuclear disarmament, anti-imperialism, anti-colonialism, and anti-racism.[1] During the initial period after independence the thoughts of leaders like Mahatma Gandhi and Jawaharlal Nehru had a profound influence on the policies of the country. Jawaharlal Nehru who was the first prime minister as well as the foreign minister of Independent India was opposed to power blocs and therefore pursued the policy of non-alignment to have full autonomy over its foreign affairs.[2] India's foreign policy can be divided into 3 distinct phases. The initial phase was from 1947 to 1962, the second phase was from 1962 to 1991 and the third phase from 1991 which continues to the present.[3]

THE IDEALISTIC PHASE (1947–1962)

The time from 1947 to 1962 was the period from which India pursued an idealistic foreign policy; during this period India voiced its concerns against some of the colonial and racial practices which existed during that time such as Dutch colonialism in Indonesia and apartheid regime in South Africa. India supported the freedom struggle of third world nations and was one of those who advocated for the greater role of the U.N in world peace and development. During this period India's voice for the third world nations earned it respect among the world community and was regarded as one of its leaders.[4] Nehru believed that due to its non violent freedom struggle India possessed a moral authority in the international system and therefore in 1954 he became the first world leader to propose a ban on nuclear tests, moreover he was widely critical about military alliances such as CEATO and SEANTO. Military build up during his tenure was largely ignored, the importance of which was realized only after the military debacle with China in 1962.[5]

REALISTIC PHASE (1962–1991)

It was only after the 1962 military defeat with China that the nation realised that however idealistic a foreign policy maybe, it should have an adequate military back up, thereafter the 1960's saw a change in India's foreign and security policies. It continued to have a non-aligned policy with a realist oriented, it has even appealed to the United States for military and economic assistance.[6] A sequence of events such as Indo-China war of 1962, the Pakistan-China border agreement of 1963, the Chinese nuclear test of 1964 and the Indo-Pak war of 1965 all paved way for India's pursuance of nuclear weapons. Some within the parliament called for an abandoning of the nonalignment and pursuance of nuclear weapons. It was after the failed attempt of Prime Minister Indira Gandhi to seek nuclear guarantee from the great powers which further culminated in India's Subterranean Nuclear Explosions Project (SNEP). Though India continued for the struggle against colonialism on the one side, on the other hand it no longer had reservations in the use of force to achieve its national means and this was evident in the important role that it had played in the creation of Bangladesh and the signing of Indo-Soviet Friendship Treaty in 1971.[7] The pro-Soviet tilt in India's foreign policy was also visible during this period as India was reluctant to condemn the Soviet invasion of Czechoslovakia in 1968 popularly known as the 'Prague Spring'.[8] During the 1980's the country began to engage more in the matters of Asia and signed several bilateral contracts and increased its UN Peacekeeping engagements. The relations with the United States improved in the latter half of 1980's.[9]

PRAGMATISM (1991-TO THE PRESENT)

Since 1990's there has been a worldview among scholars that geo-economics had replaced geopolitics. This was more evident after the publication of an article by Edward Luttwak, 'From Geopolitics to Geo-Economics' in 1990. Similar to this period elements of liberal internationalism became increasingly visible in Indian foreign and economic policy debates with a view for increased participation in the global economy and a change thus occurred in its foreign policy as a result of its economic reforms accelerating policies for trade and investment and transformed from an inward looking economy to a globally integrated economy.[10]

India's foreign policy in the post cold war has undergone a transformation and has been heavily influenced by the forces of globalisation and there has been a shift from non-alignment to what is popularly called as 'pragmatism'. The international events in the early 1990's like the collapse of the Soviet Union and the rise of the United States as the sole super power, the economic implications of the gulf war as well as the domestic crisis such as the collapse of the monopoly of the congress party, the liberalisation process, the dependence of the Indian economy on international financial institutions all lead to the way for changes in its polices.[11]

> *"Taking about foreign policies, the house must remember that these are not just empty struggles on a chess board. Behind them lie all manner of things. Ultimately foreign policy is the outcome of economic policy, and until India has properly evolved her economic policy, her foreign policy will be rather vague, rather inchoate and will be groping."*

Jawaharlal Nehru in a speech to the Constituent Assembly in December 1947.[12]

Today from the foreign policy perspective, economic prosperity is now seen as the key as India's attainment of great power status rather than being a leader of the third world in their struggle against imperialism. Trade and bilateral relations have been the cornerstone of India's relation with the world. As Finance Minister P Chidambaram stated in 2007 *"The world respects India because of its capacity to emerge as an economic powerhouse."*[13] Today Indian corporates had made significant presence among the world's leading industries and thus has put significant pressures on India's economic diplomacy to represent business interest and attract investments. The CII and FICCI has no become as two powerful lobbies in influencing India's economic diplomacy.[14]

IRAN AT THE CROSS ROADS

As of today many of the discourses pertaining to strategic affairs in the world in general and West Asia in particular finds Iran at the focal point. Being an ancient civilization situated in a geostrategic location between West, South and Central Asia with an abundant oil and gas reserves, a huge population, rentier economy and as one of the biggest military might's of the region together as the custodian of Shia Islam, Iran enjoys an important position in the region and is admired by some and feared by the others. To India, Iran is prominent due to its economic and geostrategic importance which is vital to India's interests.

INDIA-IRAN: HISTORICAL TIES

India and Iran have a long history of relations dating back to the period as far as 2000 B.C following the Indo-Aryan migration from Iran to India and thereafter both the civilizations influenced each other in the realm of various spheres such as languages, culture, religion, architecture, and literature. During the Medieval period the Safavid Empire of Persia and the Mughal Empire of India were in constant touch with each other, during this period Persian became the official language of the Mughals and the TajMahal in Agra testifies to this common bondage. Both the nations shared a common boarder until 1947. Today India hosts the second largest Shia community in the world after Iran, a large chunk of which is of Persian descent and they still maintain strong religious and cultural ties with Iran.[15]

COLD WAR PERIOD

India's Rlations with the Shah of Iran (1947–1979)

Nehru viewed that Iran was an important country in India's extended neighbourhood therefore he worked hard to maintain cordial relations with Iran. The Treaty of friendship was signed between New Delhi and Tehran on 15th March 1950. There were several high level visits on both sides. During the period of Shah of Iran until 1979 India and Iran continued to be on different camps, while India continued to pursue a non-alignment policy, Iran along with Pakistan were close allies of the United States and were members of the military alliance known as Baghdad Pact later known as CENTO in 1955. India's close ties with Gamal Abdul Nasser of Egypt and the Soviet Union was viewed with suspicion by the Shah of Iran, this along with the Pakistani factor constrained the Indo-Iranian relations. Iran was the first nation to recognize the state of Pakistan after its formation in 1947 and the Shah of Iran was the first head of the state to pay a visit to Pakistan in 1950. Though Iran was sympathetic towards India in the India-China war of 1962, when it came to matters with Pakistan, Iran sided with Pakistan on all its conflicts with India including on the matter of Kashmir. During the 1971 Bangladesh crisis the Shah provided financial and military support to Pakistan which annoyed New Delhi.[16]

The Islamic Revolution and Thereafter from 1979

The 1979 Islamic Revolution in Iran brought an end to the period of Mohammed Reza Shah and there by Iran's pro-western alliance.

Immediately after the revolution Iran withdrew from the CENTO and joined the Non Aligned Movement. India welcomed the change in regime as well as Iran's induction into the NAM. This brought India and Iran a step closer. However the subsequent Iran-Iraq war from 1980–88 and the new regimes foreign policy deeply rooted in Islam made matters more complicated. There are dual opinions regarding India's stance over the Iran-Iraq war, some scholars argue that India remained neutral where as some others argue that India was more sympathetic towards the Iraqi secular regime of Saddam Hussein with whom India enjoyed cordial ties as being one of the very few Arab leaders who supported India's cause on Kashmir. In the post revolutionary Iran Supreme Leader Ayatollah Khomeini's Islamic solidarity with the oppressed and struggles of Muslims all over the world which also includes the Muslims of India especially in the state of Jammu and Kashmir was an irritant in the Indo-Iranian relations.[17]

RELATIONS AFTER THE COLD WAR

The late eighties and early nineties witnessed increased dialogues between India and Iran. Events such as change of the regime in Iran, the Gulf war, the disintegration of the Soviet Union and economic reforms in India paved way for the increased dialogues and cooperation. After the first Gulf war India lost two of its major oil suppliers i.e. Iraq and Kuwait and this vacuum was filled by Iran thus becoming India's second largest oil supplier after Saudi Arabia.[18] There were many visits from both sides such as the visit of Indian Prime Minister P.V. Narasimha Rao to Iran on 1993 which was reciprocated by Iran's President Akbar Hashemi Rafsanjani to India on 1995. The early nineties also witnessed Iran's change in the position on Kashmir, in 1991 for the first time Iran acknowledged Kashmir to be an integral part of India. In 1994 Iran influenced Pakistan not to refer the human rights situation in Kashmir to the UN Human Rights Commission in Geneva. During this period both sides shared their mutual concerns regarding the Taliban regime in Afghanistan (1996–2001).

Though the increased dialogues in the nineties laid the foundation for a strong groundwork it was only after the visit of Indian Prime Minister A B Vajpayee to Iran in 2001 and the subsequent signing of the 'Tehran Declaration' that Indo-Iranian relations were taken to higher levels, many consider this visit as a 'turning point' among the two countries which encouraged for the 'dialogue among civilizations' as advocated by Iranian President Mohammed Khatami. In 2003 India hosted President Khatami as the chief guest of India's Republic Day celebrations. During this period the two sides shared deep concerns regarding the US preparations to invade Iraq.[19]

INDIA AND THE IRANIAN NUCLEAR CRISIS

Iran's controversial nuclear programme came to the lime light in 2002 after the findings of two new nuclear sites in Natnaz and Arak.[20] Iran's failure of disclosing theses two sites violated the transparency requirements of its safeguard agreement with the International Atomic Energy Agency (IAEA). It paved way for concerns such as Iran's intention to build a nuclear bomb. Though Iran consistently clarified that they are producing nuclear energy for civilian purposes and not for nuclear weapons which will violate its religious principles, many in the Western world and some in Asia are sceptical about this claims.[21] Although India views that Iran has the right to pursue civilian nuclear energy it insists that Iran should clarify the doubts raised by the IAEA regarding Iran's compliance with the NPT. India does not want to see another nuclear weapon state in its extended neighbourhood as it would escalate arms race in the region. India calls for resolution of the problem through negotiation rather than military means and calls for the UN to play a pivotal role in resolving the crisis. A nuclear Iran is not of India's interest. Moreover India is also worried regarding reports that Iran might have benefitted from the AQ Khan Network.[22]

THE IPI PIPELINE AND INDIA'S VOTE AGAINST IRAN AT THE IAEA

The much hyped $7 billion 2700 km Iran-Pakistan-India gas pipeline has failed to materialize. Though officials point out security reasons and transit fees to be the constraints of the project it is widely believed that it is much to the displeasure of Washington that the IPI had failed to bear fruit. Had the IPI pipeline materialized it would have been a breakthrough in India's future energy demands.[23]

The Obama administration is opposed to the pipeline as this would bring substantial revenue for Iran which is facing punitive economic sanctions due to its controversial nuclear programme. As of now if India continues to engage with Iran over the pipeline then it would be under sanctions according to the Comprehensive Iran Sanctions, Accountability, and Divestment Act of 2010 (CISADA) which will impose penalties on foreign companies that invest more than $20 million in a single year in Iran's energy sector.[24]

India's vote in the IAEA against Iran was something which was unexpected and took the Indian public as well as Iran by surprise. The first vote in 2005 in the IAEA resolution was to make Iran in compliance with the NPT safeguards and the second vote in 2006 was to refer Iran to the UNSC.[25] India further went to vote against Iran both in 2009 and in 2011 stating the reasons that Iran failed to comply with the NPT obligations. The timing of the first vote in 2005 was important for the reasons that it was the year in which the Indo-US civilian nuclear deal was given a green signal by the US Congress and the Iran vote was crucial for getting the consent of the US Congress for the nuclear deal.[26]

OPPORTUNITIES FOR INDIA-IRAN RELATIONS

India is having a tough time while engaging with Iran, on one hand it paves way for many opportunities at a comfortable level owing to its close geographical proximity with Iran. The sanctions that isolate Iran can also be seen as an opportunity for India.

Iran is crucial to India's interest in Afghanistan and in Central Asia. One of the significant dialogues has been regarding the Indian participation of upgrading the Chabahar Port in south eastern Iran. The developing of this port will jointly benefit Iran, India and Afghanistan as it will generate more revenues for Iran, give access to Indian exports to Central Asia at the same time reduce the dependence of Afghanistan on Pakistan for its exports via Karachi. Chabahar port has the immense potential to connect the business hubs of West Asia, South Asia, and Central Asia via trade. There were also talks in 2008 between India and Iran of a possible rail link between Russia and Iran. The possibility of the North-South Corridor by linking Iran with Russia has also been discussed during many of the bilateral negotiations.[27]

New sectors such as agriculture, pharma and automobiles are identified as potential areas of doing business. Recently a new production sharing contracts for exploration of oil was offered to Indian companies. Iran was India's second largest exporter of oil and now it has fell to the sixth position and the Mangalore Refinery and Petrochemicals Ltd. (MRPCL) is a client of the Iranian crude. The prospect of a new pipeline project between the two countries beneath the sea is also being discussed. The India-Iran trade during the year 2011–2012 was more than $14 billion of which the major chunk was petroleum products. The two countries had decided to increase it to $25 billion in the next four years.

Iran controls the entry and exit point of the Straits of Hormuz through which a large chunk of the oil passes which is also very crucial for India's energy needs. Any military confrontation with Iran can lead to closure of the Straits of Hormuz which will shoot up the oil prices that can badly affect developing economies like India. Though both nations share the concerns over Syria, Iran has a larger stake in Syria and has expressed the acceptance of Kofi Annan's six point plan which is also acceptable to India. The issue of Iran has also a say in the Indian public domain therefore it is important in India's domestic politics.[28]

There are some challenges which the region faces especially after the NATO pullout from Afghanistan in 2014. Iran is crucial to India's access to Afghanistan where Indian investments are said to be valued at more than $1 billion. Peace and stability as well as the fall of the Taliban in Afghanistan is crucial to both India's and Iran's interest. Infrastructure development in Afghanistan is vital due to the connectivity to Central Asia.

CHALLENGES OF ENGAGING WITH IRAN

While on the one hand there are many opportunities foreseen owing to India's engagement with Iran, on the other hand this engagement would be at a very high cost looking at the apprehension expressed by Iran's adversaries i.e. the GCC, United States and Israel with whom India' stakes are huge. A careful move without antagonizing the other is vital to India's energy, security and economic interest.

The GCC Factor

Trade and Indian diaspora are the two crucial things which form the backbone of India-GCC relations. The Gulf supplies two third of India's energy requirements. For India, Iran has been an important source of energy especially after the Gulf war when both Iraq and Kuwait who were key energy suppliers to India during these period suffered huge debacles as a result of the war. The GCC nations are under the security umbrella of the United States therefore India's engagement with Iran not only antagonises the GCC but also the United States.[29] The GCC views Iran as a difficult neighbour and threat to their regional stability. It could also be seen in the wider spectrum of power struggle between Shias and Sunnis as well as Persians and Arabs and also between Revolutionary Republic and Gulf Monarchies. Among the GCC Bahrain, UAE and Saudi Arabia has been more sceptical of Iran than the rest of the others. Bahrain consists of a

Sunni minority royal family in a Shia majority state. Therefore the royal family is always apprehensive of Iran instigating the Bahrain shias to upraise against the royal family.[30] During the uprisings which took place in the month of March of 2011 in Bahrain some observes in the GCC pointed out at Iran's involvement in instigating the unrest.[31]

Iran's tensed relations with UAE involves regarding 3 islands which is claimed by UAE but is currently under the control of Iran, i.e. Abu Musa, Greater Tunb and Lesser Tunb. UAE foreign minister Sheikh Abdullah bin Zayed Al Nahyan in a statement of 2010 compared Iran's occupation of these 3 islands with Israel's occupation of Arab lands and called for the return of these islands to UAE.[32]

The relations between Saudi Arabia and Iran deteriorated after the 1979 Islamic Revolution and the call by Iran Supreme leader Ayatollah Khomeini on GCC monarchies as unislamic and called for the overthrow of these regimes. He called the GCC monarchies as the puppets of "the Great Satan" ie the United States. The rivalry grew worse following the Saudi support to Iraq during the Iran-Iraq war of 1980–88 and there after the killing of 400 Iranian pilgrims in 1987 in Saudi Arabia. Both Iran and Saudi Arabia had been competing for the leadership in the Islamic world and for the influence in the region.

Saudi Arabia fears that Iran may mobilise the Shia population of Saudi Arabia which is mainly concentrated in the oil rich eastern region of the kingdom to rise against the royal family owing to its pro-US alliance. The GCC poses great anxiety over Iranian nuclear programme and pressurises the world community through diplomatic means not to engage with Iran.[33] A Wiki leaks cable of 2008 reveals that the Saudi King Abdullah bin Abdul Aziz has called upon the United States to attack Iran several times.[34] About 40 percent of the population of Saudi Arabia's oil producing eastern region are Shias and this worries Riyadh. The Iranian nuclear controversy has brought both India and Saudi Arabia closer. India is looking towards the GCC for huge investment opportunities especially in infrastructure therefore it cannot afford to loose out Saudi Arabia by way of getting closer with Iran.[35]

The US Factor

Ever since India became a strategic partner of the United States, engaging with Iran has been a crucial test for New Delhi and in proving its loyalty with the United States through means such as the IPI Pipeline project and the Iran vote in the IAEA. The Bush administration made it a condition for India to vote against Iran at the IAEA in 2006 for the approval of the Indo-US Civilian Nuclear deal in the US Congress. This puts the Indian foreign policy in dilemma. The United States is critical of Iran's nuclear programme and alleges Iran that it supports terrorism. The United States views that a nuclear Iran is a threat not only to the GCC but also to Israel.[36] It is widely believed that the deterioration of economics between India and Iran such as the IPI gas pipeline, non realisation of the LNG deal, substantial oil reduction from Iran and reduction in India's exports of petroleum products to Iran, and India's vote in the IAEA are largely due to the pressure from Washington.[37]

The call to attack Iran gained sufficient momentum in the Unites States when in 2011 FBI claimed that they have unearthed an Iranian plot to assassinate the Saudi Ambassador to the United States and blow up the embassies of Saudi Arabia and Israel in Washington. The anti Iran campaigns were lead by right wing congressman who had strong ties with Israel.[38] When this issue was brought before the UN on 18th November 2011 India choose to abstain before the voting. While the GCC has expressed concerns regarding Iran's growing military power India has never expressed concern about Iran's growing military might inspite of being in India's extended neighbourhood.[39]

The US pulling out from Afghanistan in 2014 is another cause of worry, while United States may not give an upper hand to India in Afghanistan which may offend Pakistan. And stability in Afghanistan is crucial to India's interest. At the same time India is not in a position to challenge the US non proliferation priorities in the Gulf.[40]

The Israeli Factor

Since 1990s both Israel and Iran has become important for India; one by means of energy security and other by means of national security. Both India and Israel are pluralist democracies and are victims of terrorism. There are significant common challenges that they face and therefore they understand each other better. Israel has serious concerns regarding India's ties with Iran. In 2003 former Israeli Prime Minister Ariel Sharon stated that he would put an end to military technology transfer to India if it is redirected towards Iran.[41] Israel accuses Iran of aiding Lebanese and Palestinian organizations like Hezbollah and Hamas who are in hostility with Israel.[42]

Though both the nations, share concerns regarding the negative implications of the Iranian nuclear bomb, India does not share the Israeli call for a military strike on Iran on the other hand India follows the resolutions of the IAEA as a military strike on Iran would endanger the whole region as well as the safety of 6 million Indian nationals working in the Gulf and affect the world economy. Cooperation with Israel is vital to India's security interest and India is trying hard to balance its relations with Israel vis-a vis Iran.[43] The accusation of both Iran and Israel against each other has kept India in a tight situation by not siding with either and this was evident in the event of the attack on the Israeli diplomat in New Delhi on February 2012, Israel accused Iran for the incident where as Iran denied the charges, after a month of investigation Indian authorities arrested a journalist named Mohammad Ahmed Kazmi from South Delhi and was accused him of providing logistics for the blast.[44] India also has not reacted to the holocaust denial statements of Ahmedinijad. Good relations with Israel for India in a way will also help to maintain good relations with the United States.[45]

CONCLUSION

Today India continues to a enjoy significant weightage in the international system and its foreign policy is more over determined by its economic interest and therefore there has to be a cost-benefit analysis regarding its relations with Iran on the one hand and with the US-GCC-Israeli axis on the other. The Iranian Nuclear issue is a crisis as well as an opportunity for India either to seal ties with Iran, thus, by becoming the dear of the other or by stepping in as a mediator and bridging the gap between the two just like the role played by Russia in the Syrian crisis, thus India would be able to protect its interests from both the sides in the long term. As far as Iran is concerned it would be the right time for India to step in and have a bargaining chip as Iran is confronting with sanctions and facing a declining economy it may make compromises on many of the demands that India puts forward. E.g., Payment of oil bills in rupees.

China has gained a strong foothold in Iran buy utilizing every crisis created by western sanctions into an opportunity to their advantage at the same time Indian companies such as Reliance are loosing out whatever stakes they have in Iran. Oil import is the major contribution to India's current account deficit and according to Petroleum Minister Veerappa Moily making payments to Iran in rupees for importing petroleum would save India up to $8.47 billion. Apart from the oil factor the geographical access to Afghanistan and Central Asia lies key to India's economic relations with Iran.

However looking at the volume of trade and the future prospects of India becoming a global power the US-GCC-Israeli axis far outweighs the India-Iran bilateral relations. Being a strategic partner to the United States and as an aspiring member to be the UN Security Council good relations with the United States is crucial for India's global power ambitions. The two countries enjoy a trade volume of $ 100 billion which is huge when compared to India's trade with Iran which is at $15 billion. India seeks significant US cooperation in its security, energy, investments, environment, higher education, counterterrorism, cyber and space technology.

The United States is looking at India as a counter weight to China and is significantly engaging with it. There are many areas of convergence and divergence in Indo-US relations and many a times economic interest has to be compromised with political decisions. The troubled relations that India has with Pakistan and China is also cited as one of the reasons that India has to have good relations with the United States as it can intervene on behalf of India and Pakistan in case of a conflict as it did in the Kargil crisis when Clinton asked Nawaz Sharif to withdraw the forces to the Loc. At the same time the rise of China has raised some concerns among the global community especially among United States, Japan and ASEAN. And all these groups look forward to India to act as a power balancer in the continent.

Today GCC as a group has emerged as the largest trading partner of India with a trade volume of $158 billion in 2012 out of which a major chunk is contributed by UAE nearly $75 billion which itself as a country is the second largest trading partner of India after China. Moreover GCC supplies more than 60% of India's oil needs and is home to 6 million Indians who in turn remit nearly $52 billion annually. Therefore decision on Iran is crucial to India's relations with the GCC as many in the GCC views Iran as a difficult neighbour. The GCC also plays an important role in the OIC were every time anti-India resolutions are taken up by Pakistan owing to the situation in Jammu and Kashmir. India's decision on Iran could also influence on GCC's condemnation of India over the human rights situation in Kashmir at the OIC summits. The recently proposed 'Nitaqat System' in Saudi Arabia is another cause of worry to the Indian migrants.

As far as Israel is concerned it has become as one of the top arms suppliers to India in recent times. It has supplied weapons to India even when there was no diplomatic relations. Apart from arms there are also trade taking place in agriculture, farm research, space technology, health, IT and tourism. The bilateral trade accounts for $ 6 billion. The recent discoveries of Tamar and Leviathan gas fields in Israel have opened up new opportunities to energy hungry nations like India. Good relations with Israel can also help in sustaining good relations with the United States. As a nation which has good relations with all these blocs i.e. Iran, US, GCC and Israel India can play the role of a mediator like which had been played by Russia in the Syrian crisis.

The recent telephonic conversation between Iranian President Hassan Rouhani and US President Barak Obama, the first of such a kind between the Presidents of two nations after the Islamic Revolution of 1979 brings optimism among the world community that tensions could be resolved. India's ties with Iran withstanding the US pressure will also be one of the points of debate in the upcoming general election in 2014. India is engaging with a nation who was once upon a time perceived as 'an axil of evil' by the United States, a difficult neighbour by the GCC and whose present President Rouhani was described by Israeli Prime Minister Benjamin Netanyahu as a 'a wolf in sheep clothing'. Taking all these into account together with the present importance attached with Iran it needs immense calculations before New Delhi makes every move and utilize the opportunity wisely to its advantage.

REFERENCES

[1] Kumar, Atul (2010). "A Historical Perspective on Indian Foreign Policy", *World Affairs Spring*, 14(1): 105.

[2] Noorani, A.G. (2001). "Indian thinking on foreign policy", *Frontline*, Chennai, 6–19, January, 2001.

[3] Ganguly, Sumit (2010). "The Genesis of Non Alignment", in Sumit Ganguly (eds.) *India's Foreign Policy: Retrospect and Prospect*", New Delhi: Oxford University Press.

[4] Tripathi, Ambikesh Kumar (2011). "Dynamics of India's Foreign Policy: Challenges of 21st Century", Working Paper, Varanasi: Banaras Hindu University.

[5] Kennedy, B. Andrew (2011). "India's Nuclear Odyssey: Implicit Umbrellas, Diplomatic Disappointments and the Bomb", *International Security*, 36(2): 120–153.

[6] Kumar, Atul (2010). "A Historical Perspective on Indian Foreign Policy", *World Affairs Spring*, 14(1): 105.

[7] Ganguly, Sumit and Pardesi, S. Manjeet (2009). "Explaining Sixty Years of India's Foreign Policy", *India Review*, 8(1): 4–19.

[8] Mohan, C. Raja (2009). "The Making of Indian Foreign Policy: The Role of Scholarship and Public Opinion", Lecture delivered on 13 July 2009 at the Institute of South Asian Studies, National University of Singapore: Singapore.

[9] Kumar, Atul (2010). "A Historical Perspective on Indian Foreign Policy", *World Affairs Spring*, 14(1): 105.

[10] Sachdeva, Gulshan (2011). "Geo-economics and Energy for India", in David Scott (eds.) *Handbook of India's International Relations,* United Kingdom: Routledge.

[11] Ramakrishnan, A.K. (2005). "Neoliberal Globalism and India's Foreign Policy: Towards a Critical Rethinking", in Rajan Harshe and K.M. Seethi (eds.) *Engaging with the World: Critical Reflections on India's foreign Policy,* New Delhi, Orient Blackswan Private Limited.

[12] Sachdeva, Gulshan (2011). "Geo-economics and Energy for India", in David Scott (eds.) *Handbook of India's International Relations,* United Kingdom: Routledge.

[13] Malone, David and Mukherjee, Robin (2009). *"Polity, Security and Foreign Policy in Contemporary India",* Princeton: Princeton University Press.

[14] Botez, Radu (2013). "India's Experiment in Economic Diplomacy", Accessed on 5 Oct. 2013, URL: *www.thediplomat.com/pacific-money/2013/08/14/india's-experi ment-in-economic-diplomacy.*

[15] Baba, Noor Ahmed (2013). "India and West Asia", *World Focus,* June 2013, 402: p. 23.

[16] Pasha, A.K. (2013). "India and West Asia", *World Focus,* June 2013, 402, p. 15.

[17] Pradhan, Bansidhar (2004). "Changing Dynamics of India's West Asia Policy", *International Studies,* 41(1): 1–89.

[18] Levaillant, Melissa (2012). "India's Foreign Policy Towards Iran: Dilemma's of an Emerging Power", *Network of Researchers in International Affairs,* November 2012: 1–27.

[19] Fair, C. Christine (2010). "Indo-Iranian Relations: What Prospects for Trans-formation", in Sumit Ganguly (eds.) *India's Foreign Policy: Retrospect and Prospect",* New Delhi: Oxford University Press.

[20] Jafarzadeh, Alireza (2007). "The Iran Threat: President Ahmadiniejad and the Coming Nuclear Crisis", New York: Palgrave MacMillan.

[21] Perkovich, George, Radzinsky, Brain and Tandler, Jaclyn (2012). *"The Iranian Nuclear Challenge and the GCC",* accessed 14th Sep. 2013 URL: http:// carneigeendowment.org/2012/05/31/iranian-nuclear-challenge-and-gcc/b67p#

[22] Pant, V. Harsh (2011). "India's Relations with Iran: Much Ado about Nothing", *The Washington Quarterly,* 34(1): 61–74.

[23] Fair, C. Christine (2010). "Indo-Iranian Relations: What Prospects for Trans-formation", in Sumit Ganguly (eds.) *India's Foreign Policy: Retrospect and Prospect",* New Delhi: Oxford University Press.

[24] Cheema, Sujatha. Ashwarya (2010). "India-Iran Relations: Progress, Challenges and Prospects", *India Quarterly,* 66 (4): 383–396.

[25] Ibid.

[26] Desai, D. Ronak (2012). "On Iran, India's Record is Better Than You Think", Accessed 14th October 2013, *URL:* http huffington post.com/ronak-d-desai/iran-india_b_1959712.html.

[27] Roy, Meena Singh (2013). "India and Iran Relations: Sustaining the Momentum", IDSA Issue Brief, p. 5.

[28] Ibid.

[29] Pradhan, Kumar Prashanth (2011). "GCC-Iran Rivalry and Strategic Challenges for India in the Gulf ", *Indian Foreign Affairs Journal,* 6(1): 45–57.

[30] Perkovich, George, Radzinsky, Brain and Tandler, Jaclyn (2012), "The Iranian Nuclear Challenge and the GCC", accessed 14ᵗʰ Sep. 2013, URL: http:// carneigeendowment.org/2012/05/31/iranian-nuclear-challenge-and-gcc/b67p#

[31] The Telegraph (2011). "*Bahrain hints at evidence of Iran protest links*", accessed 18ᵗʰ October 2013 URL: www. telegraph.co.uk.news/worldnews/middleeast/bahrain/ 8912240/Bahrain-hints- at-evidence -of -Iran-protests –links.html

[32] Khaleej Times (2010). "Iran must end occupation of Islands: Abdullah", accessed 18ᵗʰ October 2013 URL: www.khaleejtimes.com /kt–article-display-1.asp?xfile=data/ theuae/2010/April/ the uae_April 658.xml&section=the uae

[33] Perkovich, George, Radzinsky, Brain and Tandler, Jaclyn (2012). "The Iranian Nuclear Challenge and the GCC", accessed 14ᵗʰ Sep. 2013, URL: http://carneigeen dowment.org/2012/05/31/iranian-nuclear-challenge-and-gcc/b67p#

[34] Reuters (2010). "Saudi King urged U.S. to attack Iran: Wiki leaks", accessed 18ᵗʰ Oct. 2013 URL: www.rueters.com/article/2010/11/29/ us-wiki leaks-usa-idUSTRE6AP06Z20101129

[35] Pant, V. Harsh (2011). "India's Relations with Iran: Much Ado about Nothing", *The Washington Quarterly,* 34(1): 61–74.

[36] Pradhan, Kumar Prashanth (2011). "GCC-Iran Rivalry and Strategic Challenges for India in the Gulf ", *Indian Foreign Affairs Journal,* 6 (1): 45–57.

[37] Kumaraswamy, P.R. (2012). "Israel Confronts Iran: Rationalities, Responses and Fallouts", *IDSA Monograph Series,* November, 2012, No. 8.

[38] Cherian, John (2011). "Plot against Iran", *Frontline*, Chennai, 05–18, November, 2011.

[39] Kumaraswamy, P.R. (2012). "Israel Confronts Iran: Rationalities, Responses and Fallouts", *IDSA Monograph Series,* November, 2012, No. 8.

[40] Pant, V. Harsh (2011). "India's Relations with Iran: Much Ado about Nothing", *The Washington Quarterly,* 34 (1): 61–74.

[41] Blarel, Nicolas (2010). "Indo-Israeli Relations: Emergence of a Strategic Partnership", in Sumit Ganguly (eds.) India's Foreign Policy: Retrospect and Prospect, New Delhi: Oxford University Press.

[42] Frankel, D. Rafael (2012). "Keeping Hamas and Hezbollah Out of a War with Iran", *The Washington Quarterly*, 35(4):53–65.

[43] Rajiv, C. Samuel (2012), "The Delicate Balance: Israel and India's foreign Policy Practice", *Strategic Analysis*, 36 (1): 128–144.

[44] Chauhan, Neeraj (2012). "Journalist held for terror attack on Israeli envoy's car", Accessed on 20 Oct. 2013 URL: http://articles.timesof india.indiatimes.com/2012-03-08/india/31135394_1_iran-link- israeli-embassy-iranian-publication

[45] Kumaraswamy, P.R. (2012). "Israel Confronts Iran: Rationalities, Responses and Fallouts", *IDSA Monograph Series*, November, 2012, No. 8.

Chabahar Port and India's
New Strategic Outpost in Middle East

Anns George

Right from history, India had always maintained trade and commercial relations with Middle East through Arabian sea and even far off to Europe. There were close links between the Mesopotamia and Indus Valley civilization through trade and commerce. Even in the present days also India is maintaining friendly and cordial relation with the Arab world. Due to the richness in oil wealth, Middle East is India's largest oil supplier. More than 60% of our energy requirements are satisfied from West Asia. Among those middle Eastern states, Iran is the largest crude oil exporter to India after Saudi Arabia.

As a vibrant economy, India always stood to maintain friendly relations with its neighbours both near and distant. As a emerging economy, India was keen in diversifying its energy supplies. After the New Economic Reforms of 1991, Indian economy had showcased rapid growth and development. Indian textile and Pharmaceutical industries became the leading Industries in the world. Annual GDP growth rate had tremendous increase. As a result, the Indian economy has grown rapidly and steady supply of energy for feeding the economy became inevitable.

The foreign policy of India after the New Economic Reforms had started to show a growing trend in focusing on the economic aspects. With regard to this, India's relation with Iran is the most complex in recent years. Elements of economics and politics coincide with India's relation with Iran. On one hand there are western and American sanctions over Iran with regard to the issue of uranium enrichment and nuclear weapons. On the other hand India needs the oil and natural gas of Iran bypassing western sanctions. This will be consistently a hard step for India to take a decision on Iran. So it is in this context, India's strategic investment in Chabahar port is going to be a key issue of debate.

Chabahar port is located at the south eastern Iran along the Makran coast in the Oman Sea in the Sisten and Baluchistan province of Iran. Chabahar is Iran's closest and best access point to the Indian Ocean, and which is also the only Oceanic port of Iran. Chabahar is the focal point of Iran for development of the east of the country through expansion and enhancement of transit route among countries situated in the northern part of the Indian Ocean and central Asia. A port outside the Persian Gulf makes sense from a strategic and logistical viewpoint for Iran. The port of Chabahar was part of a plan to develop transportation infrastructure in Eastern Iran for many years. Initially put on hold in 1984, it revived in 2002 with Indian help, not only limited to financing and engineering assistance. India also wished to bypass Pakistan, by cooperating on a highway system that lead from the port into Afghanistan as well as a planned railroad to Afghanistan. Iranian officials state that Chabahar will become the port for trade with Afghanistan and Central Asia.

Recently India had decided to invest a $100 billion US dollar in developing Chabahar port which is considered strategically and economically important for the country's exports to landlocked Afghanistan. India, Iran and Afghanistan have an agreement on preferential treatment and low tariffs for goods moved through Chabahar port, which also has a free trade and industrial zone in its vicinity. Between India and Afghanistan, Pakistan is a major actor in the region who has a hostile relation with India. Pakistan is the key land route from India to Afghanistan and other Common Wealth of Independent States. Pakistan is continuously denying India's transit access to war torn Afghanistan where India is undergoing several development projects. A large number of Indian personals are working in various infrastructural and reconstruction developments in Afghanistan. Along with workers many Indian security personnel's are engaged in training programmes for Afghan security forces. This humanitarian assistance from the part of India is going to expand with the withdrawal of NATO forces from Afghanistan in 2014. India is serious on this issue. The peace in Afghanistan will determine the future peace and stability in the region. Once Afghanistan gets into the hands of terrorist groups, it will pose a serious security challenge to India and increase terrorist insurgency in Jammu and Kashmir. The recent militant attacks in Jammu are an example for it. So a peaceful and stable Afghanistan is vital for Indian national security. This would justify India's positive engagements in Afghanistan.[1]

India has to diversify its transit access to Afghanistan apart from the traditional route through Pakistan. Pakistan had signed a trade and transit agreement with Afghanistan in 2010, allowing Kabul to transport goods to Pakistan ports and also to Indian border. But India cannot utilize those arrangements for transporting its cargo to Afghanistan since Pakistan continues to be vehemently opposed to any Indian role in the war torn country. So India must go for alternative routes and Chabahar port in southeast Iran is the best option.

Apart from the development assistance in Chabahar along with Iranian government, India is engaged in several other projects. It works in the development of transit routes from Chabahar port to Afghanistan. The recent completion of Zaranj-Delaram highway in Afghanistan is being built with Indian assistance and this connects Afghanistan to Iranian border. Iran also completed a proposed road link from Chabahar port to Milak borders in Afghanistan. These connecting routes provide an easy access for India to the war torn Afghanistan, bypassing Pakistan.

India helped in building Chabahar a decade ago to provide Iran access to Afghanistan and Central Asia which was banned by neighbouring nuclear Pakistan. India was also involved in constructing a 560 km long line from the Zabul iron ore mines in South Afghanistan to the Iranian port. Afghanistan has huge mineral resources in which India has keen interest. It is estimated that Afghanistan has iron and other minerals resources worth almost $3 trillion. Recently India's Iron and Steel Consortium has won the mining rights in the iron ore mines of Bamiyan. Indian companies are working hard to exploit the rich mineral deposit in north and central Afghanistan. All these mineral wealth can only be exploited by a viable transit route through Iran to India. Therefore the Chabahar port has its significance in India's economic relation with Afghanistan and also for reconstruction developments in the war torn country particularly after the NATO forces withdrawal in 2014. And recently for the first time ever, Chabahar port in Iran was used by India to transport 100000 metric tons of wheat to Afghanistan as part of its humanitarian aid to war torn country.

The strategic location of Iran to the north of Persian Gulf and South to Central Asia has placed it as an important trade route between Asia and Europe. Even during the days of silk route itself, this was a major trading route between Asia and Europe. The Chabahar port in Iran is spreading out the existing or planned transportation infrastructure that leads into various economic centers and importantly for Central Asia, and towards North. Iran's geostrategic position allows it to play an important role in connecting India to central Asia both militarily and strategically. Iran is the gateway for the five Central Asian states of Kazakhstan, Kyrgyzstan, Turkmenistan, Tajikistan and Uzbekistan.

India's relations with Central Asian states are more on trade and cultural issues. India and Central Asia had strong relations during historical times itself. The Mughal emperor Babar and many others rulers and conquers of India are from Central Asia. This facilitated a strong cultural relation between India and Central Asia. Even today with all the memories of past, India's cultural relations with Central Asia are more significant. Apart from cultural relations, India has recently started to explore the trade and economic opportunities in central Asia. India's trade relation with Central Asia is over $500 US million and is on a steady increase. Among the five Central Asian States, Kazakhstan is a major trading partner of India. These Central Asian states are rich in natural gas and mineral resources which is an essential resource for the 1.2 billion people economy of India. Many Indian companies are engaged in oil exploration and extraction of minerals and natural gas. There are many proposals for linking the natural gas reserves of Central Asia with India via Iran and Pakistan. India is also engaged in joint ventures with Central Asian countries in mineral extraction. Kazakhstan has huge uranium deposits and India is working for joint mining projects with Kazakhstan. As a part of our friendly and cordial relation with Tajikistan, India was able to open its first Airforce base beyond its borders. The Farkhor Airbase in Tajikistan is assisting Indian workers and security personnel's in reconstructural projects in Afghanistan. In regard to the immense possibilities, India's relation with Central Asian states has huge potential to gain a new dimension in social, economic, political, cultural and military spheres.

Thus comes Iran and its Chabahar port as the major, viable access to this energy rich Central Asia. Trade with Central Asia can satisfy India's growing energy needs and facilitate economic growth and prosperity. Presently the most major road routes running from Chabahar to northern Iran to Uzbekistan is via Afghanistan's Heart province to Taskhant and Tajikistan. With the completion of Kerman-Zahedan railway and its connection to Chabahar port it is going to connect the port with the trans-Iranian railway which takes to Caspian Sea. And there are important sea routes to Kazakhstan and Russia and other European countries. Apart from the proposed railway line, there are many major land routes which connect Persian Gulf and Caspian Sea. India can utilize these trade routes to enhance its trade links with Eurasia.

Instead on depending on the Atlantic Ocean, India can now go for trade links with Europe especially Russia, Ukraine, Turkey, Georgia, Azerbaijan, Armenia etc... through Iran. The development of International North South Corridor (INSC) is again going to enhance India's trading potentials through Chabahar port. Thus India-Iran relation and India's strategic investment in Chabahar port is a major game winning for India by increasing its economic, political, cultural and military influence in the region despite of all the US imposed western sanctions over Iran.[2]

It is possible for India to revitalize the ancient trade routes between India and Europe in the present days. The silk route which had trade links between India and Europe can be revived through India's trading through Chabahar port and Central Asia. Before the coming of Europeans, this trading route was the prominent and easiest way to connect to Europe. The European colonizers destroyed the Arab trading routes and used Cape Town to reach Europe. With the European domination, the trade were dictated by European powers for their own interests. Now in a free independent world, each nation can choose their trade which will not be dictated by others. But instead are aimed at mutual benefits. Rebuilding the old trading routes can enlarge trade and would bring peace and prosperity to Asia and Europe.[3]

Apart from India's strategic footholds in Chabahar port, India is increasing its influence in Middle East. Recently the government of India has signed a defense cooperation pact with Qatar. Top officials labeled the agreement on joint training exercises, training of personnel and maritime cooperation as just short of stationing troops. Under the agreement, New Delhi has committed to protect assets and interests of Qatar from external threats. This landmark agreement has enabled India with several strategic advantages. With an active defense agreement with Qatar, India can increase its footholds in Qatar and also the surrounding Persian Gulf. Increasing maritime cooperation with Qatar has the potential for India to build Qatar into a listening post of Indian Naval forces or a surveillance station in the Persian Gulf. With American naval fleet all over deployed in Persian Gulf and the large oil supply through the Strait of Hormuz makes region much more significant. India's interest in the region is to make sure a steady supply of energy flow into the country which is vital for our economic development. This particular strategy was employed by Britain all over the world to increase its trade and naval dominance.[4]

Meanwhile a port in Chabahar in southeast Iran and a defense cooperation agreement with Qatar is all part of India's grand strategy to increase its influence all over the Indian Ocean littorals and beyond. Thus India's increasing role in Middle East is based on India's wish for great power status and global power. But India is not the only country which is competing for the global power. China is the major forerunner in this competition. Chinese influence in the region is also strong. China is building a port in Pakistan, the Gwadar port. China has increased its footholds in Middle East by constructing Gwadar port which is 400 nautical miles from the Strait of Hormuz and also is an international transit route from Persian Gulf to India Ocean. This will allow China a strategic location on the sea lines of communication in which China is always depended on. More than 70% of Chinese oil supply is coming from Middle East. So China's increasing dependence on Indian Ocean and Malacca strait has placed China in a vulnerable position. China had wished to get access to Indian Ocean through Gwadar port in Pakistan and Kyaukpyu in Myanmar. Thus Gwadar provided China a direct access to India Ocean through Pakistan.[5]

Thus strategic investment of China in Gwadar port is a threat to Indian investment in Chabahar, which is just 76 km far to West. The Gwadar port is both beneficial for Pakistan and China which reduce the overburden and congestion from the commercial, fishing and naval ships in Karachi port. Indeed any transportation or military problem in the Malacca strait, Strait of Hormuz, the Suez or anywhere along Asia's southern coastline will boost the importance of central Asia as a transport and trade corridor. The rising Chinese presence in Gwadar will be a threat to India and Gwadar port will be a tough competitor for Chabahar port. As if the competition increases it will not be a winner takes all outcomes but rather one port earning the greater share of trade. Both the Chabahar and Gwadar will be beneficial for Central Asia states to diversify their import and export routes as a logical economic and political step. In my perception it is likely the Chabahar port to be the winner in the competition at least in the short run. Iran is more stable than Pakistan and its relation with Afghanistan and central Asian states are better. Unlikely the Gwadar is in the tensed region in Baluchistan Province of Pakistan, the proposed road route from Chabahar port goes through relatively stable part of Afghanistan. And now it will be the technological factors and capacity of the two ports which determine the winner in the competition.[6]

To increase the strategic depth in the region, India also has defense cooperation with Oman. Indian Navy has been utilizing Oman's ports on the basis for conducting anti-piracy operations in the Gulf of Aden. The Indian Airforce has also been holding biannual joint exercises with the Royal Airforce of Oman since 2009. This provided India with a strategic advantage over the geo-strategic location of Oman in the mouth of Strait of Hormuz. With all these factors the Chabahar port which is located in the Makran coast in Oman Sea will enable Indian naval vessels to monitor the Strait of Hormuz and the two ports in the north of Arabian Sea.[7]

As an all, India's defense cooperation with Oman and Qatar will enable a significant Indian military presence in either sides of Strait of Hormuz and potential means to guarantee the security of Chabahar port and protection of our sea lines of Communication from Middle East. This will increase the trade traffic between India and Middle East and also ensure a steady supply of oil and other energy supplies to the country. The Kandla port and Jawaharlal Nehru port in the western coastlines will be the most important beneficiaries of Chabahar port and India's positive engagements in Middle East. The Indian Navy Western Command in Arabian Sea will be responsible for the protection of India's strategic assets in Middle East.[8]

With all these developments in sight in the aftermath of NATO forces, withdrawal will be an opportunity for India to establish its power structures in the region. Along with it the economic benefit of trade with central Asia and Iran will leap India forward to growth and prosperity. Indeed, with India's military capabilities and India's soft power is going to play a major role in increasing India's power and protect its strategic interests in the Middle East, and thereby project India's rising global power.

REFERENCES

[1] Tuteja, Ashok. (2013, April 14). India to develop Iran port for access to Afghanistan, Tribune India. Retrieved from http://Tribuneindia.com/2013/20130415/main5.htm. Accessed on 26/9/2013.

[2] Muzalevsky, Roman (2012, September 12). India's Eurasia strategy leverages Iranian ports. Asia Time .Retrieved from http://atimes.com/atimes/South_Asia/NI12Dfol.html. Accessed on 4/11/2013

[3] Balooch, Mahmoud (2009). Iran and India's cooperation in Central Asia, China and Eurasia Forum Quarterly, Vol. 7. Retrieved from https://www.google.co.in/#q=india+iran+cooperation+in+central+asia. Accessed on 26/9/2013

[4] DFI. (2010). India Qatar Strategic ties: CASS-India, Indian Defence Forum. Retrieved from http://defenceforumindia.com/forum/foreign-relations/19097-India-quatar-strategic-ties-cass-india-html. Accessed on 31/10/2013

[5] Bhandari, Shraddha (2013). China sniffs around Chabahar: Will India get its act right?. South Asia Monitor. Retrieved from http://southasiamonitor.org/detail.php?type=sl&nid=5700. Accessed on 14/10/2013

[6] Bleuer, Christian (2007, Augest 20). Central Asia's Seaport: Gwadar or Chabahar. Registan. Retrieved from http://registan.net/2007/08/20/central-asia-seaport-gwadar-or-chabahar. Accessed on 15/10/2013

[7] FP (2011, December 28). India, Oman ink pact on extending military cooperation. FirstPost. Retrieved from http://firstpost.com/fwire/india-oman-ink-pact-on-extend ing-military-co-operation-167802.html. Accessed on 31/10/2013

[8] Manoj, P. (2013). India's two big state run ports set for maiden overseas venture. Live mint& the Wall street journal. Retrieved from http://livemint.com/opinion/BrAFTFByPjS3IEILrnpGJP/indias-two-big-staterun-ports-set-for-maiden-overseas-vent.html. Accessed on 14/10/2013

Extra Regional Powers Dynamics in Iran: Implications for India's Foreign Policy

Sukalpa Chakrabarti

The relationship between the Islamic Republic of Iran and the extra regional big powers in the region poses a unique challenge to India's foreign policy interests and objectives. Presently the key players, viz. USA, Russia and China—are manipulating their own strategic interests in the region while taking care not to trip the delicate balance of relations. In the Indian context too, continuity of amiable relationship with Iran is of critical significance not just for protecting our national interests, but because of the serious implications for regional as well as global politics. This paper seeks to come up with policy recommendations for making necessary adjustments in Indo-Iran foreign relations that would enhance mutual confidence and also ensure that it meets the national interest without compromising favourable relations with the USA, Russia and West Asia. Built into this revision would be accommodation of energy, trade and geo-political needs. The findings would be important for both the nation states in their strategic interactions in the region and beyond and also help develop a better understanding of the vital interests for any future arrangement to bring about sustainable peace and stability in the region.

INTRODUCTION

Iran's geo-strategic location draws significant attention from all major powers. It has an appreciably long coastline on the North Arabian Sea and it dominates the entire eastern flank of the Persian Gulf. It has long borders with Iraq, Turkey, Afghanistan and Pakistan. It also borders on the residual republics of the former Soviet Union. In the North, Iran also has a coastline on the Caspian Sea and it shares borders with the republics in the Central Asian region.[1] Presently the key players, viz. USA, Russia and China—are manipulating their own strategic interests in the region while taking care not to trip the delicate balance of relations. In the Indian context too, continuity of amiable relationship with Iran is of critical significance not just for protecting our national interests, but because of the serious implications for regional as well as global politics. The enhanced focus in India's relations with Iran is largely an offshoot of its revised West Asia Policy, marking a distinct move away from ideology-based commitments to interest based relations.

IRAN IN THE CONTEXT OF CURRENT INTERNATIONAL DEVELOPMENT

Iran has been historically isolated in its international relation and even regionally—made amply clear during Iran-Iraq war of the 1980s. Despite aggressive instigation of the war by Iraq in an unabashed bid to annexing Iranian territory, Arab nations all over the Persian Gulf took to Iraq's side. This eager move was possibly backed by the consideration that Iraq would serve as an effective buffer against Iranian religious extremism. Bahrain, Kuwait, Oman, Qatar, Saudi Arabia and the UAE came up with an economic and security organization called the Gulf Cooperation Council (GCC) to promote their trade interdependence with each other and further distancing Iran. The western powers were also quick to use this opportunity to weaken Iran by supporting Iraq and contain the theocracy. For the USA it was the perfect chance to reverse its humiliation at the hands of Iran during the embassy hostage crisis. Thus while USA, France, Britain, West Germany, China and Soviet Union sold billions of dollars worth of military equipment[2] to Iraq, the number of states Iran could truly receive significant support was minimal. Support from global powers decisively affected the course of the war in Iraq's favour and highlighted the extreme extent of Iran's isolation in the wider international scene.[3] A break in this came in the wake of Iraqi invasion and annexation of Kuwait in 1990. Given the larger threat posed by the concentration of Iraqi troops near Saudi Arabia, an international coalition led by the United States was quick to move in and crush the Iraqi forces. After the destruction of Iraq's brute force by the United States during the Gulf War, Iran emerged as one of the preeminent military powers of the region.

The leadership in Iran by now appeared to be aware of the huge costs and vulnerability of the continued isolation and embraced a different approach to its international relations in order to acquire allies. So we found Iran complying with international sanctions on Iraq, while simultaneously offering to mediate in the crisis (possibly in a bid to undercut the US influence). Iran's volunteering of humanitarian support into Iraq to relieve the civilian suffering helped improve its tarnished international image. Iran also began to consciously work on enhancing its bilateral relations with the GCC member nations. Iran was particularly successful in establishing a good relationship with Oman which acted as Iran's main supporter in the GCC as well. Saudi Arabia also restored diplomatic relations with Iran.

Despite these attempts, it continued to be a major challenge for Iran's new foreign policy to overcome its negative reputation (further heightened by Iran's ties with terrorist organizations) in the eyes of the Gulf states and the larger international community. Also while Iran had sought improved relations with the Gulf states, Europe, and most of the international community, it continued to oppose the United States. The reasoning behind this opposition was a combination of domestic politics, strategic interest, and ambition to replace American leadership in the Gulf.[4] For its part, the United States views Iran as the "major challenge to stability" in the Gulf[5] and seeks to alienate Iran in the region propagating that Iran's ideology was inherently threatening and destabilizing. The early 90s Iran's push for modernization of its military and weapons, especially nuclear weapons were interpreted as a clear threat to USA's extra regional dominance in the Gulf. The neighbouring states were also sceptical of the real motives behind the up gradation of Iran's capabilities. Of course these moves were clear indications of Iran's desire to become a major player both regionally and internationally.US President, Barrack Obama has justified the establishment of the U.S. Missile Defence System in Europe to confront Iran's nuclear program by describing Iran's nuclear program as dangerous and referring to Iran and North Korea as threats of the 21st century.[6]

Seizing the opportunity of the disintegration of the Soviet Union in 1991, Iran sought to engage in diplomatic interaction with and was among the first nations to recognize the newly created Central Asian states. By joining the Economic Cooperation Organization, Iran has engaged in successful economic diplomacy with the energy resource rich states.Russia and Iran have expanded their political and military relations significantly in recent months following the escalation of violence in Syria.[7] Led by the apprehension that the offensive launched by the US and its allies in the Middle East, which has destabilised the entire region, may spread to Russia and Iran, both countries have stepped up their bilateral diplomatic, military and security engagement.

Iran has also made significant progress in Europe with Britain resuming its diplomatic ties with Iran since September 1990 and the EU emerging as Iran's largest trading partner. This explains why EU has been vocal in its objections to sanctions on Iran mooted by the USA—notably the Iran-Iraq Non-Proliferation Act of 1992 and the Iran-Libya Sanctions Act of 1996. In fact, Britain, China, France and Russia all have come to possess significant financial stakes in Iran in a variety of areas.

Iran is also active in North Africa and is found cultivating political and economic ties with the Islamic Salvation Front in Algeria, the government in Tunisia, and the National Islamic Front in Sudan. It is observed that Iran's Africa strategy significantly involves courting African countries voting in important international bodies, prioritizing outreach to African countries that mine uranium, and cementing partnerships that could give Iran access to strategic naval bases.[8] Thus Iran's diplomatic outreach to African nations is likely to challenge US aims across Africa.

West Asia in recent times has been witness to unforeseen volatile political changes, which have contributed to the rising role of Iran as a regional power in the face of new challenges and opportunities. In Syria, Iran's strategic ally in the region, we find Rouhani gravely condemning the use of chemical weapons and endorsing the US-Russia agreement on Syrian chemical weapon disarmament while expressing interest in participating in the Geneva process aimed at a ceasefire in Syria. Iran has been pursuing a diplomatic resolution to the crisis that would undercut the American initiatives and determine a road-map for the country's political transition. After a longstanding opposition, the USA has a few days back agreed to Iran's participation in the "Geneva 2" conference seeking an end to the war in Syria. However Iran has refused to accept the precondition of Iran supporting the June 2012 "Geneva Communique" sought to chart a path to a diplomatic resolution of the conflict, and was agreed to by major powers such as the United States and Russia, Gulf states, Iraq and Turkey—but not Iran, which was not invited to those talks.[9] It is believed while many Gulf states may have wanted to pursue both courses of action, the mutual animosity between the United States and Iran has made this untenable.

In the context of the nuclear standoff, Iran under Rouhani has already initiated a number of unilateral objective guarantees against stockpiling and acquisition of nuclear weapons and even categorically declared that Iran "will not pursue nuclear weapons under any circumstance".[10] Iran has reportedly slowed accumulation of enriched uranium insisting that the procurement is legal and for peaceful uses to fuel Teheran's medical reactor. This is a positive step aimed at greater nuclear transparency that would create confidence in Iran's peaceful nuclear intent. Consequently the sanctions on Iran may get gradually lifted. In addition to such "objective guarantees," Rouhani has stated that Iran is willing to register the Supreme Leader's edict against the acquisition and stockpiling of nuclear weapons at the UN in the form of a resolution.

Thus while suspected nuclear ambitions, terrorist ties (such as those with the Hezbollah) and miserable human rights records continue to limit the extent of Iran's progress in international relations, Iran has succeeded in engaging with the world economically as well as diplomatically.

FACTORS INFLUENCING INDIA-IRAN BILATERAL RELATIONS

The earlier phase in Indian foreign policy towards Iran has seen the former following the US dictum to oppose Iran on the issue of nuclear programme. Scholars have argued that India—Iran ties are viewed by the US strategists to have a potentially damaging impact on U.S. interests in Southwest Asia and the Middle East. However as India has come to consolidate a stronger stature in international relations both politically and economically, she is keen to develop an independent Middle Eastern strategy keeping in mind the strategic interests. Iran is also crucial for India because of its strategic geographic location and shared interests in the region. Current Indo-Iranian interests have converged around issues such as energy security, stability and opportunities in Central Asia, terrorism emanating from Afghanistan and Pakistan, prospects of mutual benefit from commercial ties, and the possibility of strategic ties in defence and intelligence areas.

There is a growing recognition the Indian diplomatic circle that Indo-US bilateral must be balanced against the economic and energy realities at home which necessitate the continuation of bilateral ties with Iran. India, the world's fourth-largest petroleum consumer, is Iran's second largest oil customer after China and purchases around $12 billion worth of Iranian crude every year, about 12% of its consumption.[11] Therefore, despite the tightening of sanctions, India cannot arrest the import of crude oil from Iran.In fact the subsequent US decision to exempt India from the oil embargo against Iran has come as welcome relief.

India has to engage in a tight rope walk to maintain the delicate balance of relations since a distinctly pro-Iran position would put at risk the mutually beneficial relationship she shares with the anti-Iran, US and Israel. India's strategic interest in West Asia is further complicated by the rival interests of Shiaite Iran and a Sunni GCC. The situation is further compounded by fresh violence in Syria which threatens to spill over in the region and India as friend of Syria cannot afford to stay distant. In fact by virtue of enjoying the confidence of Syria, it becomes imperative that India also use her neutral stature in international relations to convince the big powers to accept Iran as a part of the "Geneva 2" peace process and usher in a democratic and peaceful regime change in Syria, sans any politically motivated international intervention. India recognizes that without Iran's inclusion, sustaining an effective regional security architecture that would bring an end to the political uncertainty being faced in West Asia, will not be feasible.

Maintaining friendly relations with Iran also allows India to address her interest in Afghanistan and counter the threat posed by hostile neighbours. In fact as Indian and US interests coalesce in Afghanistan, it would be counterproductive for the USA to ask India to scale back ties with Iran, which consequently may result in Iran cutting Indian access to Afghanistan.

The visit of the Indian Prime Minister, Dr. Manmohan Singh to Iran on August 28, 2012 to participate in the NAM summit was a clear indication of New Delhi's desire to give new impetus to bilateral relations and enhance economic cooperation. The Prime Minister said: "there is lot of interest in doing business with India and getting Indian investment in infrastructure. There are of course difficulties imposed by western sanction, but subject to that I think we will explore ways and means of developing our relations with Iran".[12]

Iran's controversial nuclear programme has been a sore point between the two countries following India's vote against Iran at the IAEA in 2005. Iran feels that India should have been more sensitive towards Iran and not have toed the Western line. However India has been clear in the articulation that Iran has a right for peaceful use of nuclear energy while fulfilling its obligations owing to its membership of Nuclear Non-Proliferation Treaty (NPT) and has urged for resolution of the bone of contention through discussions and negotiations.

Iran's newly elected President Hassan Rouhani has conveyed to Prime Minister Manmohan Singh that developing relations with India is "one of Iran's foreign policy priorities".[13] Significant among the various inter-actions has been the recent 17th India-Iran Joint Economic Commission meeting held in Tehran on May 4, 2013. The external affairs minister of India, Salman Khurshid and his counterpart Ali Akbar Salehi, under the framework of joint commission, has discussed critical bilateral and regional issues. The key areas of cooperation identified are:

1. Regional connectivity
2. Enhancing bilateral trade and economic cooperation
3. Cooperation on regional security issues
4. Enhancing cultural and people-to-people contact.

The strategic interests of India and Iran reveal that both stand to gain from mutual cooperation and understanding. Given the increasing energy consumption, India needs a country that would help overcome its energy deficiency and Iran needs support from a powerful country having a say in international and regional affairs to achieve its own power interests in Western and Central Asia. Afghanistan and Syria are two other pivots of shared concern. Both are keen to counter any possible return of the Taliban regime in Afghanistan keeping in mind the impact for regional security dynamics.

Convergence of these interests finds reflection in the Indian pledge to support Iran on the up gradation of Chabahar port—the 'Golden Gate' to the landlocked Central Asian States and Afghanistan. By providing access to Afghanistan and Central Asian States, this port would reduce India, Commonwealth of Independent States (CIS) and Afghanistan's dependence on Pakistan as the link to the troubled region. India and Iran have also agreed to establish regional transport networks such as a rail link between Iran and Russia and the International North South Transport Corridor, which will help connect South, Central and West Asia to Europe and give a boost regional trade and investment. While these do sound positive, there are also fears of sabotage in the hands of Taliban which is stalling the immediate execution of the projects. Other than the Taliban angle, the future of India- Iran relations is also contingent upon:

(a) Iran's foreign policy dialogue with the European powers, China and Russia
(b) India's foreign relations dynamics with USA, Israel and GCC.

CONCLUSION

It is obvious that Iran is vital to India's foreign policy interests. Whether it is energy security or enhanced trade or countering Taliban, India needs Iran as a geo-strategic ally. If India has to retain influence in Afghanistan beyond 2014, India must rely on Iran's cooperation. However any attempt to implement infrastructural projects to enhance connectivity or trade is likely to be jeopardized given the strong presence of anti-India and anti-Iran forces in the region. The response of Pakistan to the Indo- Iran partnership the region would also have to be weighed in, since the alliance would reduce Pakistan's importance for the region. Throughout the last decade, Iran, India and Russia coordinated extensively to contain Pakistan's involvement in Afghanistan and its support to the Taliban. Caution must be exercised to prevent Afghanistan from becoming a battleground for extended proxy war among Iran, Pakistan and India. Therefore the foremost task before the two countries is to contain the Afghan issue through collective diplomacy and inclusion of all stakeholders, ensuring a smooth political transition next year.

Another hindrance to a smooth Indo-Iran bilateral relation is the Gulf Cooperation Council (GCC) countries that are ideologically opposed to Iran and are suspicious of Iran's power aspirations for the region. India's relationship with the GCC represents varied economic and strategic interests in the region and the bilateral trade had crossed the $124 billion mark in 2011–12. Iran and the GCC are not only at odds over territorial disputes, but Iran's nuclear program is also viewed with suspicion by the other regional power Saudi Arabia. In the event of any conflict between the GCC and Iran, Indian diplomacy will find itself in a tricky situation.

Most significantly, India cannot afford to overlook the US policy in West Asia and specifically Iran—more so with the USA declaring India as the lynchpin for its "Asian pivot and the enhanced bilateral ties. History is witness that under the American pressure India had voted against Iran at IAEA. Thus if in future if US-Iran nuclear standoff gets worse, then India is likely to stand by the United States. Another regional stakeholder, Israel is a major supplier of arms and military equipment to India and would never want Iran to become a nuclear weapon state or get stronger economically with the help of any other country. Given the bilateral strategic negotiations that are on between India, the USA and Israel, it would be diplomatic suicide for India to antagonise the US and other countries in nuclear suppliers group for Iran. Finally with Iran, China, and Russia building closer ties to offset the geopolitical dominance of the US, it becomes even more uneasy for India to choose a side.

Therefore the future of Indo-Iran relations is ultimately dependent on how best India manages to balance the interest of the extra and intraregional players and her own increasingly diverse foreign policy interests that often conflict with one another.

On a realistic assessment of the current situation of the region, it appears that Afghanistan can provide the way forward in bringing the about a change of relations between the Western powers (specially USA) and Iran, thus providing much relief to Indian diplomacy which has been walking the tightrope walk for quite some time. All the big powers have a major stake in the stability of Afghanistan. In past, India-Iran and Russia have jointly cooperated on Afghanistan with a focus on stability and security challenges that a possible return of Taliban would bring. With the 2014 retreat of US forces from Afghanistan round the corner, this might be an opportune moment for India to spearhead collective diplomacy efforts involving all the extra and intraregional stakeholders to help Afghanistan in rebuilding the country. Together India, Iran, USA and USSR can combine efforts to build infrastructure connecting Afghanistan with Central Asia via Iran, and bettering the opportunities for trade and commerce. Another key area of cooperation could be to share and pool information to neutralize the Taliban forces.It is only by working together on common issues of concern can Iran clear the air of mistrust surrounding its political intentions among the international community members. Iran's new president, Hassan Rouhani, has been proactive in heralding a distinct change in Iran's foreign relations and bringing about many unilateral moves to promote a more transparent image of Iran before the world community as the country tries to tackle humanitarian abuse and economic crisis brought forth in the wake of sanctions. India as he rightly recognizes, would have a key role to play as an ally to help Iran push ahead the agenda of regional peace, stability and economic prosperity.

REFERENCES

[1] Alterman, J.B. and Garver, J.W. (2008). *The Vital Triangle: China, the United States, and the Middle East.* New York: Center for Strategic and International Studies. Burman, E. (2009*). China and Iran: Parallel History, Future Threat?* The History Press.

[2] Reynolds, Paul. "How Saddam Could Embarrass the West." BBC News16 Dec. 2003. Retrieved from: http://news.bbc.co.uk/2/hi/middle_east/3324053.stm, accessed on 26.10.2013

[3] Lee, Sean, "The Second Iranian Revolution: Why Iran's modern radicalism should ease US fears", Stanford Journal of International Relations, Vol 10, No. 1; Retrieved from http://sjir.stanford.edu/pdf/Iran_REAL_final.pdf; accessed on 12.10.2013

[4] Ibid.

[5] Ibid.

[6] Andrew, Futter, "Obama's Nuclear Weapons Policy in a Changing World"; Retrieved from www.lse.ac.uk/IDEAS/publications/reports/pdf/SR009/futter.pdf; accesed on 12.10.2013.

[7] Clara, Weiss, "Russia and Iran deepen political and military cooperation", wsws.org, 8.8.2013;Retrievedfromwww.wsws.org/en/articles/2013/08/08/russ-a08.html? view=print;accessed on 15.10.2013

[8] Michael, Rubin, "Africa: Iran's final frontier", American Enterprise Institute (AEI) for Public Policy Research, No. 2, April 2013,Retrieved from http://www.aei.org/files/2013/04/16/-africa-irans-final-frontier_145228692703.pdf;accessed on 15.10.2013

[9] Iran rejects US precondition for participating in Syria peace conference—By Reuters 10/09/2013 10:32; retrieved from -http://www.jpost.com/Iranian-Threat/News/Iran-rejects-US-precondition-for-participating-in-Syria-peace-conference-328237; accessed on 20.09.2013

[10] Rebooting US-Iran relations-By Nader Entessar and Kaveh Afrasiabi, September 24, 2013; retrieved from http://www.bostonglobe.com/opinion/2013/09/23/iran-rouhani-obama-foreign-policy-litmus-test/WwWy0LHc3e9lhwbiG6a8oL/story.html;accessed on 01.10.2013.

[11] Retrieved from http://www.indianexpress.com/news/india-a-foreign-policy-priority-says-rouhani/1140364/; accessed on 24.10.2013.

[12] Sandep, Dikshit, "India, Iran to work around sanctions", The Hindu, 21.09, 2012; Retrieved from http://www.thehindu.com/news/international/india-iran-to-work-around-sanctions/article3844996.ece; accesse on 15.10, 2013

[13] Retrieved from http://www.indianexpress.com/news/india-a-foreign-policy-priority-says-rouhani/1140364/; accessed on 16.10.2013

Energy and Nuclear Security

Iran's Nuclear Weapons Programme— How Real is the Threat

Rajeev Agarwal

As the world is fine tuning and adapting to the future of the West Asian region after the so called "Arab spring" toppled decades old dictatorships in Egypt, Libya, Yemen and Tunisia, another interesting duel continues to foster in the region. This battle pitches Iran against the Western lobby led by the US which accuses Iran of running clandestine nuclear weapons programme which not only undermines the security of the region but also threatens its closest ally Israel. Iran, on the other hand repeatedly claims that it has no nuclear weapons programme and that the nuclear programme is for peaceful purposes, medical research and energy and that it has a sovereign right towards it under the NPT regime. With none of the warring sides relenting, West Asia has been brought to the cusp of war more than once in recent times. The battle lines continue to be drawn with each side perhaps waiting for the other to call the bluff.

The geo-political realm of West Asia would undergo a drastic change if any of the leading country (Iran and Saudi Arabia) obtains a nuclear weapon. The Iranian effort to obtain a nuclear weapon could serve as the Shiá axis's ultimate shield against any attempts to curtail its progress in the region. The Sunni ruled states of the Arab World led by Saudi Arabia fear that if there is an Iranian nuclear weapons umbrella, they are the ones who will be subject to pressure and blackmail difficult for them to resist. There is also a lurking apprehension that the US and possibly Israel(?) in such a scenario would stop short of responding militarily in order to avoid a nuclear war. Hezbollah, Hamas and other proxies of Iran will gain much more courage to act.

So far neither the IAEA nor the US intelligence community has been able to prove that Iran is developing, manufacturing or testing any nuclear weapon devices. Various assessments indicate that Iran could have nuclear weapon capability ranging from a few months up to two years. It appears quite clear that Iran is going to continue with its nuclear enrichment program. This is a red line that Iran is not going to allow other nations to trespass over. A large portion of its budget is specifically allotted to the nuclear program. The nuclear programme has become a sensitive issue for Iran and a major cause for nationalism.

Is it however, the nuclear weaponisation that Iran yearns for or is it a manifestation of a bigger fear that is threatening it? When seen from an Iranian perspective, it is the survival of the Islamic Regime that dominates the security perspective and strategic aims of present day Iran. On the other hand, when seen from a regional perspective, nuclear weaponisation of Iran is just one part and maybe, the public part of this strange conflict. At the core of this issue is the concern in the region over Iran's growing sphere of influence in the region which now stretches across the Levant from Afghanistan towards the Mediterranean.

This paper attempts to highlight various facets of this very interesting duel in West Asia and argues that it is not merely the nuclear programme that has led to Iran being targeted by majority of the international community. In fact there are other countries in the region (like Pakistan) which have declared nuclear weapons, could be seen as more unreliable and less responsible nations in their conduct in international affairs and have initiated military conflicts in recent times (including after acquiring nuclear weapon status) but, far from being targeted by severe economic sanctions like Iran, enjoy patronage of global powers.

THE IRANIAN NUCLEAR PROGRAMME

It may sound ironic in present circumstances when we see that the Iranian nuclear programme was born out "Atoms for Peace" programme sponsored by the US in 1950s. The US supplied the Tehran Nuclear Research Center (TNRC) with a small 5MW research reactor (TRR), fuelled by highly enriched uranium (HEU), in 1967. In 1968, Iran signed the Non Proliferation Treaty (NPT) in an effort to speed up its negotiations for nuclear agreements, particularly with the United States. This was ratified in 1970 and its obligations went into force. In 1973, the Shah of Iran established Atomic Energy Organisation of Iran (AEOI) and announced plans to install 23,000 MW of nuclear power in Iran by the end of the century. In the next five years, Iran concluded several contracts for the construction of nuclear plants and the supply of nuclear fuel: with the United States in 1974; Germany in 1976; and France in 1977. In 1976, Iran also purchased a stake in Eurodif's (the European consortium) Tricastin uranium enrichment plant in France and purchased a stake in the RTZ uranium mine in Rossing, Namibia. Also in 1976, the government signed a $700 million contract to purchase uranium yellowcake from South Africa.

By the time of the Islamic Revolution in January 1979, its nuclear program was considered one the most advanced in the Middle East. However, in the immediate aftermath of the Revolution, Iran's ambitious nuclear program fell apart due to the opposition by the Khomeini government to nuclear technology which led to the withdrawal of foreign suppliers from Iran and the abandonment of nuclear cooperation agreements. Iran's only nuclear power plants in 1979 were the two plants under construction at Bushehr, under contract with Germany's Siemens.

The outbreak of war with Iraq in 1980 and fear that Saddam Hussein might be developing a nuclear weapon, forced Iran to think that it needed a nuclear deterrent. As per reports, in 1984, at a top-level meeting, current supreme leader Ayatollah Ali Hosseini Khamenei and then president endorsed a nuclear weapons programme, saying "a nuclear arsenal would serve Iran as a deterrent in the hands of God's soldiers".[1] Towards the end of war with Iraq and thereafter, Iran took steps to revive its nuclear programme. It signed long-term nuclear cooperation agreements with Pakistan and China, in 1987 and 1990 respectively. In 1990, it began negotiating the Soviet Union over the completion of the Bushehr reactors and signed a bilateral nuclear cooperation agreement in August 1992. In January 1995, Russia formally announced that it would complete the construction of the Bushehr reactors and signed an agreement with Iran to build three additional reactors at the site.

Despite concerns expressed by the US on Iran's nuclear programme, it lumbered on till 2002 when a sensational disclosure by an exiled dissident Iranian group, the National Council of Resistance of Iran (NCRI) on 14 August 2002[2] revealed the existence of undeclared nuclear facilities in Iran, including pilot uranium enrichment plant at Natanz and a heavy water production plant under construction at Arak. In addition, Iran was continuing work on a 1,000 megawatt nuclear reactor at Bushehr under Russian help.

Between September and October 2003, the IAEA carried out a number of facilities inspections and met with Iranian officials to determine the history of Iran's nuclear program. To avoid referral to the UN Security Council, Iran entered into negotiations with the EU-3 (France, Germany, and the United Kingdom), and agreed in October 2003 to cooperate with the IAEA, sign the Additional Protocol, and temporarily suspend conversion and enrichment activities. Faced with sanctions threats, Iran concluded the Paris Agreement with the EU-3 on 15 November 2004. Iran agreed to continue the temporary suspension of enrichment and conversion activities, including the manufacture, installation, testing and operation of centrifuges, and committed to working with the EU-3 to find a mutually beneficial long-term diplomatic solution.

Diplomatic process however broke down on 1 August 2005, when Iran notified the IAEA that it would resume uranium conversion activities at Esfahan and on 5 August, Iran rejected the EU-3's Long Term Agreement prompting the IAEA Board of Governors adopting a resolution that found Iran in non-compliance with its Safeguards Agreement. In February 2006, Tehran ended its voluntary implementation of the Additional Protocol and resumed enrichment at Natanz. The IAEA Board of Governors subsequently voted to report Iran's case to the UN Security Council. Iranian President Mahmoud Ahmadinejad responded through a speech in April 2006 in which he acknowledged Iran's second uranium enrichment facility with P-2 centrifuges at Natanz. In June, the EU-3 together with the United States, China and Russia (P5+1) offered to provide Tehran with advanced civilian nuclear technology if Iran suspended enrichment activities and resumed implementation of the Additional Protocol to which Iran failed to respond clearly. In response to Iranian defiance, the UNSC unanimously passed Resolution 1696 in July, which demanded that Iran suspend enrichment activities, banned the international transfer of nuclear and missile technologies to Iran, and froze the foreign assets of twelve individuals and ten organizations involved with the Iranian nuclear program. Iran ignored the UNSC resolution and in the same month, inaugurated a heavy water production plant at Arak.

The next important timeline in this controversial programme came On 21 September 2009 when, under threat of public disclosure by the US, France, and the United Kingdom, Iran disclosed to the IAEA that it was building a second pilot enrichment facility at Fordow known as the Fordow Fuel Enrichment Plant (FFEP) near the holy city of Qom. Thereafter, Iran and the P5+1 (Five permanent members of UN Security Council and Germany) commenced talks; first in Geneva and then in Vienna. During the talks, Iran agreed to IAEA inspections at the FFEP and, in principle, to send 1,200 kg of LEU to Russia for further enrichment and to France for fuel plate fabrication. P5+1 and Iran tentatively agreed to this fuel swap arrangement. Iran, however, subsequently rejected the deal and proposed instead to conduct the exchange in phases, with the first phase involving the swap of 400kg of LEU for fuel on the Gulf island of Kish. The proposal was dismissed by the IAEA and the US as inconsistent with earlier negotiations. With the Tehran Research Reactor expected to run out of 19.7% enriched LEU fuel soon after 2009, Iranian President in

December 2009 announced that Iran will enrich Uranium to 20% itself[3] and on 09 February 2010 announced that Iran had produced its first batch of 20% enriched uranium.[4] Tensions with the international community further increased after President Ahmedinejad announced that Iran intended to construct 10 additional uranium enrichment facilities.

In a letter dated 19 February 2010, Iran informed the IAEA that it was still seeking to purchase the required fuel for the TRR on the international market and would be willing to exchange LEU for fuel assemblies "simultaneously or in one package inside the territory of Iran." It was followed by a new nuclear fuel swap proposal brokered by Brazil and Turkey. On 17 May 2010, Brazil, Turkey and Iran issued a joint statement in which Iran agreed to export half of its LEU stock (1,200 kg) to Turkey as a confidence-building measure, in return for 120 kg of 20% enriched uranium for use in its medical research reactor. The deal, however, was not accepted by Western countries, which saw Iran's agreement to the removal of only 1,200 kg of LEU from its territory as too little, too late. In June 2010, the UN Security Council approved another set of sanctions under UNSCR 1929, primarily aimed at Iran's nuclear-related investments; three affiliates of the state-owned shipping company the Islamic Republic of Iran Shipping Lines (IRISL) and the Iranian Revolutionary Guard Corps. These sanctions were followed by unilateral and multilateral sanction by the US, EU, Canada etc which not only targeted Iran's nuclear industry but its entire banking, financial, oil and gas sectors thus crippling the entire Iranian economy.

Efforts to resume talks continued throughout 2010 and 2011. On 13 July 2011, Russian foreign minister Sergey Lavrov proposed a phased approach to addressing the nuclear dispute with Iran which was not accepted by the west. The most damming report against Iran's nuclear programme came out in November 2011 by the IAEA[5] wherein the Agency presented a lengthy, detailed account of "possible military dimensions" to Iran's nuclear program. After the November 2011 IAEA report, the US and the EU launched a series of unprecedented unilateral sanctions. For the first time, the US designated the Government of Iran and all financial institutions in the country as entities of money laundering concern, warning financial institutions around the world that doing business with Iranian banks entailed significant risks.

The 'Arab Spring' protests took away some of the focus from Iran nuclear talks in 2011–12 but attempts continued during the period through talks at various levels. In January and February 2012, an IAEA team visited Iran to discuss ways to resolve outstanding issues but was unable to agree on a plan including grant of access to the IAEA at the Parchin military complex. On 14 April, 2012, Iran and the P5+1 countries met in Istanbul to re-open discussions about Iran's nuclear program followed by another round of talks on 23 May 2012 in Baghdad. Despite 'positive atmosphere', there were no signs of any common meeting points. The US presidential elections in November 2012 and the Iranian Presidential elections in June 2013 ensured no major talks or breakthroughs. The election of Hassan Rouhani as the President however has brought some cautious optimism regarding the future trajectory if nuclear talks. Riding on his main pledge to try to ease international sanctions imposed on Iran over its nuclear programme, he signaled greater engagement with Western powers in his victory speech in June 2013 where he said: "This victory is a victory for wisdom, moderation and maturity... over extremism.[6] "In his speech at the UN General assembly in September, he has given clear signals that Iran is ready to engage in constructive talks and seek a mutually acceptable resolution soon. He emphasized that he is prepared to engage in "time-bound and results-oriented" talks on his country's nuclear programme. He called the "so-called Iranian threat" as imaginary and added that Iran poses absolutely no threat to the world and that nuclear weapon and other weapons of mass destruction have no place in Iran's security and defence doctrine.[7] Talks have re-commenced in October with a preliminary meeting in Geneva on 15–16 October[8] which is to be followed by a detailed meeting on 07–08 November likely to formulate a roadmap for possible resolution of the issue.

NUCLEAR PROGRAMME AND IRANIAN REGION

The nuclear programme and the Iranian regime have been very closely associated, often drawing support from each other. In order to better understand the mutual relationship between the nuclear programme and the regime, it is necessary to have a look at the structure of Iranian regime too. The regime in Iran is based on an extremist interpretation of Shia Islam. The theological ideology establishes the supremacy of religion over governance. In the words of the regime's founder, Ayatollah Ruhollah Khomeini, "In Islam the legislative power and competence to establish laws belongs exclusively to God Almighty. The sacred Legislator of Islam is the sole legislative power. No one has the right to legislate and no law may be executed except the... ruling of the [Divine] Legislator. "[9] The regime structure is based on a complex democratic model with various intertwined and overlapping layers, working on parallel levels of governance and rejects the idea that religion and politics can be separated. The formal level is led by the democratically elected President and is responsible for routine governance of the nation. The other level is that of clerics headed by the Supreme Leader which decide on critical issues of national policy.

Thus, although the president is the nominal head of government, he takes direction from and reports to the Supreme Leader ensuring that there is a well-defined clerical oversight over governance issues and that the Supreme leader wields true power, the nuclear programme being one of them. It is however ironic in the sense that the current regime in Iran, immediately after the Iranian revolution in 1979 disapproved of the nuclear programme and shelved it. It was the eight year war with Iraq in the 1980s and Iraq's use of chemical weapons on Iran that forced Iran to think of a strong deterrent against future misadventure by Iraq and thus came about the revival of the nuclear programme in 1984.

Emerging from eight years of war, the nuclear programme was seen as an instrument towards self-reliance in energy and technology. Slowly the programme became a by-product of Iran seeking its rightful place in the region as well as at home. It became a consistent tool for the legitimacy of the theocratic regime around which it could rally national support against all other odds. The regime fed on people's perception that Iran was being denied the nuclear technology over which it had legitimate rights having signed the NPT. It fed on public minds that just because Iran had fought and got rid of autocratic regime under the Shah who was considered pro West, Iran was being targeted by the global community. Drawing from the glorious past of Persian empires, people were convinced that Iran could not be subjugated to the discriminatory policies of the West.

The sudden disclosure about secret nuclear programme in Iran in August 2002 and the entire process thereafter brought the regime and the nuclear programme closer. The international sanctions in the past decade has brought about economic and social hardships for the nation. In midst of growing dissent over the negative effect of the nuclear programme, the Iranian regime has come under frequent pressures. However, as mentioned earlier, it has skillfully rallied public support behind the programme making it appear that the sanctions on Iran are unfair and that it is being denied its legitimate right for nuclear enrichment. The election of Mahmoud Ahmadinejad as the President in 2005 just when the nuclear programme and the resultant international sanctions were becoming critical assumes importance. Many say that he was picked up by the

Supreme Leader to ratchet up public support in favour of the regime. His eight years in office not only ensured regime stability but gave a perception to the Iranian people that the entire world was conspiring against it and they needed to stand shoulder to shoulder to protect the nation. It is because of this stature that the occasional public protests against economic hardships were subdued. Even the Green Movement which stood up against the fraudulent Presidential elections in 2009 was carefully managed and kept under control.

The nuclear programme has thus been a rallying point for the regime domestically. However, the possibility of weaponisation of the nuclear weapons programme and its effect on regime needs a totally separate consideration. As regards nuclear weapons, the Supreme Leader has frequently said that it is un-Islamic and that Iran is not in pursuit of nuclear weapons. Iran, in fact gains little from possessing nuclear weapons. In case Iran get nuclear weapons, it is almost a given that Saudi Arabia and possibly Egypt and Turkey could be forced to do the same, thus dramatically altering the security situation in Iran's neighborhood. In a region infested by terrorism, the chances of a rogue group getting hold of a nuclear weapon and threatening its use could further endanger existing regimes. Being a theological state, Iran has very few friends. Possession of nuclear weapons could further alienate it as also force nations neutral to Iran to look at Iran with fear and suspicion. Also, the international community including US and Israel could seek legitimate right to bomb Iran. With very few friends and possible lack of retaliatory capability, Iran could face major damage. However keeping the threshold well beyond nuclear weapons capability keeps Iran's position ambiguous and in many ways strong enough to ward off external pressures.

It would thus seem clear that although nuclear programme has been a rallying point for the regime, the possession of nuclear weapons does not favour Iran in any manner. Iran would thus be served better if it reaches and maintains a level of 'nuclear latency' with the ability of break out in shortest possible time when required.

IRAN AND ITS INCREASING REGIONAL INFLUENCE: THE REAL THREAT?

West Asia bridges the area from the Arabian Sea to the Mediterranean Sea covering the land between Turkey in the north, Afghanistan in the east, the Persian Gulf in the south, and the Mediterranean Sea in the west. The three important powers in the region; Iran, Israel and Turkey dominate this zone, while Syria, Lebanon, Jordan and Iraq complete the complex geopolitical matrix. This region which contains almost 50 percent of the world's known oil and gas energy reserves, is a major centre of religious and ethnic rivalry, is home to the Arab-Israeli dispute, international terrorism and the supposed proliferation of weapons of mass destruction. Couple this with Saudi Arabia led Gulf countries to the south of Persian Gulf, there is a ready mixture of conflict and intrigue. Also, the battle lines between the Wahabi Sunni and Shia become more pronounced.

Of all the countries in the region, Iran is the only country which has a direct interface with Central Asia, West Asia and South Asia. Iran's centrality, its commanding position in the Persian Gulf, domination of the Strait of Hormuz, geographical position for oil and gas pipelines emanating from the Central Asian Republics and the energy rich Caspian Sea makes it a fulcrum of West Asia. This position gives Iran a chance to carve out a bigger sphere of influence in the region.

Withdrawal of US forces from Iraq further increased Iran's sphere of influence in the region. The withdrawal had two immediate consequences. First, it created a vacuum the Iraqis themselves cannot fill, Iran willingly stepped in. The withdrawal of US forces from Iraq without a strong Iraqi government and military also created a crisis of confidence on the Arabian Peninsula. Saudi Arabia, in particular, unable to match Iranian spread of influence and doubtful of US intentions to restrict Iran, is increasingly pressured, out of necessity, to find a political accommodation with Iran.

Iraq turning into an extension of Iranian sphere of influence has extended Iran's sphere of direct influence upto Syria (its close ally), has effectively brought Iran to the borders of Kuwait, Saudi Arabia and Jordan, has effectively extended Iran's border with Turkey and has brought it in close proximity to its major adversary in the region; Israel.

Amongst the countries in the region, the AKP led government in Turkey over the past decade has not only built ties with Iran steadily but has also exerted its independence in policies over its relations with the US. Despite being a NATO ally, it did not permit US troops to launch operations through its territory in 2003 into Iraq. Even thereafter, it's breaking off ties with Israel in 2010 after the Gaza Flotilla incident and taking the initiative along with Brazil to be the interlocutor on Iran nuclear talks has not gone down well with the US. US thus feels that Turkey could go out of its sphere of influence and the benefit could go to Iran. Although there has been some strain in their ties due to their opposing stance on the current Syrian crisis, it is unlikely to adversely affect Iran's ties with Turkey in the long run.

As regards Afghanistan, the US is determined to pull out its combat mission by end of 2014. Iran with historical and cultural ties in Afghanistan, especially the western provinces could become influential. The Hazara population in Afghanistan swears allegiance to Iran and Iran with the history of supporting the Northern Alliance in overthrow of Taliban regime in 2001 could play a major role in post 2014 Afghanistan.

Given its historical links from the times of the Persian Empire and the significant Shiite Muslim population, Iran enjoys significant support in some of the Central Asian Countries like Tajikstan, Uzbekistan and Turkmenistan. It has funded several welfare and education projects there and enjoys goodwill in the region.

As regards major powers, Iran enjoys good support from Russia and China. Both have stood by Iran not only on the nuclear issue in the past but also the present Syrian crisis. Trade and defence ties have increased manifold and China, especially has been one of the major source of oil exports for Iran despite international sanctions.

Despite its adversarial relationship with the Saudi Arabia led GCC, Iran enjoys cordial relations with Oman and Bahrain. In Yemen Iran supports the Shiite Houthi rebels in the North and is involved in proxy war with Saudi Arabia. In Israel-Palestine issue, Iran supports the Palestine cause and has been especially supportive of Hamas and Hezbollah in their conflict with Israel.

It would thus seem that Iran has steadily increased its sphere of influence in the region. Given its declared anti US and anti-Israel stance, it is definitely not a very comfortable situation for the US and its allies. It gets even more pronounced when seen in the context of waning US interest in the region and its declaration of 'Asia Pivot', which would lead to shift in focus towards the Asia Pacific. The signs are already there as the US has been very reluctant to be drawn into any regional conflict directly as seen in the case of Libya and Syria as well as its drawing down in Afghanistan soon. In such a situation either the US and its allies accept Iran's spreading influence in the region or do something to counter it. Accepting Iran as a regional hegemon is not acceptable due to concerns of Israel as well as the GCC. Military strikes on Iran may not yield the required pay offs given its military might and Iran's influence across the region (especially through its proxies in Hamas, Hezbollah, etc). Nuclear issue is therefore an issue on which Iran can be pinned down and kept under check.

CONCLUSION

Iran's nuclear programme therefore is a story of several interesting paradoxes. A programme which was built by the US is today being threatened by it. The Iranian regime which shunned the nuclear programme in 1979, today identifies its survival with it. Although the world accuses Iran of running a clandestine nuclear weapons programme, it has yet to establish any concrete evidence despite numerous opportunities which various teams in IAEA had in the past decade while visiting and inspecting various sites in Iran. Also, till December 2009, Iran enriched Uranium only upto 3.5% which is well below weapons grade. It was the denial of higher grade enriched Uranium to Iran which prompted Iran to publicly declare enrichment up to 20%.

Also, the history of nuclear weapons clearly demonstrates two clear facts; firstly, no nation has yet been prevented from becoming a nuclear weapons power if it sets it sights on it whether it was India, Pakistan, North Korea or Israel and secondly, there has yet been no incident of a nuclear weapon nation using its nuclear weapons in a conflict. Iran, despite its traditional belligerence has conducted itself with restrain and is yet to be directly involved in any military conflict in a region riddled with intra and inter regional conflicts. Finally, as discussed, it is in Iran's interest to maintain a level of 'nuclear latency' and it has no need to declare a nuclear weapons programme.

REFERENCES

[1] Iran capable of building nuclear bomb, is working on missile to carry atomic warhead: IAEA report, AP News, 18 September 2009, available at http://www.nydailynews.com/news/world/iran-capable-building-nuclear-bomb-working-missile-carry-atomic-warhead-iaea-report-article-1.379898#ixzz2iLYbyCiJ

[2] Remarks by Alireza Jafarzadeh on New Information on Top Secret Projects of the Iranian Regime's Nuclear Program, http://www.iranwatch.org/library/ncri-new-information-top-secret-nuclear-projects-8-14-02

[3] Iran President Says Nuclear Enrichment Will Grow, New York Times, 02 December 2009, http://www.nytimes.com/2009/12/03/world/middleeast/03nuke.html?_r=0

[4] Iran produces first batch of 20% enriched uranium: president, http://news.xinhuanet.com/english2010/world/2010-02/11/c_13172471.htm

[5] Implementation of the NPT Safeguards Agreement and relevant provisions of Security Council resolutions in the Islamic Republic of Iran, http://www.iaea.org/Publications/Documents/Board/2011/gov2011-65.pdf

[6] Hassan Rouhani wins Iran presidential election, BBC News 15 June 2013, http://www.bbc.co.uk/news/world-middle-east-22916174

[7] Full text of Hasan Rouhani's speech at the UN, http://www.timesofisrael.com/full-text-of-hasan-rouhanis-speech-at-the-un

[8] 'Substantive' talks over Iran's nuclear program, CNN News 16 October 2013, http://edition.cnn.com/2013/10/16/world/meast/iran-nuclear-talks

[9] Ruhullah al-Musawi Khomeini, Islam and Revolution, trans. Hamid Algar (Berkeley: Mizan Press, 1981), p. 55.

India-Iran Energy Ties: Problems and Prospects

Abhimanyu Behera

INTRODUCTION

India and Iran have shared close historical and civilizational ties which have bound the two countries together more than a millennium. The two nations have also long influenced with each other in the fields of culture, art, architecture, and language, especially during the 1526–1757 period, when the Mughals ruled India. India and Iran also shared a border until 1947. Notwithstanding these connections, Iran's alignment with the West during Cold War and India's nonalignment policy prevented the two countries from closely interacting with each other. In the post-independence period, Indo-Iran relations have gone through many ups and downs. But, after the Iranian Revolution in 1979, their relations have entered into a new phase of engagement between the two countries with high level visit of heads. Iran is one of the most important countries in the West Asian region with which India has maintained fairly and extensive relations in various fields. Both countries came closer after India and Iran signed a treaty of friendship on 15 March 1950, known as the perpetual peace and friendship period (Pasha 2009: 115).

Indo-Iranian relations were first boosted by the visit of the then Indian Prime Minister P.V. Narasimha Rao to Iran in 1993 which was followed by a reciprocal visit of Iranian President Rafsanjani to India in 1995 by a tripartite agreement among India, Iran and Russia to establish a North-South Transportation Corridor linking India through Iran to Russia and then to Europe. However, the most important milestones for Indo-Iranian relations came up when Indian Prime Minister Vajpayee visited Tehran in 2001, followed by the reciprocal visit of Iranian President Khatami to India in 2003 during India's Republic Day celebrations. Both India and Iran have strong motives for courting the other. Iran sees India as a strong partner that will help Tehran to avoid strategic isolation, particular at a moment when Tehran has been designated a member of the "Axis of Evil" (Berlin 2004). For India, the establishment of a strong relationship with Iran is part of a wider effort to pursue Indian interests pragmatically and patiently with all significant states and especially with those in India's neighbourhood. It has been part of a broad effort in recent years to transform Indian foreign policy towards Iran.

SIGNIFICANCE OF IRAN FOR INDIA

Iran's paramount importance is its hydrocarbon resources, as it holds 10 percent of the world's proven crude oil reserves and 15 percent of the world's proven natural gas reserves. Its location on the Persian Gulf coast allows it to control the Strait of Hormuz and to threaten to block maritime traffic in the strait. Iran has also one of the largest armed forces in the West Asian region, with significant maritime capabilities and ballistic missile capabilities. Another factor that largely affects bilateral relations is that, like Iran, India too has a large muslim population of 160 million, the second largest Shiaite population in the world. However, the importance of Iran to India is based on two relevant factors i.e., energy and geostrategic location.

Energy

In the light of steady economic growth, since the 21st century the Indian Government has positioned energy security as a key foreign policy consideration to sustain economic and social development which is crucial to India's rise in international system (Pant and Super 2013). The imports of oil from Iran are often cited as the most important factor behind India's need for healthy relations with the Islamic Republic. India has been undergoing rapid growth for two decades and is thirsty for energy. India's main importance is Iran's hydrocarbons, as it holds huge amount of oil and gas reserve. Today's energy ties between India and Iran are on the brink of a crisis. While India is under heavy political pressure to stop the imports entirely, it would be hard pressed to find alternative sources of crude oil, in terms of both quality and shipping costs.

Geostrategic Location

For India, Iran serves as a land bridge both to countries in the Caucasus and to the nations of Central Asia, and through them, to North and Central Africa. Since the subcontinent was divided between India and Pakistan, India has been blocked from direct access not only to Central Asia, but also to Afghanistan. Iran is the only bridge that allows India access to Afghanistan and Central Asia for economic or security purposes. India needs Iran to achieve its varied objectives in Central Asia. Both the governments are optimistic about the commercial benefits of Central Asia markets and hope to share the benefits of the North-South Transit Corridor. Iran will require massive infrastructure investments to extract maximum benefits from it, and India is lined up to provide cost-effective intellectual and material assistance in the development of information technology networks, ports, roads, and rail projects (Balooch 2009: 25–29). However, several large projects have been designed out of which the most important is the Chabahar port and the North-South corridor.

ENERGY FACTOR IN INDO-IRAN RELATIONS

India and Iran are two important players in Asia and world today. There is a great potential for meaning full cooperation between them in energy, trade and economic sectors. Energy is one of the most important and efficacious elements in the strategic collaborations between Iran and India (Roy and Lele 2011). India's large population and the need for fast economic growth, India is in need of new energy sources. In the field of energy, Iran is known as India's one of the most important oil trade partner. It imports 12% of total crude oil and the second largest after Saudi Arabia. The most important capacities and potentialities for the relationship between Iran and India lie on energy and trade collaborations. These two countries are of great importance in Asia and in the realm of regional powers. There isalso a good opportunity between them to expand their mutual relations (Sisakht and Mahmoudi 2012: 9267). Nevertheless, energy can be one of the most consequential fields for the expansion of ties between the countries.

Since the end of the Cold War, India has been slowly forging a comprehensive relationship with Iran based on energy and commercial cooperation, infrastructure development. Iran holds particular importance for India as it provides unique access to Afghanistan and Central Asia, two theatres in which India seeks to project greater influence (Fair 2007: 14,5–159). Iran and India have an explicit interest in advancing commercial and energy ties. With the world's sixth-largest oil reserve second-largest proven gas reserve, Iran is anxious to get its hydrocarbons out of the ground and into new markets, while energy-starved India wants to access into those resources. Nevertheless, India is likely to presence it's grow in Iranian energy sector not only has Pakistan signed the pipeline deal with Iran but China is triggering to make its presence in Iran in big way (Pant 2010).

India's international energy strategy has been two-fold: diversifying sources of supply and increasing India's stake in overseas production facilities. Although oil is not India's primary energy source, 70 percent of India's energy needs are met by coal and oil is still India's major energy import.

India imports over 70 percent of its oil, and some experts believe that this number will rise to 90 percent in the next two decades. Iran is a major supplier of energy to India. According to the Planning Commission of India (2005), India imported approximately 9.61 metric tons of oil from Iran in 2004–2005. This accounts for approximately 10 percent of India's total oil imports, making Iran India's fourth-largest source of imported oil. India's phenomenal economic growth and limited coal reserves are going to fuel an exponential increase in dependence on imported oil, therefore energy supplies will remain a major economic and strategic issue in India's engagement with Iran (Planning Commission report 2005).

ENERGY COOPERATION

Energy cooperation between Iran and India has been the major incentive for two states to come closer. In this regard, According to the New Delhi Declaration in January 2003, "India and Iran had a complementarity of interests in the energy sector which could develop as a strategic area of their future relationship. Iran with its abundant energy resources and India with its growing energy needs as a rapidly developing economy are natural partners" (New Delhi Declaration 2003). This complementarity of interests was recognised in the Tehran Declaration, stated that "The geographical situation of Iran and its abundant energy resources along with the rapidly expanding Indian economy and energy market on the other hand, to create a unique complementarity which the sides agree to harness for mutual benefit." Thus energy cooperation between Iran and India has forged as a producer-consumer relationship that promises to serve both countries' immediate and long-term needs (Tehran Declaration 2001).

India, in recent years, has emerged as one of world's largest consumers and importers of petroleum products. It has experienced a growing energy supply-demand gap as its domestic production of oil and gas has failed to keep pace with rising consumption needs. For India, energy relations are even more vital in that energy security is seen as absolutely essential if India is to achieve great power status. Thus, India's quest to diversify its foreign sources of supply (Recknagel, 2004). On the other hand, Iran is endowed with enormous energy resources, and is therefore keenly interested in exporting its surplus natural gas to India. Iran has 5 percent of world's crude oil and 14 percent of world's natural gas reserves. In fact, it has the second largest natural gas reserves in the world after Russia, estimated at 23 trillion cubic meters. Therefore, Iran has figured prominently in India's strategy to establish and expand its energy relationship with the Gulf countries. As far as the practical dimension of energy cooperation between the two sides established a Joint Working Group (JWG) on energy transport in 1999, with a view to determining how to make this complementarity work to the advantage of both sides.

Anothersignificant development took place in June 2005, when India and Iran signed a multi-billion dollar deal under which Iran will supply India with 5 million tons of liquefied natural gas annually for 25 years in the beginning of 2009. The deal also envisaged Indian participation in the development of the Yadavaran and Jufeyr oilfields in Iran. Besides, India and Iran have been discussing the construction of a gas pipeline via Pakistan since early 1990s. However, the idea has not come to fruition, initially due to India's reluctance to have the pipeline pass through Pakistani territory, Pakistan's assurances regarding the security of the pipeline notwithstanding. More recently, Indian interest in the project seems to have waned, which many attribute to the US offer of civil nuclear energy to India. The US is believed to have demanded the abandonment of the project as one of the quid pro quos for the civil nuclear deal. The Indian stance has led Pakistan and Iran to decide to go ahead with the project even without India (Kiani, 2006). Although, India still maintains that it is determined to implement the pipeline project and will continue efforts to reach a tripartite agreement on the project, there is a perception that India does not want to categorically abandon the project until the Indo-US nuclear deal is passed by the US Congress. India, therefore, participated in the Iran-Pakistan-India Joint Working Group's meeting in Islamabad from May 22–23, 2006 (Ibid).

Energy is undoubtedly the common meeting point for India and Iran. Iran, with its huge hydrocarbon resources, and India, with its increasing demand for energy, can be partners to carryforward the existing cooperation in the energy sector to more meaningful levels. According to Energy Information Administration (EIA 2006) report, Iran's oil reserves increased by five percent from 125.8 billion barrels (bb) in 2005 to 132.5 bb in 2006 EIA (2006) and as per 2009 EIA reports, Iran has 136.2 bb of oil reserves, with Saudi Arabia having the most at 266.7 bb and Canada the second largest at 178.1 bb. Iran holds the second largest gas reserve estimated at 992 trillion cubic feet (tcf) after Russia, making it the largest natural gas producer in West Asia. The largest natural gas development project in Iran is the offshore South Pars fields discovered in 1990, estimated to contain between 350 tcf and 490 tcf of reserves. Iran has set a goal to raise natural gas production to between nine tcf and 10 tcf per year by 2010. This amounts to more than double its 2006 marketed production of 4.4 tcf (EIA 2009). However, given the sanctions imposed on Iran, this target may be difficult to achieve. In addition, Iran has the second largest deposits of copper, the largest deposit of zinc and the ninth and tenth largest deposits of iron ore and uranium, respectively (MEA 2008).

Iran's importance for India's energy security is undisputable. India's imports of crude oil and petroleum products in 2007–2008 were worth US$ 10.96 billion and its export of gasoline to Iran was worth US$ 850 million (Agence News Irna 2008). India is the third largest buyer of Iranian crude oil. More than 12 percent of India's oil imports come from Iran. India has signed an agreement with Iran to purchase five million tonnes of liquified natural gas (LNG) per annum for 25 years from the second half of 2009. This agreement, however, could not be implemented due to a dispute over prices. According to BBC media reportsIndia's vote against Iran at the IAEA as the cause for non-implementation of the LNG deal. However, Indian and Iranian officials are of the view that this deal can be renegotiated. During the recent visit of Iran's national security chief Sa'id Jalili to Delhi, prime minister Manmohan Singh said that energy cooperation was the most important area for expanding economic ties between India and Iran (BBC 2009).

INDIA'S THIRST FOR ENERGY

India imports more than two-thirds of its hydrocarbon requirements and any further escalation would adversely affect its energy security. Placing current import dependency at 72 percent, a Planning Commission report warns that the country faces 'formidable challenges' in meeting its energy needs and that our 'import dependence is growing rapidly' (Planning Commission 2006: 9). In this scenario, India's policy makers are well aware of the need to diversify the sources of energy supply. This is where Iran comes into play in the Persian Gulf nation accounts for roughly 10 percent of the world's total proven petroleum reserves (Country Analysis Briefs January 2010). Iran in 2007 accounted for 17 percent of India's crude oil imports making it the second-largest supplier of oil after Saudi Arabia at 23 percent. In addition to seeking new suppliers for energy, India is also looking for energy resource diversification. This accounts for the increasing use of natural gas, largely driven by demand in the power sector. The power and fertilizer sectors account for nearly three-quarters of natural gas consumption in India. Although India's natural gas production has consistently increased, demand has already exceeded supply and the country has been a net importer of natural gas since 2004.

Iran is the second largest reserve of natural gas, according to (EIA 2013) estimate stands second only to Russia. It has 1, 187 tcf of gas reserve. Iran's tremendous potential as a source of natural gas for India is yet to materialise. Talks have been underway between Iran and India to build a pipeline via Pakistan to transport Iran's abundant natural gas to India. The plan, also known as the Iran-Pakistan-India (IPI) pipeline project, envisages the transportation of Iranian natural gas through a 2,600-kilometre pipeline from the South Pars fields in Iran via Pakistan to Gujarat in India. Even though the project appears beneficial for all the concerned parties, several commercial and political issues have delayed an agreement. Indian security officials have questioned the wisdom of importing a commodity as critical as natural gas through the Pakistani corridor. They insist that the gas pipeline passing through Pakistan should be accompanied by clear security guarantees from Islamabad. Moreover, there is still no agreement, for example, between India and Iran on the price of the gas or between India and Pakistan on the tariff to be paid for transportation across latter's territory. Due to the uncertainties involving this pipeline, the Indian government's 11th Five Year plan does not project any gas supply from this route. In mid-2009, Pakistan signed an agreement with Iran to secure 750 million cubic feet of natural gas per day through the pipeline, without India's participation in the negotiations. The message from this development seems to be that India could join the deal as intended but it would not wait infinitely for New Delhi to make up its mind. India's hesitation in reaching an agreement on the proposed deal is no less influenced by US opposition to it (Mafinezam and Mehrabi 2008: 78).The Bush administration opposed the project because of the crucial revenue it would give to Iran, which is facing punitive economic sanctions for its controversial nuclear programme. Even though Washington is no longer actively opposing the pipeline project, India's negotiations with Iran over the pipeline could now trigger sanctions under the Comprehensive Iran Sanctions, Accountability, and Divestment Act of 2010 (CISADA). This Act provides for the imposition of penalties against foreign companies that invest more than $20 million in a single year in Iran's energy sector.

IPI Gas Pipeline

On the Iran-Pakistan-India (IPI) gas pipeline, India continues to reiterate its interest to take part in the project. Due to technical, security, political and pricing problems, the deal has been on freeze for almost three years. India has not been attending trilateral meetings since 2007. In this context, the Iranian ambassador in India said in February 2010 that while the doors are open to India to join the IPI, Iran will not wait indefinitely (Dikshit 2010). Iran and Pakistan have signed the final agreement in Turkey in May 2010 to launch the Iran–Pakistan gas pipeline, with a provision for India to join the project at a later stage. Both countries have signed the operational agreement and the heads of agreement. Under this provision, Pakistan will have the right to charge transit fees for transportation of gas to India calculated in accordance with international practices (The Hindu 2010). In March 2010, India indicated its willingness to hold talks on the IPI project. On the sidelines of the 12th International Energy Forum, India's petroleum minister Murli Deora met Iran's deputy minister of international affairs H. Noghrehkar Shirazi and proposed bilateral talks in May 2010. India proposed the meeting of the Joint Working Group of both the countries on the pipeline project and is waiting for Tehran to decide the dates (Ibid). Tehran has yet to respond to this proposal. During the foreign minister's visit in May 2010, it was conveyed to the Iranian officials that India's main concerns on the project relate to security of the pipeline that will pass through the volatile Baluchistan province in south-western Pakistan, as well as differences over pricing (Hindustan Times, 2010).

Investment

In the oil and gas sector, India's ONGC Videsh Ltd (OVL) has successfully executed a contract to explore the Farsi oil block. It was awarded the development contract for this block in November 2008 and it submitted the development plan in 2009. OVL is interested in exploration and development of Phase 12 of the South Pars and Azadegan oilfields. In December 2009, after tough negotiations, Iran signed an agreement with OVL and ALPS (Hinduja Group) combined, providing a 40 percent stake in this project. ONGC and ALPS, along with Petronet LNG, have also signed a pact to buy a 20 percent stake in Iran's LNG, and building a $4.32 billion plant on the southern coast to convert gas from SP-12 into LNG for export. In addition to phase 12 is the largest of 28 phases in which the South Pars gas field in the Persian Gulf is divided. According to some media reports, SP-12 is expected to produce three billion cubic feet of gas per day and two-thirds of this will be converted into LNG for exports. However, according to IEA report of 2009 indicates that each phase is expected to produce one billion cubic feet per day (IEA 2009).

Iran has offered to sell six billion tonnes of LNG per year to India. Petropars is a subsidiary of the National Iranian Oil Company, which will hold a 40 percent stake in SP-12 and the remaining 20 percent will be with Sonangol of Angola (Business Standard 2010). However, a consortium of three Indian companies—ONGC Videsh Ltd., Indian Oil Corporation Ltd. and Oil India Ltd. has plans to invest about US$ 5 billion to develop Iran's Farzad gas field in the Persian Gulf (The Hindu 2008). The oil and gas sector offers possibilities of setting up mutually beneficial projects. India and Iran have successfully collaborated in setting up the Madras Refinery project, the Kudremukh iron ore project and the Madras Fertiliser project, as well as the Irano-Hind Shipping Company. Iran can possibly invest in the energy sector in India, such as in an oil storage facility. Thus, these two countries have good collaborations in the field of energy as follows: Natural gas pipeline, LNG import from Iran, Investment of Indian companies in energy in Iran (Roy and Lele, 2011).

It is worthwhile that India-Iran cooperation in the energy sectors is based on the solid logic of supply and demand. Iran is anxious to sell its abundant hydrocarbon resources and India is an eager buyer. The complementary interest of India and Iran in this area was recognised in the New Delhi and Tehran declarations in 2003. India envisages energy as a strategic area in the bilateral relationship, whereas Iran emphasises mutual benefits that would accrue from enhanced cooperation. With high rates of economic growth and over 17 percent of the world's population, India has become a significant consumer of energy resources. The government hopes to maintain an annual Gross Domestic Product (GDP) growth rate of about 8–10 percent over the next quarter century to meet its goals for poverty eradication. This level of growth will require India to at least triple its primary energy supply (Zissis 2007). In 2006, India was the sixth largest oil consumer in the world and some observers believe that by 2025, India become the fourth largest consumer of crude oil following the US, China and Japan (Tuli 2006).

INDIA'S ENERGY STRATEGY

India's international energy strategy has become a key ingredient of its foreign policy. Its strategy to acquire stakes in energy production facilities in Iran, in order to ship back Liquefied Natural Gas (LNG). India's investment in Iran's energy sector stands around $100 million. In November 2009, the overseas arm of state-run Oil and Natural Gas Commission (ONGC), ONGC Videsh Limited (OVL) and Ashok Leyland Projects Services, a private company, signed agreements to take 40 percent stake in South Pars field-phase 12 (SP-12), offered by the state-run National Iranian Oil Company (NIOC). OVL has also submitted a

$5.5 billion plan to bring to production the Farzad-B gas find in Farsi gas fields in the Persian Gulf. Besides, in December 2009, OVL agreed to take 20 percent stake in the LNG gas export facility that Iran LNG (a subsidiary of NIOC) is building at the southern Iranian coast. Though this plant is to turn gas produced from phase-12 into LNG for exports, India is eying on it for turning gas from the Farzad-B gas field into LNG. The Indian company is expected to receive up to 6 million tonnes per annum of LNG for its efforts in both the gas fields (Business Standard Report 2009). Natural gas is set to become the major component of India's import from Iran, especially as domestic demand rises and India begins to face higher prices in the international market.

MAJOR PROBLEMS AND CHALLENGES

Iran and Sanctions

Iran is still facing sanctions from US, EU and United Nations. In the beginning of 2012 the United States and the European Union imposed harsh sanctions on Iran's energy and financial sectors with the goal of preventing other countries from purchasing Iranian oil and conducting transactions with Central Bank of Iran (Mahajan, 2013). Along with, it also forbids Europe insurance companies from insuring shipments of crude oil from Iran. However, the EU and US sanctions go into effect, insurance services for oil imports from Iran will be restricted. As most of the ship insurance companies and their reinsurers are American and European, refiners will import crude carried over by Iranian ships. It remains be seen how much India can rely on Iranian transportation. Iran will not be able to dedicate its oil cargo fleet to India due to competing needs like storing its excess supply of oil. Moreover, because of sanctions India has reduced its oil imports 26.5% in 2012–13 where it was carrying 18.1 million tons reduced to 13.1 million tons of crude oil (The Hindu, 2013).

Payment Mechanism

Payment Mechanism is another pertinent issue as the US sanctions on Iranian Central Bank for carrying out transactions in US dollar and Euro have made it difficult for India to make payments directly. But the actual problem started when Reserve Bank of India withdrew Asian Clearing Union (ASU) in 2010 through which India was paying Iran directly all oil transactions. Moreover, another problem under this mechanism is the increasing volatility of currencies in global market.

Difficulties in Investment

Oil exploration was stocked because of investment constraint in Iranian energy sector. However, the difficulty in investment sector has signalled a major energy problem between the two countries. In addition, it has also lack of foreign technology which has severely impacted on investment.

Tension between US and Iran

Prolonged Tension between the US and Iran and their inability to resolve mutual differences since 1979 largely impeded India's energy security through Iran. The historical grievances between the US and Iran were far too painful for either country to seek accommodation with other (Kumaraswamy, 2013).

Poor Business Environment in Iran

Business environment in Iran is not favourable. As per Doing Business Report of World Bank 2012, Iran ranked 140 out of 183 countries in 2011 still lower at 144 in 2012 slipped to 145 in 2013 out of 185 countries. However, this study clearly indicates that the Iran's business climate has not been conducive to external trade and investment as it is seen as a result of economic sanctions (World Bank 2012).

SUGGESTIONS

In order to bring harmony among them and the issues can be solved by taking the following steps. First of all, developing the trans-Afghan transit routes to Russia, Central Asia and Afghanistan which was discussed with the Iranian Foreign Minister in 2009 led the prospects of closer cooperation in the energy sector. Secondly, developing the IPI project because India is very much keen on the integrated development of Iranian Chabahar Port and building a railway line from there to Bam on the Iran-Afghanistan border (The Hindu 2009). Along with we are also looking at reenergising international north south transport corridor (INSTC) to Europe. Thirdly, India should participate in joint exploration and production sharing Agreement in any oil block of Iran. Fourthly, Development of Insurance Fund, India has been preparing a $34 million insurance fund to cover future imports as India insures declined to cover refineries process Iranian oil. In combating sanctions Iran has made a conscious effort to orient its trade and commercial ties. In this regard, by the first quarter of 2013, 75 percent of Iran's trade has been channelled to Asia (Aneja, 2013). Finally, Iran is the only opportunity to dump billions of dollars into various economic sectors. However, the two countries prepare the grounds for further cooperation at the international level.

CONCLUSION

Being a major player in the hydrocarbon sector, Iran is both an opportunity and challenge for India. On one level, Iranian energy could partly address India's growing enthusiasm for oil and gas on the other level, geographic proximity, resource diversity and political dividends are extra leverage for India. Moreover, India's willingness to transform its energy ties with Iran beyond purely commercial transactions unfortunately coincides with its desire to negotiate a civil nuclear deal with the US. As a result, it has brought India within the ambit of US-Iran tensions. Nevertheless, the relation between Iran and India is of great importance in the 21th century. These two countries need each other's help and assistance by virtue of their geographical proximity, cultural background, and coordination in strategic profits, geopolitical and geostrategic condition. India and Iran have got copious mutual advantages for investment and strengthening their relations particularly in the energy sector. India owns all the prerequisite components and potentialities to become the regional and global power and can be a pioneer country in economy, military and nuclear fields. But to reach to these long term goals India needs a stable energy especially gas. Nonetheless, energy security is the most important components in the global issues today. Iran with the extensive gas resources is the choice for India. But here there is a problem that India has extensive relations with the United States and European countries. Large population and other countless problems made India to establish great relations with other countries but these relations should not be considered as anti-Iranian relations. However, common profits, reciprocal vulnerability, tertiary players in recent years were very influential to the relations between India and Iran. These influences brought the capacities and limitations in mutual relations between the two countries.

REFERENCES

[1]   Aneja, A. (2013). "Deepening of India-Iran Energy Ties, a win win outcome". The Hindu, August 21, 2013.

[2]   Balooch, M. (2009). Iran and India's Cooperation in Central Asia", *China and Eurasia Forum Quarterly*, Vol. 7(3): 25–29.

[3]   BBC (2009). 'Regional Problems Unresolved Without India, Iran-Indian PM', *BBC Monitoring Global News line-South Asia Political*, March 29, 2009.

[4]   Berlin, Donald L. (2004). "India-Iran Relations: A Deepening Entente", Special Assessment, Asia-Pacific Centre for Security Studies.

[5] Blank, S. (2010). "Will China Join the Iran-Pakistan-India Pipeline?", *China Brief*, Volume: 10 Issue: 5, March 5, 2010, Jamestown Foundation, http://www.jamestown.org/programs/chinabrief/single/?tx_ttnew

[6] Business Standard (2010). 'ONGC, Hindujas Spar over Stake in Iran Gas Field', Business Standard, January 25, 2010, Iran.

[7] Country Analysis Briefs (2010). 'Iran', Energy Information Administration Official Energy Statistics from the US Government. Retrieved 15 February 2010, from http://www.eia.doe.gov/emeu/cabs/Iran/Full.html

[8] Dikshit, S. (2010). 'Can't Wait Indefinitely on Pipeline Project: Iran', *The Hindu* (Delhi), February10, 2010.

[9] EIA (2009). Energy Information Administration /International Energy Outlook 2009, at http://www.eia. doe.gov/oiaf/ieo/pdf/0484(2009).pdf (accessed May 19, 2011).

[10] EIA (2009). Energy Information Administration /International Energy Outlook, No. 26, 39.2009.

[11] EIA (2013). Energy Information Administration "Iran", Country Analysis Brief, 2013.

[12] Hindustan Times (2010). 'Krishna Heads to Tehran; Afghanistan, Pipeline on Agenda', Hindustan Times, May 13, 2010.

[13] Khan, M.N. (2008). "Vajpayee's Visit to Iran: Indo-Iranian Relations and Prospects of Bilateral Cooperation", Strategic Analysis, 25(6): 765–779.

[14] Kiani, Khaleeq (2006). "Pakistan To Get 33pc More Gas: India Almost Out of Iran Pipeline Project", *Dawn*, May 1, 2006.

[15] Kumaraswamy, P.R. (2013). "India's Energy Dilemma with Iran", Journal of South Asian Studies, Vol. 36 (2): 288–296.

[16] Mafinezam, Alidad and Mehrabi, Aria. 2008. *Iran and its place among nations*. Westport, CT and London: Praeger.

[17] Mahajan, Anilesh S. (2013). "Oiling the wheels", Business Today, Accessed online 29th September 2013.

[18] MEA (2008). Fact Sheet on Iran, Indian Embassy in Tehran, Ministry of External Affairs, India, November 2008.

[19] New Delhi Declaration (2003). "For the text of the New Delhi Declaration", Accessed online 29th September 2013, http://meaIndia.nic.in/event/ 2003/01/25 events01.htm#1 Pdf.

[20] Pant, Harsh V. (2010). "Security Multipolarity: Iran's role in India's energy calculus", *Journal of Energy Security*, 1–4.

[21] Pant, H.V. and Super, J.M. (2013). "Balancing Rivals: India's ran and United States", Asian Policy, No. 15, 2013.

[22] Planning Commission (2006). "Integrated energy policy: Report of the Expert Committee", New Delhi: Planning Commission. Retrieved 15 February 2010, from http://planningcommission.gov.in/reports/genrep/rep_intengy.

[23] Recknagel, Charles (2004). "Iran: India Deepens Strategic Partnership", at ww.rferl.org/nca/features/2001/04/13042001120322.asp

[24] Retrieved 15 February 2010, from http://www.ris.org.in/dp112_pap.pdf 15 February 2010, from http://www.cfr.org/publication/12200/indias_energy_ crunch.html

[25] Roy, M.S. and Lele, A. (2011). "Engaging Iran in the new Strategic Environment: Opportunities and Challenges", *Strategic Analysis*, 35 (1): 88–105.

[26] Shapir, Y.S. (2013). "Walking a Fine Line: Israel, India and Iran", Strategic Assessment, Vol. 16 (1): 2013.

[27] Sisakhat and Mahmoud (2012). "The Role of Energy in Iran-India Relations", Journal of Basic and Applied Science Research, Vol. 2(9): 9267–9274.

[28] Tehran Declaraion (2003). "Text of the Tehran Declaration", at Http://pib.nic.in/archive/pmvisit/pm_visit_iran/pm_iran_re14.html

[29] Tehran Times (2010). "India reiterates interest in IPI", *Teheran Times*, December 30, 2010, News Irna (2008) 'Iran-India Trade up 80 pc in 2007–08', *Agence News Irna*, October 31, 2008.

[30] The Hindu (2008). Submits Feasibility Report on Iranian Block', *The Hindu*, December 13, 2008, p. 16.

[31] The Hindu (2009). "India-Iran Explore Closer Ties in Energy Sector", Accessed November 14, 2009.

[32] The Hindu (2010). 'India Proposes Dialogue with Iran on IPI Pipeline', *The Hindu*, March 31, 2010.

[33] The Hindu (2010). 'Under this agreement, Iran will provide Pakistan with 750 million cubic feet of gas per day for the next 25 years. In Atul Aneja, 'Iran, Pakistan Clinch Gas Pipeline Deal', Accessed online March 18, 2010, p. 11.

[34] The Hindu (2013). "India cuts oil imports from Iran by 26.5% in FY' 13", Business Line, April 24, 2013.

[35] Tuli, Vipul (2006). "Regional Cooperation for Asian Energy Security", *RIS Discussion Paper*, No. 112, p. 2.

[36] World Bank (2012). "Iran Trade", Doing Business Report, World Bank.

[37] Xinhua News Agency (2008). "Ahmadinejad Would Welcome Chinese Role in Gas Pipeline", *Xinhua News Agency*, Accessed September 28, 2013.

[38] Zissis Carin (2007). 'India's Energy Crunch', *Council on Foreign Relations Publication.*

Economic and Trade Cooperation

Changing Dynamics of India-Iran Relations: An Assessment of Trade and Investment

M. Mahtab Alam Rizvi

INTRODUCTION

The Persian Gulf economy including Iran is mainly based on its oil revenues that have increased largely in recent years. However, due to international sanctions Iran's oil revenues decreased sharply. Due to the uncertainty regarding sustaining high oil prices in the long run, all Persian Gulf countries have been working towards the diversification of their economies. Due to the diversification process ongoing in the Persian Gulf region and the increasing trade and economic profile of India, their economic engagement is growing sharply. India's increasing dependence on the Persian Gulf region for energy supplies and other oil-based products like petrochemicals and fertilizers and the demand for manufactured goods in the Gulf region provide a significant prospect for a stronger and mutually advantageous economic relationship between India and the Persian Gulf region. However, despite century's old civilisational, cultural and commercial linkages, and geographical proximity, India currently does not figure in the list of top trading partners of the Persian Gulf region including Iran. In the recent past, however, there has been a noticeable rise in high-level interactions between the two sides. A number of agreements and memoranda of understanding (MoU) have been signed in the last few years covering a wide range of trade and investment items and infrastructure projects.

India's relations with Iran is very old, its spans centuries and has continued to increase despite couple of hardship between the two nations. India and Iran have been trading partners for a very long time. Trade relations between India and Iran have witnessed a significant growth during the last decade, with India's total trade with Iran growing from US$ 1.185 billion in 2003–04 to US$ 14.95 billion in 2012–13.[1] This buoyant trend has been continued by both increase in India's exports to and imports from the Islamic Republic of Iran. The exports to Iran have risen from US$ 918.11 million in 2003–04 to US$ 3.35 billion in 2012–13. India's imports from Iran have also grew as well. In 2003–04, India's import from Iran was

266.82 million only however, it increased by 11.6 billion in 2012–13[2] due to imports of large amount of crude oil by India from Iran. Though, the trade balance is still in favour of Iran due to huge oil imports by India from the Islamic Republic. In order to limit trade imbalance the emphasis of India's trade with Iran needs to be shifted to exports more Indian goods, investment and joint ventures. India should also focus on increasing trade in commodities, manufacturing as well as in services. Despite huge growth in bilateral trade between India and Iran, the total trade is declined in last financial year (2012–13). One of the reasons in declining of total trade between the two countries is the international sanctions including United States of America (USA) and the European Union (EU) economic sanctions against Iran (Table I). According to ministry of commerce (Government of India) Iran is India's eighteenth largest trading partner, with a share of 1.89 percent of India's total trade in 2012–13. During the year 2011–12 growth rate of bilateral trade was 28 percent between the two countries.[3] In light of current development especially under the leadership of new Iranian president, Hassan Rouhani, it is argued that the time is ideal for promoting the India-Iran trade and investment relationship considerably in the coming years based on mutual complementarities and better political ties. In this context, this chapter studies the changing dynamics of India-Iran relations with special focus on Trade and Investment between the two. This chapter also tries to examine contours and prospects for improving trade and investment relations between India and Iran.

Table 1: India-Iran Bilateral Trade

Figures in US$ Million

	2008–09	*2009–10*	*2010–11*	*2011–12*	*2012–13*
India's Exports to Iran	2,534.01	1,853.17	2,492.90	2,411.33	3,351.07
India's Imports from Iran	12,376.77	11,540.85	10,928.21	13,556.71	11,603.79
Total Trade	14,910.78	13,394.01	13,421.12	15,968.03	14,954.86
% Growth		–10.17	0.20	18.98	–6.35

Source: Government of India, Ministry of Commerce and Industry.

TRADE RELATIONS BETWEEN INDIA AND IRAN

Iran's economy is based on oil, which provides the most of government revenues about 80 percent. Price controls system, subsidies, and other rigidities consider down grade the economy, denting the capability for private-sector-led development. Private sector is only working in small-scale sectors such as farming, and services. Though, in December 2010, the then president, Mahmoud Ahmadinejad had implemented a law known as Targeted Subsidies Law (TSL) to reduce state subsidies on food and energy. This law was also approved by the parliament of Iran. This was the significant economic reform since the government implemented gasoline rationing in 2007. Over a five-year period the bill will phase out subsidies that previously cost Tehran US$ 60-$ 100 billion annually[4] and mainly helped Iran's upper and middle classes. Although expansionary fiscal and monetary policies, government mismanagement, the international sanctions including US and EU sanctions, and a depreciating currency are fueling inflation rate,[5] and GDP growth remains stagnant. Iran also continues to challenge from double-digit unemployment and under-employment. Even in recently held presidential election, June 14, 2013, the key agendas of the all presidential candidates including Hassan Rouhani (who won the election)—were high inflation rate and increasing unemployment.

India's trade linkages with Iran is not new, it has been began since civilizational period. The Indus people, and their ancestors, had strong trade linkages with Iran. During that period India had been imported silver, copper, turquoise and lapis lazuli from Persia in return for ivory. India had also been exported spices such as black pepper to Iran. The grape, first time presented by Persia with the almond and walnut, was cultivated in the Hindukush and western Himalayas. Bam, in south-east Iran, was a major commercial and trading hub on the well-known Spice Road, a major offshoot of the Silk Road that connected trade routes from India through Iran to Central Asia and China.

Even in changing global milieu India and Iran which enjoy civilisational and cultural linkages are trying to strengthen their relations in various sectors including trade and investment. Undoubtedly Iran is a significant country for India especially for trade and investment. Good trade and economic relations with Iran are in conformity with India's strategic interests. Business delegations have played a significant role in consolidating business ties between India and Iran. Recently in May 2012, Iranian delegation visited India and has signed deals to buy shipment of rice, sugar and soybean from India. Both countries are also agreed to strengthen their annual trade to US$ 24 billion in the medium term from US$ 14 billion now.

JOINT MECHANISM TO BOOST BILATERAL TRADE

One of the means by which both countries are increasing their bilateral trade is the Joint Business Council (JBC), set up by the Indian Chambers of Commerce and Industry and the Iran Chamber of Commerce, Industries, and Mines.[6] Both India and Iran hold JBC meetings regularly. The 10ᵗʰ meeting of the JBC was organized by the Federation of Indian Chambers of Commerce and Industry (FICCI) in New Delhi on November 13, 2009. Iranian delegation was headed by Iran's Chamber of Commerce, Industry and Mines president, Mohammad A. Nahavandian. He stated that the time was ripe "to move away from oil to the non-oil sectors such as agricultural machinery, food processing, pharmaceuticals, auto and auto components, telecommunications, mining, physical infrastructure, IT and ITeS and biotechnology. This is also the time to move from just trade to cooperation in investment and R and D by pooling our assets for the common good of the people of Iran and India."[7] He also proposed to upgrade the JBC into a Joint Business Chamber which could be helped to prepare an action plan to promote business relations.

Another means of interface between India and Iran especially in economic and trade areas, is Joint Commission Meeting (JCM). The JCM provides a good platform to discuss all issues including contentious issues related to trade and investment. It also helps in removing all barriers in the two-way trade and allow smooth flow of investments. The JCM also provides a forum to examine bilateral economic and cultural co-operation between the two nations. The two countries hold regular bilateral meeting of the JCM on economic, trade and investment. The JCM was set up in 1983. The 16ᵗʰ JCM was held in New Delhi on July 8–9, 2010. A 30-member delegation of Iran led by Shamseddin Hosseini, Minister of Economic Affairs and Finance of Iran attended the meeting. The meeting was also co-chaired by the then Indian External Affairs Minister S.M. Krishna. The following MoUs/Agreements were signed during the Meeting:

(i) Air Services Agreement; (ii) Agreement on Transfer of Sentenced Persons; (iii) MoU on Cooperation in New and Renewable Energy; (iv) MoU on Cooperation in Small Scale Industry between National Small Industries Corporation (NSIC) and Iranian Small Industries and Industrial Parks Organisation (ISIPO); (v) Programme of Cooperation on Science and Technology and (vi) MoU on Cooperation between Central Pulp and Paper Research Institute of India (CPPRI) and Gorgan University of Agricultural Science and Natural Resources (GUASNR).[8]

The 17th Joint Commission meeting was held in Tehran on May 4, 2013. The meeting was co-chaired by the then Iran's foreign minister, Ali Akbar salehi and Indian External Affairs minister, Salman Khurshid. The main focus of the meeting was how to expand bilateral ties and mutual co-operation between the two countries especially in economic and trade sectors. Both sides also agreed to work on a trilateral transit agreement involving India, Iran and Afghanistan.[9] Both leaders also discussed and reviewed the development on the proposed International North-South Transport Corridor (INSTC) which will link Russia with Iran.

However, despite strong historical and cultural linkages between India and Iran, India does not figure in the list of Iran's top trade partners. It has been also observed by the two sides that the level of trade was not reflective of the close relations between the two countries and should be strengthened. In this regard, agriculture and pharma products and aeronautics were among the areas identified where cooperation could be enhanced. At the meeting the two sides also discussed the importance of enhancing cooperation in expanding trade and banking relations and agreed to study the prospects of joint investment in both countries. Both countries are also agreed to diversify their cooperation in this regard. India and Iran are making robust efforts to renew and strengthen the bilateral economic and trade relations. The relationship between the two countries has evolved into a significant partnership in the economic and commercial sphere.[10] At the same time, Indians have emerged as important investors in the Iran, and India as an important export destination for the Iran manufactured goods.

INDIA'S EXPORTS TO IRAN

India's exports to Iran have grown by 40 percent over the past year and estimated to increase further. India's exports to Iran include petroleum products, rice, cereals, machine tools, automobile parts, steel, metals, primary and semi-finished iron, drugs/pharmaceuticals and fine chemicals, processed minerals, manmade yarn and fabrics, tea, organic/inorganic/agro chemicals, rubber manufactured products, etc.[11] Rice and textile exports have seen the largest jump. Indian officials mentioned that a liberalized visa policy for businessmen from both sides is implemented soon. This will help in enhance the exports and imports from both sides.[12] During 2001–2010, India's exports to Iran have grown around ten-fold, from US$ 253.3 million in 2001 to US$ 2.5 billion in 2010. The main reason of India's exports to Iran grown during this period was; growth in exports of inorganic chemicals, cereals, iron and steel and articles of iron or steel to

Iran. These items accounting for 50.6 percent of India's total exports to Iran in 2010.[13]

Recently, the head of the Federation of Indian Export Organizations, Rafeeque Ahmed says the latest measures to liberalize trade with Iran will result in sizeable growth in exports this year. India's exports amounted to less than US$ 3 billion last year, while its oil imports totaled about US$ 11 billion. Ahmed said India's exports is diversified into new areas such as textiles, machinery and consumer goods. Ahmed also stated "We feel that certain chemicals, automobile parts, some light engineering items, and home needs can exports to Iran." He added "With this facility they can set up projects... And there are companies in India which are capable of it, but they had to import certain parts from outside. That can be done now."[14]

IMPORTS BY INDIA

This is also the fact that India-Iran trade relations are dominated by Indian imports of Iranian crude oil. India always maintains that Iran is an important partner for hydrocarbon resources. India's imports from Iran include crude oil, urea, Petroleum products, Saffron, Dry Fruits.[15] In 2012 Iran was second largest supplier of crude oil to India. However, due to the US and EU sanctions, Iran position is replaced by Iraq. Iran is also a major source for India's imports of plastics as well as fertilizers, ores slag and ash.

ENERGY

India-Iran economic and trade relations have traditionally been buoyed by Indian import of Iranian crude oil. The importance of Iran's energy resources has also to be seen in the milieu of India's increasing demand for energy. Recently Indian oil minister Veerappa Moily said India plans to import 13 MT of Iranian crude oil in the current financial year and save US$8.5 billion in valuable foreign exchange. However, it can't be raised to 22 MT, as it was five years ago. This will also help to control India's currency crisis. Analysts believe that Veerappa Moily understands the significance of Iran, particularly because refiners have told him that they save about US$2 a barrel when they buy Iranian crude.[16] Importing more Iranian oil means, will also help India to maintain the balance of payments position, skewed heavily in favour of Tehran. India has also proposed facilities of routing imports from other countries through India. Both countries are also working for setting up a number of projects, which include the Iran-Pakistan-India (IPI) gas pipeline project, a long term supply of 5 million tons of LNG, development of the Farsi oil and gas blocks, South Pars gas field and other LNG project.[17]

However, the recent economic sanctions imposed by the US and the EU on the Iranian oil and financial sectors have led to the more isolation of Iran from the international community. Iran enjoyed to be India's second largest supplier of crude oil. Now Iraq become the second largest supplier of oil after Saudi Arabia as has been discussed above. India imported 16.083 million tonnes of oil in 2010–2011 and 14.689 million tonnes of oil during 2011–2012 from Iran.[18] India's imports of Iranian oil have dropped to 194,000 barrels per day (bpd) for January-September, down from 324,000 bpd in the same period last year. However, in September India's oil imports from Iran increased to 296,100 bpd from 151,000 bpd in August, partly because Indian Oil Corp importing 2 million barrels of oil from Tehran. Refiner Mangalore Refinery and Petrochemicals Ltd was the largest importer of Iranian oil in September, replacing Essar Oil by shipping in 133,000 bpd. MRPL resumed imports from Iran in August after a four month halt over the insurance issue, while Hindustan Petroleum Corp Ltd has started to buy Iranian oil in the fiscal year that began 1 April 2013. Iran also became the fourth biggest crude oil supplier to India in September 2013, improving its ranking from ninth place in August 2013.[19]

Despite huge pressure by the US and the EU, and a significant reduction in oil imports from Iran in 2012, Indian officials have clearly indicated that they are not willing to stop trade relations altogether with Iran. India also pushes the exports of textiles, pharmaceuticals, engineering goods and cars to Iran for balance of oil payments.[20] Iran is also looking deals to use its rupee balances to buy equity in the Indian refining sector.

The rupee swap agreement between India and Iran also help in balance of trade between two countries especially India's exports. India's imports around 10 percent of its oil demands from Iran, which is now being paid in Indian rupee. This offers an interesting tailwind for exports, since Iran is rather much limited to taking exports from India with its rupee. Last fiscal India's trade deficit with Iran was about $11–12 billion and as a positive implication of this rupee swap deal, in the current fiscal this number could fall to $6–8 billion.[21]

INVESTMENT

Recently, India had announced several investments in Iran. These include a railway project from Chabahar to Bam that has a free trade industrial zone. This is potentially a big investment for India at a time Iran needs friends and is likely to reward those who stand by it. The Chinese and Russians have similarly invested in Iran. Similarly, the Zaranj-Delaram road that India is helping to build links up with Afghanistan and is important for the Indian geo-strategic perspective.[22] India is one of the largest foreign investors in Iran's oil and gas industry. Due to strategic importance of Iran for India and India importance for Iran, both are working for the setting up for number of projects including the International North-South Transport Corridor (INSTC) project, the Chabahar container terminal project.

The INSTC was established in September 2000 by India, Iran and Russia in order to promote transportation cooperation among the members. Later Azerbaijan, Armenia, Kazakhstan, Kyrgyzstan, Tajikistan, Turkey, Ukraine, Belarus, Oman, Syria and Bulgaria joined the corridor. The INSTC connects India to Central Asian Republics (CARs) through Iran, and will also reduce the logistics of moving goods and diminish travel time and transport costs. This corridor also connects India Ocean and Persian Gulf to the Caspian Sea via Iran, and then is connected to St. Petersburg (Russia) and North Europe via Russia.

The primary step towards trade enhancement between India and Iran, was signing of Memorandum of understanding between the two countries over the development of Chabahar Port and transhipment facility at Bandar Abbas. The Chabahar Port in Iran along with a railway link offers India direct access to Afghanistan and the CARs. Through this project Islamic Republic of Iran will also enable to access Central Asian countries including Afghanistan. The Chabahar port has been jointly financed by India and Iran. Recently India is also agreed to participate in the upgradation of the Chabahar port and announced for the investment of around US$100 million[23] in the project in the initial stage. On the other hand Tehran has also offered Indian Public Sector Undertakings (PSUs) like ONCG Videsh, OIL and Indian Oil Corporation production sharing contracts for developing the Farzad B gas field.

INTERNATIONAL SANCTIONS AND ITS IMPACT ON BILATERAL TRADE

Iran nuclear programme and economic sanctions on Iran have had its impact on the India-Iran bilateral trade and investment as well. The recent US and EU sanctions on the Iranian oil and financial sectors also impacted on bilateral trade relations between the two countries. However, the US recently renewed six-month waivers on sanctions for India, China and seven other countries in exchange for their agreement to reduce oil purchases from Iran. It is noteworthy that India has made it very clear that it will continue to import crude oil from Iran. Because India is not bind by US unilateral sanctions. The then Indian Finance Minister, Pranab Mukherjee, has said that "It is not possible for India to take any decision to reduce the imports from Iran drastically, because among the countries which can provide the requirement of the emerging economies, Iran is an important one."[24] The then Foreign Secretary Ranjan Mathai has also stated that India will only accept sanctions imposed by the UN.

However, after decades of enmity and distrust between Iran and the USA, President Barak Obama and President Rouhani talked on telephone during his recent visit to New York. This was clearly taking many especially Iranians and westerners by surprise. This was the first highest-level contact between the two countries in three decades and an indication of rapprochement and co-operation and about reaching a deal on Iran's nuclear programme. Obama said "Resolving this issue, obviously, could also serve as a major step forward in a new relationship between the USA and the Islamic Republic of Iran, one based on mutual interests and mutual respect."[25] From his side Rouhani also mentioned in his Twitter account "We're hopeful about what we will see from" the US and other major powers "in coming weeks and months." Regarding his trip to New York, Rouhani mentioned "I expect this trip will be the first step and the beginning of constructive relations with countries of the world."[26] He went on to say that he hoped the visit would also improve relations "between two great nations, Iran and the US," adding that the trip had exceeded his expectations. The conversations between the two leaders were focused on the nuclear issue. The US-Iran tension is an important factor in the political, trade, economic and strategic ties between India and Iran. Though the tension is likely to continue in the foreseeable future, it is pertinent for India to understand that there is a possibility that the present hostility may change to some kind of rapprochement anytime in future especially in the light of recent development,under the leadership of President Rouhani.

CONCLUSION

India's trade relations with Iran has observed a robust trend in recent years. Iran will continue to be an important partner for India even as New Delhi underlines the necessity for Tehran to come clean on its nuclear programme. Increasing trade and investment relations between India and

Iran will no doubt have spilt over effect in the political and security arenas. With improvement in political ties between the two sides, it appears that the situation is ideal for taking the India-Iran trade and investment relationship to a higher orbit. A large number of Agreements and MoUs have been signed in the last few years covering wide ranging areas including trade and investment. India being a US$ 100 billion market is very significant to Iran. It is not simply the import of crude oil and gas by India that supports India-Iran economic relations but also the trade in other petro-products and fertilizers and manufactured goods. With the likelihood of US involvement with the region decreasing and muted economic growth in Europe in the next two decades, Iran will be looking forward to a higher level of trade and economic relationship with India. There are a host of issues on which the two countries can cooperate to each other such as INSTC, Chabahar project, economic, trade and investment.

The global economic crisis and the US and EU economic sanctions on Iran have had its impact on the India-Iran bilateral trade as has been argued above. From India's perspective, better Iran-US relations would also provide India an opportunity in completing other long pending energy, trade and investment projects that it has signed with Iran, but gone slow on, due to international sanctions against Iran. However, despite India's historical and cultural linkages with Iran, India is not exploiting the opportunities presented by the Islamic Republic, especially in the trade and investmentsectors. Although it's worth to mention here that Iran is a radiant and vibrant market and India look forward to larger engagement by the Indian corporate in various sectors apart from oil and gas. However, recent economic and trade data indicates that India and Iran trade and investment are growing despite couple of hindrances.

REFERENCES

[1] Government of India, Ministry of Commerce and Industry, Department of Commerce, 2013, available at http://commerce.nic.in/eidb/iecnt.asp (accessed on 7 October 2013).

[2] Ibid.

[3] Ibid.

[4] India-Iran Economic Relations, FICCI, 2013, available at http://www.ficci.com/international/75186/Project_docs/India-Iran-Economic--Relations.pdf (accessed on July 11, 2013).

[5] "Iran's Inflation Rate Rises To 32.6%", *Middle East Economic Survey*, June 28, 2013, available at http://www.mees.com/en/articles/7928-irans-inflation-rate-rises-to-32-dot-6-percent (accessed on June 28, 2013).

[6] Government of India, Ministry of External Affairs, May 2004, available at www.mea.gov.in, (accessed on June 12, 2012).

[7] The Financial Express, November 14, 2009. Also see http://www.mea.gov.in/mystart.php?id=50044479

[8] Government of India, Ministry of External Affairs available at http://www.mea.gov.in/mystart.php?id=50044479 (accessed on June 29, 2013).

[9] "Salman Khurshid in Tehran; India, Iran decide to give major push to bilateral ties", *Times of India,* May 4, 2013, available at http://articles.timesofindia.indiatimes.com/2013-05-04/india/39026313_1_two-sides-salmankhurshid-indian-cultural-centre (accessed on July 30, 2013).

[10] India-Iran Economic Relations, FICCI, 2013, available at http://www.ficci.com/international/75186/Project_docs/India-Iran-Economic--Relations.pdf (accessed on July 11, 2013).

[11] Ibid.

[12] "Iran, India boost trade ties", *Press TV,* July 6, 2013, available at http://www.presstv.ir/detail/2013/07/06/312454/iran-india-boost-trade-ties/ (accessed on July 13, 2013).

[13] "Potential for Enhancing India's Trade with Iran: a Brief Analysis", Working Paper No. 18, Export-Import Bank of India, July 2012, p.12.

[14] Anjana Pasricha, "India Takes Steps to Boost Trade With Iran", *Voice of America,* June 15, 2013, available athttp://www.voanews.com/content/india-trade-iran/1682636.html (accessed on July 16, 2013).

[15] "Potential for Enhancing India's Trade with Iran: a Brief Analysis", Working Paper No. 18, Export-Import Bank of India, July 2012, p.12.

[16] "Crude Imports: India must trade more with Iran to contain rupee crisis", *Economics Times,* September 13, 2013, athttp://articles.economictimes.indiatimes.com/2013-09-13/news/42041962_1_iranian-crude-crude-oil-imports-gholamhossein-nozari(accessed on September 17, 2013).

[17] "Potential for Enhancing India's Trade with Iran: a Brief Analysis", Working Paper No. 18, Export-Import Bank of India, July 2012, p. 13.

[18] Department of Commerce, Export Import Data Bank Country Wise all commodities available at http://commerce.nic.in/eidb/Icntcom.asp (accessed on May 12, 2013).

[19] "India's Iran oil imports drop as refiners await insurance fund," *Live Mint and the Wall Street Journal,* October 31, 2013, available at http://www.livemint.com/Industry/T8mcOlioXFktgzjZKOJJPJ/Indias-Iran-oil-imports-drop-as-refiners-await-insurance-fu.html (accessed on October 31, 2013).

[20] "Rupee trade logic gains momentum", *Telegraph,* September 3, 2013, available athttp://www.telegraphindia.com/1130904/jsp/business/story_17308933.jsp#.UnJWf2frbIV (accessed on September 17, 2013).

[21] "Better US-Iran relationship can benefit Indian economy, rupee: Saurabh Mukherjea", *Times of India,* September 25, 2013, available athttp://timesofindia.indiatimes.com/business/india-business/Better-US-Iran-relationship-can-benefit-Indian-economy-rupee-Saurabh-Mukherjea/articleshow/23018126.cms (accessed on September 26, 2013).

[22] "A tightrope walk with Iran", *Indian Express,* June 13, 2013, available at http://newindianexpress.com/opinion/A-tightrope-walk-with-Iran/2013/06/13/article1631836.ece (accessed on July 20, 2013).

[23] Harsh V. Pant, "India-Iran relations: A tangled web", May 14, 2013, available at http://www.rediff.com/news/column/india-iran-relations-a-tangled-web/20130514.htm (accessed on June 30, 2013).

[24] "India won't scale down oil imports from Iran: Pranab", *Indian Express*, January 30, 2012, available at http://www.indianexpress.com/news/india-wont-scale-down-oil-imports-from-iran-pranab/905547 (accessed on June 13, 2012).

[25] "President Obama Announces New Diplomatic Efforts with the Islamic Republic of Iran", *White House*, The USA, September 2, 2013, available at http://www.whitehouse.gov/blog/2013/09/27/president-obama-announces-new-diplomatic-efforts-islamic-republic-iran (Accessed on October08, 2013).

[26] "Analysis: Skepticism Amid Hope for Iran Solution", *ABC News,* September 29, 2013, available at http://abcnews.go.com/Politics/wireStory/analysis-skepticism-amid-hope-iran-solution-20410498(Accessed on October 08, 2013).

Trade Relations between Persia and India (1796–1859)

Seyed Hossein Hosseini

INTRODUCTION

In this article, trade relation between Persia and India between 1796 and 1859 has been studied and the reason why I chose this period was because the East India Company practically had no role in trade between Persia and India after 1859 because of the changes made in the Indian government. From the 1860's decade with opening of the Suez channel and the changes which happened after the silk export crisis of Persia, a great change was made in trade model of Persia which affected the trade between Persia and India. This article focuses on the history of trade relations between Persia and India but implicitly covers the domestictrade of Persia and political matters that had effects on this trade relation were also studied.

In Persian resources there is nothing available on commercial relations and trade between Persia and India, only political happening and people are covered in these resources. Main resources for this research are trade reports and statistical data extracted from documents of the East India Company which were released as monthly and annual note. Also, consular documents that cover the trade between Persia and India and statistical notes on foreign trade printed by the government of India and reports written by travelers and British government officials.

For a better understanding of trade between Persia and India at the beginning of Qajar dynasty (1796), the report from East India Company is of much importance. In this report its stated that the annual average of sales of the company in Bushehr was only £2,680, average loss per year was £123, and also adding £1375 for the Bushehr factory costs and £340 for the staff of the Bombay ships. The total annual loss was around £1838. Trade situation of the company was such that they were planning to stop all their trade in the Persian Gulf but unlike the East India Company Indian merchants, who were acting independently due to their experience with Persia were successful even in this period.[1]

It is clear from the report that the main problem of trade between Persia and India during this period, was lack of a suitable market for Persian products in Indian market. Therefore, Persia had to pay a high percent in specie (coins). In the late 1790's, 9/10th of the payment of the goods exported to Persia from India were paid in specie[2] which shows a decrease of 10% in exports of Persia to India in this decade. With consolidation of Qajars and the revival of trade of Persia some major changes were made in trade. According to a report from Sir J. Malcom in 1801 around 40 to 50% of trade of Persia was specie.[3]

According to Figure 7 it is clear that in 1801, Persia was facing a deficit in its foreign trade. The highest trade deficit of Persia was with India. In this year around 35 lakh rupees (£350,000) worth specie was exported. Unfortunately in this report trade with Russia and Central Asia is not mentioned, but Persia always had a trade surplus with both Russia and Central Asia till mid 1860's which could recompense a part of this trade deficit with India. In this year the total trade with India as the third trade partner of Persia is 60 lakh rupees with 270 lakh rupees as the total trade of Persia, trade with India is around 22% of the total trade of Persia in this year. If we compare this with the total trade between Persia and India through Persian Gulf which is 40 lakh rupees, we see that 2/3 of this trade was done through Persia's harbors in Persian Gulf.[4]

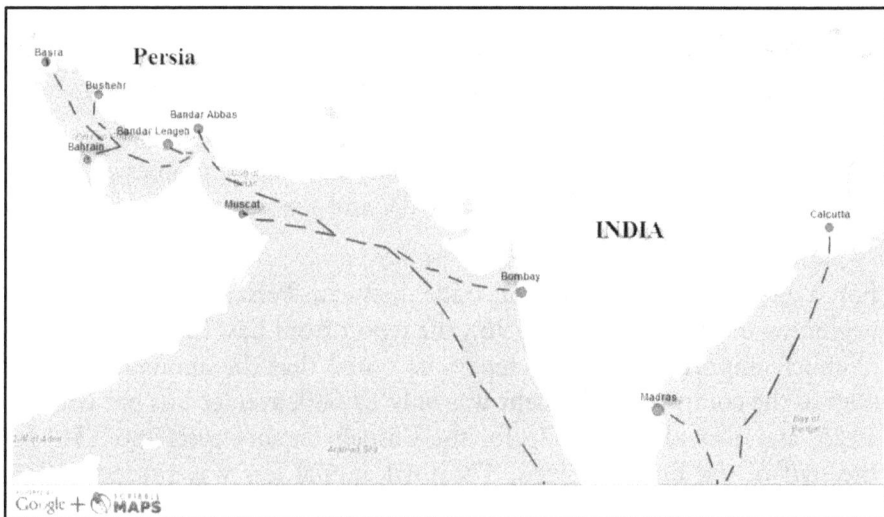

Fig. 1: Maritime Trade Routes between Persian Gulf Harbors
and Indian Harbors from 1796 to 1859

Sir J. Malcom in his first travel to Persia in 1801 from Wellesley in Massachusetts (U.K), the Ruler of India, had a mission to sign a political agreement with Persia and a trade treaty. One of the concessions that

Indian and English merchants gained through this was a fixed tax and treating them as a local Persian merchant as well as a rule of not taxing the goods again in other provinces or cities by their governors or government officials.[5] This agreement was practically on hold until 1841 that the trade agreement between Britain and Persia was signed, and before that things had their usual procedure. In fact the government of Britain intentions were more political and trade with Persia did not have as much importance, if they were showing interest in signing an agreement with Persia's government, it was because of the competition between its political rivals like France and Russia.[6]

The data we have on trade between Persia and India during this period including reports from the Company officials or consuls of Britain are from travelers who travelled to Persia like Scott Warring who visited the southern region of Persia between Bushehr harbor and Shiraz in 1802, he states that the export made through Bushehr to India done by English brokers only is 3.5 lakh rupees, including 1.5 to Calcutta and 1.5 to Bombay in addition to 0.5 drugs sent through the Company to India.[7] He also states that different kinds of pearls and Rose water and Shiraz wine are among the important goods exported to India. One of the important things that he points out is the 5% import tax in Bushehr and a 2.5% tax in Shiraz, he also writes about 9 *Rahdarees* (Toll Taxes) between Bushehr and Shiraz that charge half a *piaster* (coin of Turkey) percent from the goods.[8] If we add the transportation fee of impassable routes to this, the price of the good multiplies by times of its worth in source. When the southern routes became safer, the trade in the south expanded. Sir Harford Jones in year 1807 was sent to Persia from India for signing a contract, confirms this trade growth between Persia and India. He states that in one of his travels to Persia a few years ago only 6 Indian chintz bales were imported in that year, but now it's 500–600 bales.[9]

With the growth in trade of Persia, which was the main hub in trade of Persian Gulf, trade with India also grew in a way, that the total trade of Persian Gulf reached 158 lakh Co. Rupees (New Bombay Rupees) in 1806. But with the start of the first Persia and Russia wars, the trades decreased dramatically. When the war ended in 1813 a growth can be seen in a way that the trade increased from 137 lakhs in this year to 290 lakhs in 1817, which means the trade grew by 2.1 times in this short period of 5 years. Practically, the total annual trade never got lower than 200 lakh rupees (see Figure 2) and even in the years 1857 and 1858 which are the final years of this research the total annual trades where 240 and 257 lakh rupees.

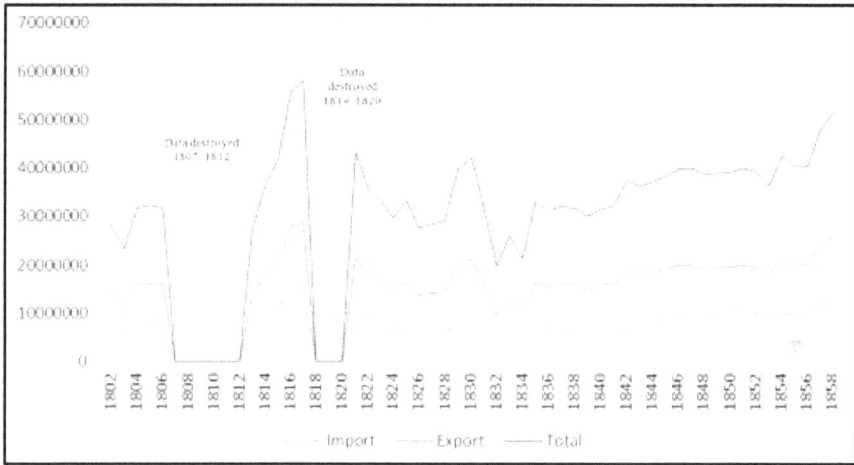

Fig. 2: Import and Export between Iran and Persian Gulf (1802–1859) (Co. Rupees)
Source: Table 1.

After the company's report in 1792, Fraser has written two reports on Persia's trade in 1820 and has mentioned the foreign trade of Persia in the part of it. He believes the whole amount of exports in the year ending in May 31, 1821 from Persia to India at the port of Bushehr, according to official reports was around £305,000 which is equivalent to 35,94,000 New Bombay Rupees. This amount is around 25% of total trades of Persia since the total trade was around £1,225,000.[10]

India in this year is the greatest destination for the goods exported from Persia, even with this growth Persia had to pay £290,000 or 34,17,999 New Bombay Rupees worth treasuries to India due to trade deficit.[11]

Between the years 1817 and 1823, before the second war between Persia and Russia (1826–1828) which were among the years with high expansion in trade between Persia and India, a complete and detailed report was written by Willog. According to this report it can be seen even when the total trade of Persian Gulf with India decreases from around 290 lakh rupees in 1817 to 172 lakh in 1823, total trade of Persia and India reached around 137 lakh rupees in 1823 from 45 lakh rupees in 1817. This shows a 3 times growth rate in these years, in these years the trade portion of Persia with India through Persian Gulf increased from 15% in 1817 to 80% in 1823.[12]

The causes of this notable increase can be listed as follows, first the chaos in southern shores of Persian Gulf and made them unsafe for trade. Therefore, the ships docked in Bushehr instead of Muscat and Bahrain, second was presence of British fleet of ships and destroying the pirate ships and making the sea routes safer; and the final reason was the economic growth of Persia and the roads were secured after the first Persia and Russia war in 1913 which resulted in transit of goods to the north of Persia as well.[13]

After the second war of Persia and Russia we see an increase in trade of Persia and India, but for various reasons from the early 1830's the importance of trade of Persian Gulf and India started decreasing and this process continued till 1860's and the opening of Suez channel and a dramatic decrease in trade of the silk which resulted in Persia changing their strategy in foreign trade. In the year 1832–1833 based on a report from the Bushehr broker, the total export of India to Bushehr was equal to 42,51,524 Bombay rupees and import to India from Bushehr was equal to 20,27,544 Bombay rupees which shows a deficit of over 50% against Persia which Persia had to balance it using specie. In the next year (1833–1834) we see a dramatic decrease in trade from Bushehr in a way that import from India to Bushehr decreased to 14,46,938 Bombay rupees and export to India from Bushehr decreased to 7,10,677 Bombay rupees.[14]

Among the reasons that resulted in a decrease in trade between Persia and India in this period, these can be stated. Firstly, Persia and Russia wars resulted in a great reduction of Persia's gold resources and a £2,500,000 as a recompense for the war practically emptied the treasury and there was nothing left for the trade deficit with India. Secondly, opening of the new trade route from Trabzon harbor in Turkey and its lower distance with the north market reduced the transportation costs and on the other hand an easier way was chosen for exporting the silk of Persia through Bushehr—Bombay sea route instead of the south route. Another reason was the chaos after the death of Fath Ali Shah in 1834 and safety problems of the ground routes in south of Persia and plague and cholera in the early 1830's which resulted in death of many people, and finally, the change of direction of ships from Bushehr to Muscat and Bandar Abbas due to lower customs.[15]

In 1850, Consul Abott writes in his report on south of Persia that imports from India through Bushehr is around £500,000. He believes that around £400,000 to £480,000 specie are imported to India from this harbor per year. He estimates the imports from India to Bandar Abbas around £300,000 which only £35,000 to £40,000 of it were sent to India in goods and the rest was sent in specie.[16]

If we compare the report of Abott with Bloe who has written the average of trade of Persia and India between 1847 and 1856 in his report. He takes the annual average import from India to Persia around £400,000 and the missing amount was paid in specie. He estimates the missing amount to be around £314,285 (Look at Figure 6) which shows that Abott's estimating is higher than Bloe.

After the Sir J. Malcom's report on 1801 which has a small mention of the goods being imported and exported to Persia or India,[17] Fraser's report shows a detailed figure of the goods being imported and exported between these two countries. Most important ones of the ones being imported to Persia from India were:Sugar and Sugar Candy, Spices, Coffee, Indigo, Cotton Yarn, Rice, Grain, Textile, And the most important exports of Persia to India were, Asafetida, Resins, Pistachio, Almond, Gum, Ammoniac, Sulfur, Saltpeter.[18]

An important thing about goods exported to India from Persia is that there was no change in them until 1914 which from that time petroleum was added to exports of Persia and these goods changed. In the goods imported to Persia from India there was an important change between 1800's and 1850's. Tea was not among the goods imported to Persia but in the report from May to October of 1856 we see that tea is one of the most important goods imported to Persia. Tea exported to Persia from India in these 6 months weighed 188,665 (lbs) and was worth 1,07,395 rupees. Piece goods and Sugar are still among the important goods exported to Persia but there is a change made in these goods from what the report shows.[19]

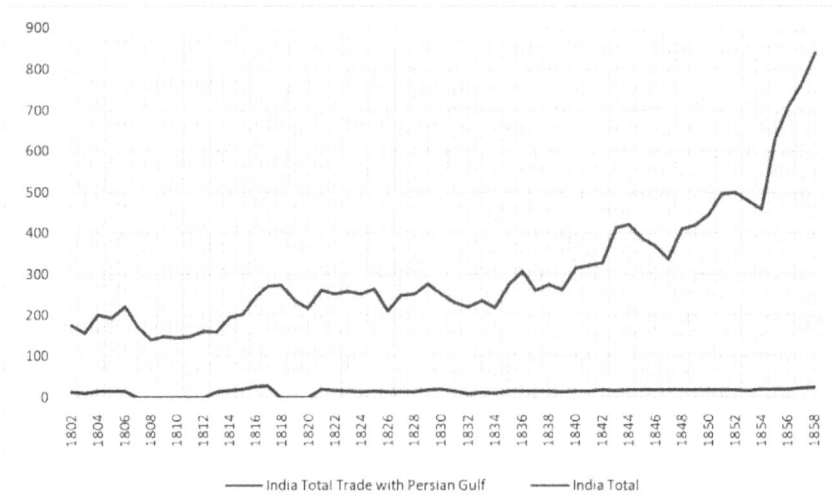

Fig. 3: Comparison of Total Trade of India with Total Trade of India with Persian Gulf (in Million Rupees)

Source: Table 1.

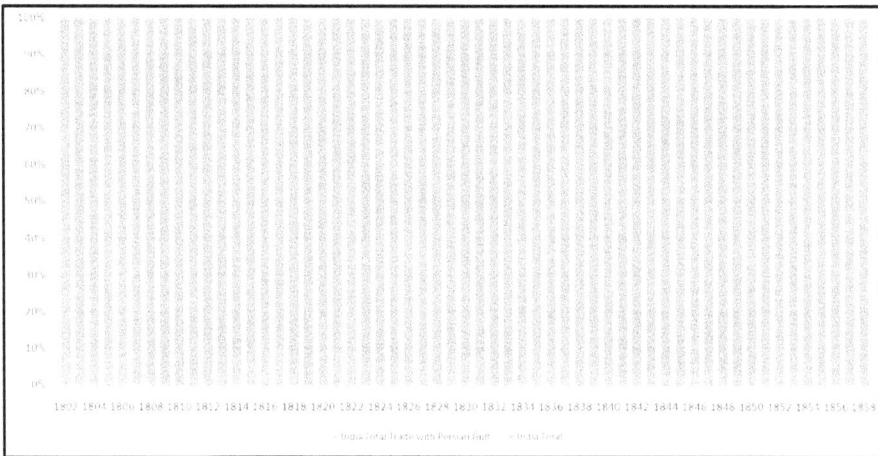

Fig. 4: Comparison of Total Trade of India with Total Trade of India with Persian Gulf in Percents.

Source: Table 1.

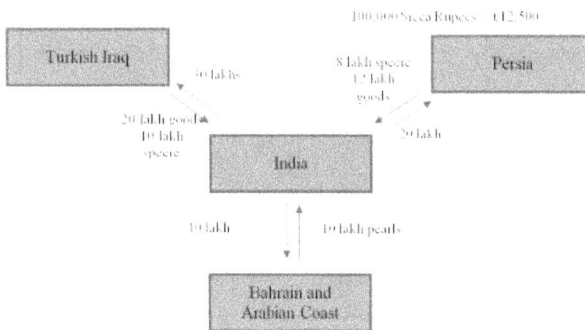

Fig. 5: Trade of India and Persian Gulf in 1801

Source: Lorimer, John Gordon Gazetteer of Persian Gulf: (Vol I, Part I) Calcutta, 1915. pp. 165–168.

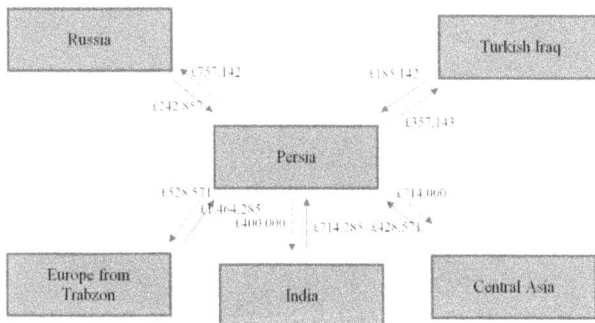

Fig. 6: Annual Estimatation of Trade of Iran (1847–1856)

Source: Issawi, Charles, Economic History of Iran (1800–1914), Translated by Yaghoob Azhand, pp. 201–204.

100,000 Sicca Rupees = 112.500

Central Asia

India

Russia

5

30

1$ specie = 15

Persia

20

30 goods
10 specie

35   35 goods = 10
specie

4.2

40

Arabia and Red
Sea

Kabul

Turkish Iraq

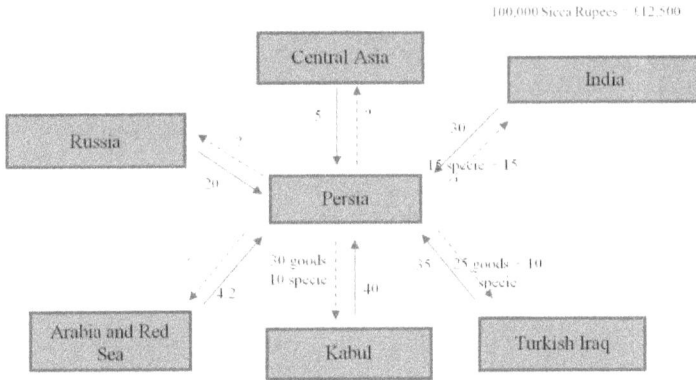

Fig. 7: Trade of Iran in 1801 (Sicca Lakh Rupees)

Source: Issawi, Charles, Economic History of Iran (1800–1914), Translated by Yaghoob Azhand, pages 404–409.

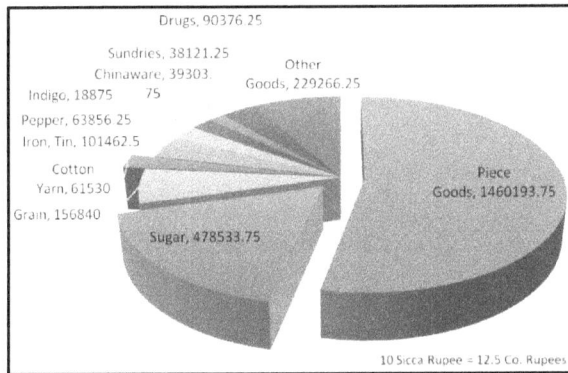

Drugs, 90376.25

Sundries, 38121.25

Chinaware, 39303.75

Other Goods, 229266.25

Indigo, 18875

Pepper, 63856.25

Iron, Tin, 101462.5

Cotton Yarn, 61530

Piece Goods, 1460193.75

Grain, 156840

Sugar, 478533.75

10 Sicca Rupee = 12.5 Co. Rupees

Fig. 8: Articles Imported to Persian Gulf from Madras and Bombay in 1805 (Co. Rupees)

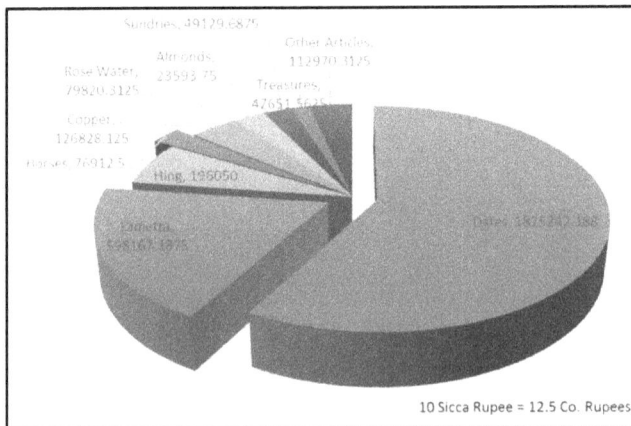

Sundries, 49129.6875

Almonds, 23593.75

Other Articles, 112970.3125

Rose Water, 79820.3125

Treasures, 47651.5625

Copper, 126828.125

Hing, 196050

Dates, 382549.4375

Lighetta, 498167.1875

10 Sicca Rupee = 12.5 Co. Rupees

Fig. 9: Articles Exported to Madras and Bombay form Persian Gulf in 1805 (Co. Rupees)

Source: Mac Gregor, John, Commercial Statistics, p. 389.

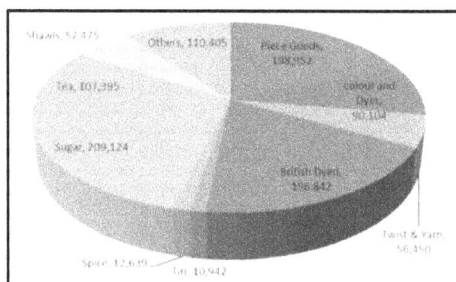

Fig. 10: Value of Articles Exported from Bombay to Bushehr from May to October 1856 (Co. Rupees)

Source: Foreign Department, Political Branch, 29 Jan, 1858, No. 1–12.

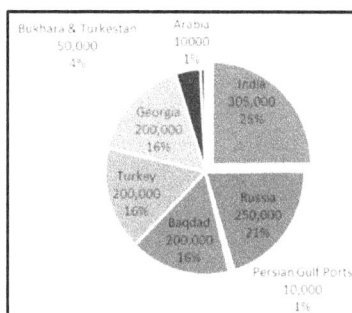

Fig. 11: Persia's Exports in 1820 (Sterling Pounds)

Source: Fraser, An Historical Account of Persia, London, 1834, p. 291.

Table 1: Total Trade of Harbors of Persian Gulf and India and Foreign Trade of India

	Total Trade of Harbors of Persian Gulf and India			Foreign Trade of India		
	Import from Persian Gulf	Export to Persian Gulf	Total	Import	Export	Total
1802–03	71,83,403	69,16,217	1,40,99,621	8,01,46,381	8,09,37,238	16,1083620
1803–04	64,06,292	52,48,155	1,16,54,447	6,87,08,056	7,62,97,011	14,5005067
1804–05	91,47,612	67,44,933	1,58,92,546	9,41,10,366	9,05,95,776	18,4706142
1805–06	84,83,281	76,80,390	1,61,63,671	8,81,98,955	8,85,96,383	17,6795338
1806–07	70,31,993	87,89,645	1,58,21,638	11,24,12,985	9,24,40,771	20,4853756
1807–08	–	–	–	8,31,33,620	8,72,19,215	17,0352835
1808–09	–	–	–	7,07,18,508	6,93,14,211	14,0032720
1809–10	–	–	–	8,38,07,360	6,43,66,520	14,8173880
1810–11	–	–	–	7,24,76,476	7,17,88,148	144264625
1811–12	–	–	–	6,91,09,603	7,95,16,760	14,8626363
1812–13	–	–	–	7,77,63,480	8,28,73,973	16,0637453
1813–14	53,78,456	83,84,276.	1,37,62,732	6,46,33,145	8,12,92,532	14,5925677
1814–15	84,88,981	99,06,167	1,83,95,148.	8,26,86,211	9,30,40,427	17,5726638
1815–16	1,06,32,560	1,01,94,328	2,08,26,888	7,93,86,010	10,26,32,541	18,2018551
1816–17	1,49,43,293	1,29,39,640	2,78,82,933	10,96,52,235	10,77,63,748	217415983
1817–18	1,55,67,101	1,34,65,311	2,90,32,412	12,73,75,211	11,38,68,610	241243821

(Table contd...)

(*Table 1 contd...*)

	Total Trade of Harbors of Persian Gulf and India			Foreign Trade of India		
	Import from Persian Gulf	*Export to Persian Gulf*	*Total*	*Import*	*Export*	*Total*
1818–19	–	–	–	15,85,48,215	11,60,39,923	274588138
1819–20	–	–	–	12,26,30,895	11,34,14,532	236045427
1820–21	–	–	–	10,16,52,628	11,46,02,300	216254928
1821–22	88,79,046	1,27,38,883	2,16,17,930	10,91,47,098	12,98,70,136	239017235
1822–23	96,86,408	83,01,532	1,79,87,941	10,51,14,005	12,79,87,221	233101226
1823–24	70,76,242	95,36,547	1,66,12,790	10,30,88,566	13,80,00,070	241088636
1824–25	67,22,286	81,40,900	1,48,63,186	10,34,42,600	13,38,70,191	237312791
1825–26	68,72,596	98,24,442	1,66,97,038	10,23,74,607	14,60,72,463	248447071
1826–27	57,33,456.	81,06,663	1,38,40,120	7,25,93,367	12,33,15,275	195908642
1827–28	67,00,837	75,58,230	1,42,59,067	11,60,00,525	11,88,39,138	234839663
1828–29	62,00,000	83,00,000	1,45,00,000	7,40,30,000	11,58,90,000	18,99,20,000
1829–30	70,00,000	1,29,00,000	1,99,00,000	7,20,00,000	13,42,00,000	83,62,00,000
1830–31	80,00,000	1,31,00,000	2,11,00,000	7,32,00,000	11,14,00,000	18,46,00,000
1831–32	63,00,000	97,00,000	1,60,00,000	5,59,00,000	11,57,00,000	17,16,00,000
1832–33	31,00,000	68,00,000	99,00,000	5,38,00,000	11,44,00,000	16,82,00,000
1833–34	52,00,000	78,00,000	1,30,00,000	5,95,00,000	11,92,00,000	17,87,00,000
1834–35	49,00,000	58,00,000	1,07,00,000	6,27,00,000	10,29,00,000	16,56,00,000
1835–36	61,00,000	1,05,00,000	1,66,00,000	6,84,00,000	13,90,00,000	20,74,00,000
1836–37	66,00,000	91,00,000	1,57,00,000	7,43,00,000	15,98,00,000	23,41,00,000
1837–38	59,00,000	1,02,00,000	1,61,00,000	7,46,00,000	12,17,00,000	19,63,00,000
1838–39	64,00,000	95,00,000	1,59,00,000	8,06,00,000	12,77,00,000	20,83,00,000
1839–40	58,00,000	92,00,000	1,50,00,000	7,61,00,000	12,23,00,000	19,84,00,000
1840–41	73,11,230	84,27,920	1,57,39,150	10,20,21,930	13,82,20,700	24,02,42,630
1841–42	71,72,510	90,36,590	1,62,09,100	9,62,99,010	14,84,02,940	24,47,01,950
1842–43	67,71,990	1,18,90,550	1,86,62,540	11,04,68,940	13,76,76,210	24,81,45,150
1843–44	71,33,900	1,10,44,370	1,81,78,270	13,61,24,760	17,99,95,540	31,61,20,300
1844–45	87,02,340	99,05,630	1,86,07,970	14,50,65,370	17,69,70,520	32,20,35,890
1845–46	90,69,820	1,01,58,270	1,92,28,090	11,58,34,380	17,84,47,020	29,42,81,400
1846–47	93,06,240	1,05,99,870	1,99,06,110	11,83,65,870	16,06,93,070	27,90,58,940
1847–48	91,29,960	1,08,96,370	2,00,26,330	10,57,10,080	14,73,84,350	25,30,94,430
1848–49	93,34,310	1,00,23,560	1,93,57,870	12,54,93,070	18,62,82,440	31,17,75,510
1849–50	1,01,73,560	93,77,830	1,95,51,390	13,69,66,960	18,28,35,430	31,98,02,390
1850–51	1,09,62,020	85,99,760	1,95,61,780	15,37,05,980	18,70,54,390	34,07,60,370
1851–52	1,07,27,900	93,02,280	2,00,30,180	17,29,25,490	20,79,83,420	38,09,08,910
1852–53	98,08,270	97,95,560	1,96,03,830	16,90,22,400	21,51,98,830	38,42,21,230
1853–54	83,37,830	98,26,020	1,81,63,850	15,99,46,130	20,77,84,350	36,77,30,480
1854–55	1,02,77,650	1,10,17,420	2,12,95,070	14,77,09,270	20,19,42,550	34,96,51,820
1855–56	98,63,280	1,03,88,980	2,02,52,260	25,24,47,820	23,63,94,350	48,88,42,170
1856–57	88,10,860	1,13,95,230	2,02,06,090	28,60,82,840	26,59,18,770	54,20,01,610
1857–58	1,20,41,270	1,19,68,720	2,40,09,990	31,09,30,650	28,27,84,740	59,37,15,390
1858–59	1,20,10,490	1,37,57,799	2,57,68,289	34,54,56,500	30,53,22,980	65,07,79,480

Most important reasons that prevented the growth of trade between Persia and India are as follows:

1. Lack of a modern banking system in Persia before establishment of Foreign Banks in Persia in 1888 resulted in all the monetary transactions to be done by Moneychangers and merchants and this made the transactions slow and high in price.[20]

2. Lack of a proper route system and high distance between the northern cities which were the richest and most fertile parts of Persia and the Persian Gulf shores which was the main route of trade with India made the goods expensive, even the cost would multiply by a few times higher than what's the good's worth. Caravan routes from important harbors in Persian Gulf to cities in north of Persia, like Mashhad, Tehran, Tabriz used to take around 75 to 90 days. Practically, due to long distances an Indian merchant was only able to use his wealth only once a year for a trade.[21]

3. It can be said that the most important difficulty of trade of Persia and India in this period, is trade deficit of Persia which in the East India Company's report in 1792 it's stated that this deficit is caused because the export products of Persia have no market in India and the exports of Persia to India only covers 20% of the import to Persia from India. Therefore, Persia had to cover the rest 80% with specie. It is also stated that the most important and most valuable product of Persia which was silk has no market in India. Morier in 1809 states that 350,000 Tooman equivalent to £350,000 is sent to India to cover the trade deficit every year and this amount could not be covered by exporting silk, the most important export product of Persia to Russia and Turkey.[22]

4. This problem in trade relation of Persia and India continues during the years of this research and Persia was only able to get a positive trade balance when petroleum was added to the list of their exports. Policies of the British government in preference of their political interests rather than commercial ones and sacrificing the potential of trade of India and Persia.[23]

CONCLUSION

Due to the political situations in both countries, situation of colonization of India and a semi colonial condition in Persia, the two countries were not able to play an effective role for their own national interests and practically were in a game of colonialism of European countries like Britain and Russia and lack of an infrastructure to increase the foreign trade of Persia. Lack of modern harbors and ports, railways, proper roads, modern banking system and disproportion of needed goods and export of specie from Persia, were among the reasons that made the trade of Persia and India grow slowly and does not go as the same level as global trade growth or even India's foreign trade. (See Annexures)

SOURCES

Third report from the select committee appointed to consider of the means of improving and maintaining the foreign trade of the country, House of Commons, 1821, Appendix (H.), Page: 398 (For Years 1802– 1817) *Note:* 100 Sicca Rupees equals 125 Company Rupees.

Finance and account—trade part II-commercial. Appendix to the report from the select Committee of the house of commons on the affaire of the East India Company, London,1833, Appendix, No. 14. Page: 862 (For years 1821–1828) Note: 100 Sicca Rupees equals 125 Company Rupees.

K.N. Chaudhuri, The Economic Development of India under the East India Company 1814–58 (A Selection of Contemporary writings), Cambridge University Press, London, 1971, pages 46– 50 (for years 1829–39).

G.E., Eyre and William Spottiswoode, Statistical Abstract relating to British India, from 1840–1865, London, 1867. (For years 1840–59) Note: 10 Company Rupees equals 1 Sterling Pound.

BIBLOGRAPHY

Statistical Sources

Eyre, G.E. and William Spottiswood, Statistical Abstract relating to British India, from 1840–1865, London, 1867 (For years 1840–59). *Note:* 10 Company Rupees equals 1 Sterling Pound.
Finance and Account, Trade Part II, Commercial. Appendix to the report from the select Committee of the House of Commons on the affaire of the East India Company, London, 1833, Appendix, No.14.
First, Second and third reports of the Select Committee, 1793.
Third report from the select committee appointed to consider of the means of improving and maintaining the foreign trade of the country, House of Commons, 1821, Appendix (H.).

Documents in National Archive of India

Foreign Department, 5, Mar, 1853, No. 17.
Foreign Department, Political Branch, 29 Jan 1853, No. 6, 7.
Foreign Department, Political Branch, 29 Jan 1858, No. 1, 2.
Foreign Department, Political Branch, 29 Jan 1858, No. 3, 4.
Foreign Department, Political Branch, 29 Jan 1858, No. 5, 6.

Others

Berared, V., Revolutions de la Perse, Translated by S.Z. Dehshiry, Tehran, 2535.

Chaudhuri, K.N., The Economic Development of India under the East India Company 1814–58 (A Selection of Contemporary writings), Cambridge University Press, London, 1971.

Curzon, George N., Persia and Persian Question Vol. II, Translated by V. Mazandarani, Tehran, 1380.

Dutt, Romesh Chunder, Economic History of India, Vol. II, Delhi, 1970.

Floor, Willem, The Rise and Fall of Bushehr, Translated by Hasan Zanganeh, Tehran, 1387.

Fraser, An Historical Account of Persia, London, 1834.

Fraser, James B., Travels and Adventures of the Persia, Provinces on the Southern Bank of the Caspian Sea, London, 1826.

Harford Jones, An Account of the transections of his Majesty's Mission to the Court of Persia in the Years 1807–11, Vol. I, London, 1834.

Issawi, Charles, The Economic History of Iran, 1800–1914, Translated by Yaghoob Azhand, Tehran, 1362.

Kelly, J.B., Britain and the Persian Gulf 1795–1880, Oxford, 1968.

Kumar, Dharm, The Cambridge Economic History of India Vol. 2 (1757–1970), First Edition Published 1982, Cambridge University Press, Printed in India.

Lambton, Ann, Qajar Persia, Eleven Studies, Translated by Fasihi, Mashhad, 1375.

Lorimer, John Gordon, Gazetteer of the Persian Gulf: Historical Vol. I, Calcutta, 1915.

Mac Gregor, John, Commercial Statistics, A digest of the productive resources, Commercial legislation, Customs and Tariffs, Shipping, Import and Exports, All Nations, Vol. II, London, 1850.

Morier, James, A Journey through Persia, Armenia and Asia Minor to Constantinople, in the years, 1808–1809, London, 1812.

Polak, *Safarnameh Polak*, Translated by K. Jahandari, Tehran, 1968.

Thomas, R. Hughes, Treaties, Agreements and Engagements, between the honorable East India Company and the native Princes, chiefs, and states, Bombay, 1851,

Warring, Scott, A tour to Shiraz, London, 1807.

REFERENCES

[1] First, Second and third reports of the Select Committee, 1793, pp. 42–46.

[2] Lorimer, John Gordon, Gazetteer of the Persian Gulf: Historical Vol. I, Calcutta, 1915 (pp. 165–168).

[3] Lorimer, Gazetteer of the Persian Gulf (p. 165–168), Issawi, Charles, The Economic History of Iran, 1800–1914, Translated by Yaghoob Azhand, Tehran, 1362, pp. 406–407.

[4] Look at Trade report between Persia and Russia (1750–1910), K.A. Ter Goskav, in Issawi, Economic History of Iran, pp. 220–224.

[5] Thomas, R. Hughes, Treaties, Agreements and Engagements, between the honorable East India Company and the native Princes, chiefs and states, Bombay, 1851, pp. 454–456.

[6] Warring, Scott, A tour to Shiraz, London, 1807, p. 8.

[7]   Ibid, p. 77.

[8]   Ibid, p. 79.

[9]   Jones, Harford, An Account of the transections of his Majesty's Mission to the Court of Persia in the Years 1807–11, Vol. I, London, 1834, p. 433.

[10] Fraser, An Historical Account of Persia, London, 1834, p. 291.

[11] Ibid, p. 292.

[12] Issawi, Economic History of Iran, pp. 134–137, Finance and Account, Trade Part II, Commercial. Appendix to the report from the select Committee of the House of Commons on the affaire of the East India Company, London,1833, Appendix, No. 14, p. 862 Third report from the select committee appointed to consider of the means of improving and maintaining the foreign trade of the country, House of Commons, 1821, Appendix (H.), p. 398.

[13] Lorimer, Gazetteer of the Persian Gulf Vol. I, Part II, P. 1955 Kelly, J.B., Britain and the Persian Gulf 1795–1880, Oxford, 1968, p. 137.

[14] Foreign Department, 5, Mar, 1853, No. 17.

[15] Lambton, Ann, Qajar Persia, Eleven Studies, Translated by Fasihi, Mashhad, 1375, p. 179. Kelley, Britain in Persian Gulf, pp. 250–251 Issawi, Economic History of Iran, pp. 139–140. Floor, Willem, The Rise and Fall of Bushehr, Translated by Hasan Zanganeh, Tehran, 1387, p. 34–35.

[16] Issawi, Economic History of Iran, p. 413.

[17] Issawi, Economic History of Persia, pp. 406–407.

[18] Mac Gregor, John, Commercial Statistics, A digest of the productive resources, Commercial legislation, Customs and Tariffs, Shipping, Import and Exports, All Nations, Vol. II, London, 1850, pp. 370–371. Fraser, James B., Travels and Adventures of the Persia, Provinces on the Southern Bank of the Caspian Sea, London, 1826, pp. 363–365.

[19] Foreign Department, Political Branch, 29/Jan/1858, No.: 1–2 Compare Figures (9) and (10) Dutt, Romesh Chunder, Economic History of India, Vol. II, Delhi, 1970, p. 380.

[20] Polak, *Safarnameh Polak*, Translated by K. Jahandari, Tehran, 1968, p. 377.

[21] Issawi, Economy of Iran, p. 299–303, Berared, V., Revolutions de la Perse, Translated by S. Z. Dehshiry, Tehran, 2535, P. 144. Curzon, George N., Persia and Persian Question Vol. II, Translated by V. Mazandarani, Tehran, 1380, p. 680.

[22] Morier, James, A Journey through Persia, Armenia and Asia Minor to Constantinople, in the years, 1808–1809, London, 1812, p. 239.

[23] Political interference of Britain in Persia's matters sometimes ended up in harming the trade between Persia and India. After the military confrontation of Persia and Britain because of Herat in 1857 we see that exports from Bombay to Bushehr decreases from 10, 50, 328 rupees during May and October of 1856 to 4,56,584 rupees from November of 1856 until April 30 of 1857. For further information check these documents available at National Archive of India: Foreign Department, Political Branch, 29 Jan 1858, No. 1, 2 and No. 3, 4.

Prospects and Possibilities of Indo-Iran Trade Relations

Radha Raghuramapatruni

INTRODUCTION

India and Iran are the two oldest countries in Asia and both are the transition countries in the world. The two countries shared a border till 1947 and also share several common features in their language, culture and traditions. Iran, located by the Persian Gulf, OmanSea, and Central Asia, is in the centre of a perpetual "hot spot" in the world affairs. It is situated at the eastern end of the oil-rich Persian Gulf and a possible export route for the natural resources of Central Asia. India views Central Asia and Iran, situated at the crossroads of overland trading routes, as potential consumer markets for Indian products and for Iran, India is a cost-effective source of high-technology inputs. The two-way trade between the two countries has shown good growth in the recent years as it has grown more than 25% during the last five years from US$ 12,887.52 mil in 2007–08 to US$ 15,968.03 mil in 2011–12 also both the economies, India and Iran are making robust efforts to renew and strengthen the bilateral economic and trade relations. The relationship between the two countries has evolved into a significant partnership in the economic and commercial sphere. At the same time, India has emerged as an important investor in the Iran's economy and also emerged as an important export destination for the Iran's manufactured goods. However, this potential has yet to translate into major economic benefits. In this context the present paper would attempt to assess the trade patterns and in particular the export and import intensity of trade relations between the two countries.

To have a better understanding of trade relations between the two countries, a few studies have been reviewed. According to *Meena Singh Roy (2013)* views that in past few years both India and Iran have been working towards managing its energy and economic cooperation under the shadow of the US and European Union (EU) sanctions. Despite the tightening of sanctions, India cannot halt the import of crude oil from Iran given its dependence on Iranian oil. Iran was India's second largest supplier of oil but now it has slipped to sixth position. India imported 16.083 million tones of oil in 2010–2011 and 14.689 million tonnes of oil during 2011–2012. Though India reduced oil imports from Iran, It is trying to expand trade in other commodities like tea, pharma, automobile, electronics, spare parts and agricultural products. Whereas, *Mahmoud Balooch (2013)* finds that Iran's geostrategic position allows it to play an important role in connecting India to Central Asia militarily and strategically. India sees Central Asia and Iran, situated at the crossroads of overland trading routes, as potential consumer markets for Indian products. Meanwhile he views that, Iran sees in India a cost-effective source of high-technology inputs and this potential has yet to translate into major economic benefits. According to *Mohammad Sadegh Avazalipour (2011)*, finds that India and Iran are two of the oldest countries in Asia and both are the transition countries in the world. Both the countries have had several Five-Year Plans for increasing the real per capita income, growth rate of GDP etc. in his study he has focused on Consumption Function between Iran and India as a comparative study and has shown that although the Iran's MPC and Consumption-GDP ratio were lower than India's during the last three decades, but in the future decades this situation of consumption will change so that Iran's Consumption-GDP ratio will be higher than that of India's. in an another study by *Meena Singh Roy and Ajey Lele (2011)*, observes that in recent years, Iran has come to acquire a significant place in the West Asian region with the ability to influence regional politics. For India, relations with Iran are vital. In the changed strategic environment, both India and Iran have been working towards improving their bilateral relations. However, there are several challenges, especially for India, in this regard. If the Iran-US confrontation intensifies, for example, India may find it difficult to pursue a smooth relationship with Iran. They looks at various facets of India-Iran relations and examines the opportunities and challenges that lie ahead.

The present study aims at observing the extent of trade relations between India and Iran and further explores the possibilities for future trade co-operation among these countries. The success of any bilateral cooperation between the economies is largely influenced by the nature of harmony that is induced at national, regional and international levels. The objectives of the study are a) To analyze the trend and pattern of growth of India's trade with the Iran's economy. b) To estimate the extent of Intensity of trade relations between India and Iran. c) To identify the commodities with trade potential, which could further enhance the trade relations between the nations. d) To further explore the areas of emerging trade opportunities and to assess the future prospects of trade between the nations under study. The following methodology is adopted to understand the possible relationships and future potentialities of trade between the two nations. One of the basic pre-requisites for economic cooperation is the existence of complementarity among the partner countries signing the bilateral trade pact. If the production structure of the partner country is different from the other and if one country exports goods which the other country imports, then we can say that there is a strong trade complementarity between the nations.

For the purpose the Revealed Comparative Advantage Index and Trade Dependency Index are calculated with respect to 16 distinct commodity categories for both the nations respectively. The values of RCA index (Revealed Comparative Advantage Index) are matched with the RID (Trade Dependency Index or Revealed Import Dependency Index) individually for both the countries to explore the potential areas of trade between them.

REVEALED COMPARATIVE ADVANTAGE INDEX

The paper identifies the pattern of revealed comparative advantage using the Balassa's (1965) index for export data. Measures of Balassa's Index of Revealed Comparative Advantage (RCA) has been used to assess country's export potential. The index has been calculated for each of the sixteen commodity category. The RCA indicates whether a country is in the process of extending the products in which it has a trade potential, as opposed to situations in which the number of products that can be competitively exported are static. It can also provide useful information about potential trade prospects with new partners. Countries with similar RCA profiles are unlikely to have high bilateral trade intensities unless intra industry trade is involved. RCA measures, if estimated at high levels of product disaggregation, can focus attention on the other nontraditional products that might be successfully exported. The RCA index of country i for the product j is often measured by the product's share in the country's exports in relation to its share in the world trade:

$$RCA_{ij} = (X_{ij}/X_{it})/(X_{wj}/X_{wt})$$

Where X_{ij} and X_{wj} are the values of country's exports of product j and world exports of product j and where X_{it} and X_{wt} refer to the country's total exports and world total exports. A value of less than unity implies that the country has a revealed comparative disadvantage in the product. Similarly, if the index exceeds unity, the country is said to have a revealed comparative advantage in the product.

REVEALED IMPORT DEPENDENCE INDEX

The index identifies the commodities, which have import dependence on the partner countries, the Revealed Import Dependence (RID) index also been called as Revealed Comparative Disadvantage index (Joh Gilbert, 2010). The RID index will give us the commodity-wise structure of imports in the countries. The RID is defined as commodity 'i's share in country's total imports vis-à-vis its share in total world imports. The RID index can be computed as follows:

$$RID\ i = (M_{ia}/M_a)/(M_{iw}/M_w),$$

Where Mia is equal to imports of commodity 'i' from a country 'a', Ma is equal to total imports of a country 'a', M_{iw} is equal to total value of the world imports of commodity i and M_w is equal to total world imports. As in the case of RCA index, an RID index exceeding one suggests a strong dependence of the country on the import of a specific item in a reference period and vice-versa.

The RCA and RID values for Iran and India were calculated and matched to assess the commodity potential for commodity trade between the nations.[a]

INTENSITY INDICES

Prof A.J. Brown (1947) first developed and applied trade intensity ratios to measure trade relationship among different countries. The Export-Intensity and Import-Intensity ratios are called trade-intensity indices. These ratios help us to assess the extent of trade relations that exist between the nations. Trade Intensity Index can be divided into Export-Intensity Index (EII) and Import- Intensity Index (III) for looking the pattern of exports and imports. Following A.J. Brown (1947) they can be defined as follows.

---

[a] While an RCA analysis will tell us about the comparative advantage that a country enjoys in the export of a certain commodities in general, its does not necessarily tell us about the specific import requirements of the countries being focused for exports. So, although India may have a comparative advantage in the export of certain commodities, it may not be necessary that Iran have a requirement for the same commodities. A comparison of the RCA of commodities in India with the RID of commodities in Iran will give a more reliable picture of the export potential of the Indian goods in Iran and Vice versa. If for a certain commodity India has a RCA index greater than one, and for the same commodity Iran has a RID greater than one, than such a commodity is considered to have a strong export potential in that particular country.

Export-Intensity Index

The ratio of export share of a country/region to the share of world exports going to a partner. Export-Intensity Index (EII) can be defined as,

$$XII_{ij} = \frac{x_{ij} / X_{iw}}{x_{wj} / X_{ww}}$$

Where x_{ij} is the dollar value of exports of country/region i to country/region j, X_{iw} is the dollar value of the exports of country/region i to the world, x_{wj} is the dollar value of world exports to country/region j, and X_{ww} is the dollar value of world exports. An index of more than one indicates that trade flow between countries/regions is larger than expected given their importance in world trade.

Import-Intensity Index

The ratio of import share of a country/region to the share of world imports going to a partner Import -Intensity Index (III) can be defined as,

$$III_{ij} = M_{ij} / M_{iw} / M_{wj} / M_{ww}$$

Where M_{ij} is the dollar value of imports of country/region i to country/region j, M_{iw} is the dollar value of the imports of country/region i to the world, M_{wj} is the dollar value of world imports to country/region j, and M_{ww} is the dollar value of world imports. An index of more than one indicates higher import intensity between the nations.

INDIA-IRAN BILATERAL TRADE

India and Iran are making robust efforts to renew and strengthen the bilateral economic and trade relations. The relationship between both the countries has evolved into a significant partnership in the economic and commercial sphere. At the same time, India has emerged as important investor in the Iran, and also as an important export destination for the Iran's manufactured goods.

Trade relations between both the economies have witnessed a significant rise especially during the last decade, with India's total trade with Iran rising from US$ 773.6 million in 1995 to 16.5 bn in 2012. This buoyant trend has been supported by both rise in India's exports to and imports from Iran showing a much higher Compound Annual Growth Rate (CAGR) as compared to India 's exports to Iran (Table 1).

Since 1995 to 2001 India had a trade deficit with Iran from 2001 till 2005 India enjoyed a positive trade balance. India's trade balance with Iran which showed a surplus of US$ 221.71 US$ million in the year 2005, turned into a deficit of US$ 3.4 billion the next year, owing to sharp increase in oil imports. By the year 2010 the trade deficit of India with Iran was registered at 6.3 billion and by the year 2012 this rose to 11.2 billion.

In 2012, Iran emerged as thirteenth largest trading partner with a share of 2.1% of India's total trade. During the same year Iran was the seventh largest source of imports for India, with a share of 3% of India's total imports, and the twenty fourth largest export markets with a share of 1.1% of total India's exports.

Table 1: India's Bilateral Trade with Iran: 1995–2012

Year	Export	Import	Total Trade	Trade Balance
		(US$ Million)		
1995	154.58	619.09	773.66	−464.51
1996	194.96	864.73	1059.70	−669.77
1997	171.69	519.60	691.29	−347.91
1998	159.06	402.78	561.83	−243.72
1999	151.93	862.14	1014.07	−710.21
2000	187.34	555.65	742.99	−368.31
2001	253.28	314.30	567.57	−61.02
2002	492.19	306.78	798.96	185.41
2003	892.99	327.03	1220.02	565.96
2004	1185.00	504.93	1689.93	680.06
2005	1072.99	851.27	1924.26	221.71
2006	1617.34	5099.89	6717.23	−3482.55
2007	1845.26	9486.64	11331.90	−7641.38
2008	2335.91	13913.48	16249.39	−11577.57
2009	1949.09	10886.27	12835.35	−8937.18
2010	2509.26	8844.84	11354.10	−6335.59
2011	2462.29	9607.78	12070.08	−7145.49
2012	2572.13	13857.68	16429.81	−11285.54

Source: www.unctad.org

Iran is one of the world's major oil exporters, with hydrocarbon related exports accounting for around three-fourth of the total export revenue. Iran's total trade increased over four-fold during the last ten years, it was 42 US$ billion during 2001 rose to 136 US$ billion by the year 2012, aided by growth in both exports and imports. This can also be observed in its annual merchandise export and import growth. During the year 2001 the annual merchandise export growth was at 10.6 percent and import growth was at 20.2 percent, by the year 2012 Iran registered an annual merchandise increase in the export growth by 21.2% but the import growth was negative by –7.5% (Table 2). The total trade declined in the year 2012 (136 US$ bn) mainly reflecting sharp fall in export demand compared to the previous year 2011 (222 US$ bn).

Table 2: Annual Merchandise Growth: 1995–2012

Year	India		Iran	
	Export	*Import*	*Export*	*Import*
1995	22.413	29.297	–5.526	0.784
1996	8.081	9.322	21.955	17.231
1997	5.748	9.197	–17.909	–12.769
1998	–4.488	3.736	–28.633	0.895
1999	6.668	9.305	60.314	–6.975
2000	18.820	9.672	36.657	4.308
2001	2.316	–2.195	–10.613	20.226
2002	13.581	12.155	9.919	23.389
2003	19.722	28.382	19.524	20.279
2004	29.995	37.512	23.547	28.946
2005	29.965	43.192	34.907	25.222
2006	22.277	24.876	36.905	1.826
2007	23.275	28.563	15.220	10.228
2008	29.748	39.962	28.101	27.722
2009	–15.357	–19.883	–30.649	–11.556
2010	37.258	36.171	28.525	28.829
2011	33.822	32.615	30.285	–5.572
2012	–2.888	5.427	–21.212	–7.558

Source: www.unctad.org

India's annual merchandise export growth was registered at 22.4 percent by the year 1995 and import growth at 29.2 percent (Table 2, Figure 1) with a total merchandise trade of 691 US$ bn. This has fallen drastically in the following years, India registered a negative export growth rate in the 1998 (–4.48) and import growth rate stood at 3.73 percent. This was revived by the year 2000 where the annual merchandise export growth was at 18.8 percent and import growth rate 9.67 percent. Following the impact of Global Economic Crisis India's total trade in the year 2009 declined to

416 US$ million from the 490 US$ million in the previous year 2008. The export and import trade also suffered a decline compared to the year 2008 which can be seen in the declined growth rates. By the year 2012 once again the country experienced a set back with respect to export and import trade mainly due to external crisis, fluctuating exchange rates and huge inflationary trends in economy where the annual merchandise export and import growth rates were –2.88 and 5.4 percent respectively.

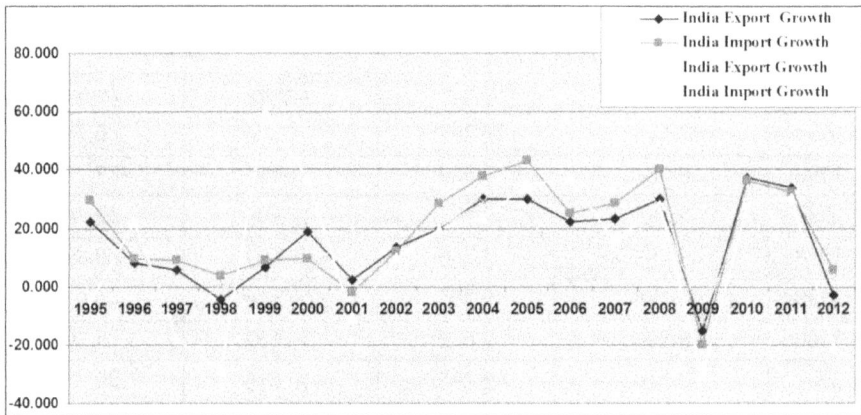

Fig. 1: Annual Merchandise Growth
Source: Author's Calculations.

INTENSITY INDEX

India's Export Intensity Index with Iran

India needs Iran to achieve its varied objectives in Central Asia. Iran, for its part, sees a tremendous complimentarity of interest with India. Both governments are optimistic about the commercial benefits of Central Asia markets and hope to share the benefits of North-South Transit Corridor. In view of the mutual benefits both the economies are committed to intensify their economic and trade relations and hold regular bilateral talks on economic and trade issues at the Indo-Iran Joint Commission Meetings (JCM). As a result the intensity of trade relations (Export Intensity and Import Intensity) between the countries has been on rise (Annexure 1 and Figure 2). During the initial period of the study India's Export Intensity Index was 1.84 and Import Intensity Index was 8.12 and these indices has been gradually on rise, as both the economies have been making progress on their commitment to build a North-South corridor with the participation of Russia. This is one of the "strategic projects" to intensify India's relations with Iran during September 2000 and they have also entered into an agreement to open up a transportation route with Turkmenistan. This agreement provides a legal framework for the multi-model movement of goods from India to Iran and Turkmenistan which would further reduce the transportation cost and helps to enhance the volume of trade between the countries. During the year 2000 the Export Intensity Index (EII) is 2.010 and Import Intensity Index (III) is 5.66, this gradually rose to 4.48 (EII) by the year 2003, whereas there was a decline in the Import Intensity Index which stands at 1.41 during the year. Largely, India has a trade deficit with Iran as the major import commodity that dominates India's import basket is oils and mineral fuels which accounts for 84.5 percent of India's total imports from Iran. In the year 2010, Iran was the third largest source of imports of mineral fuel and oils for India, accounts for 8.2 percent of India's total exports. India's exports to Iran in the year 2012 stood at US$ 2572.13 and imports were at US$ 13857.68 which was 1 percent of India's total exports and 3.16 percent of India's total imports respectively, and the value of Export Intensity Index was 2.85 and Import Intensity Index was registered at 12.60. One significant observation has been that there was a gradual fall with respect to the EII of India with Iran after the year 2005 and the III has been on rise till the year 2008, there after there was a gradual decline and it stood at 12.60 by the year 2012 where India ranked as the fifth largest export destination for Iran.

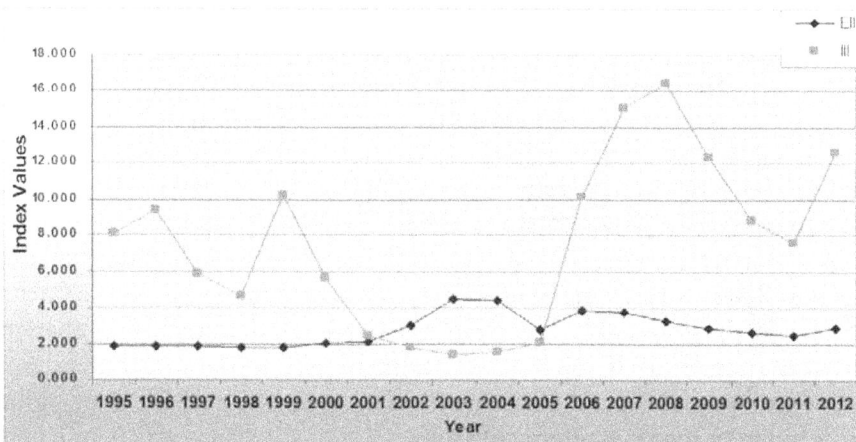

Fig. 2: India's Export Intensity Index and Import Intensity Index with Iran
Source: Author's Calculations based on data from Unctad.org

Iran's Export Intensity Index with India

Trade relations between India and Iran have witnessed a significant rise, with India's total trade with Iran rising from US$ bn 18 to US and bn 290 by the year 2012. This buoyant trend has been supported by both rise in India's exports to and imports from Iran, with India's imports showing a much higher growth as compared to India's exports to Iran. The Export Intensity Index (EII) and the Import Intensity Index (III) of Iran with India (Annexure 2, Figure 3) presents that these indices from Iran's perspective have been lower than India's Intensity Indices. The Export Intensity Index (EII) of Iran with India was registered at 4.02 in the initial period of study and the Import Intensity Index (III) was registered at 5.02. This has gradually declined to 2.15 and 3.33 respectively by the year 2000 where Iran's export and import share with India was 1.18 and 0.39 respectively. Iran's Export Intensity Index with India was to a large extent stable around 5 during the period 2006, 2007, 2008 and 2009 and by the year 2012 the Export Intensity Index was registered around 7.94 respectively.

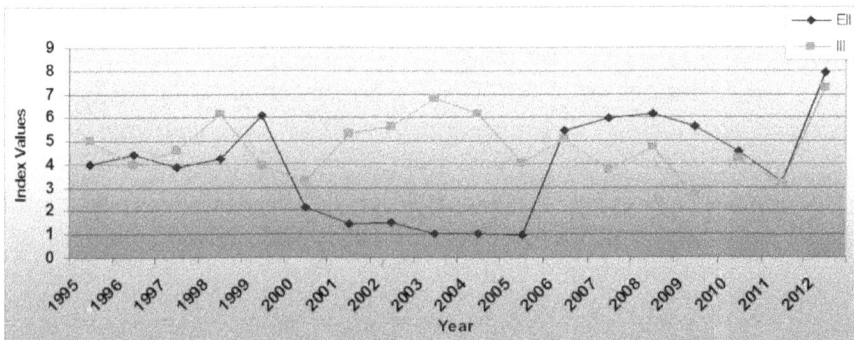

Fig. 3: Iran's Export and Import Intensity Indices with India
Source: Author's Calculations based on data from Unctad.org

India's share in the top four items in Iran's import basket is very low, which indicates a large scope for enhancing India's exports to Iran. The Import Intensity Index (III) of Iran with India saw a gradual decline after the year 2004 (6.14), it stood at 4.73 by the year 2008 and finally registered at 7.24 by the year 2012. The main reason for the declining trade share of Imports from India is the huge rise with respect to the prices of oil and petroleum products in the international market and the effect of global crisis in the domestic economy of India.

REVEALED COMPARITIVE ADVANTAGE

While India's overall exports to Iran have depicted a robust trend in recent years, an analysis of the share of India's major exports to Iran vis-a-vis Iran's global imports of these items would reveal the tremendous scope to enhance India's exports to Iran. For the purpose this Section aims at ascertaining the possibility of commodity tradebetween India and Iran. The study tries to identity the broad product groups in which India has a revealed comparative advantage and which also form the major import items for Iran and vice versa. Thus identifying the complementary or competitive nature of such product groups produced within India vis-à-vis China, which reveals the extent of the export opportunities between the nations. For the purpose of the analysis Balassa's Revealed Comparative Advantage Index (RCA) and Revealed Import Dependence (RID) were used. The RCA is a measure of the natural advantage enjoyed by a country in the conduct of its trade in an environment constrained by regulatory policies and administrative controls perpetuated by the system. The identification of commodities which enjoy Revealed Comparative Advantage would enable the policy makers to formulate an appropriate strategy, which would help to accelerate exports of the specified items and allocate resources to develop those industries, with the potential to earn maximum foreign exchange for the country.

The Revealed Import Dependency (RID) has also been called as Revealed Comparative Disadvantage, which will give us the commodity-wise structure of imports in the countries. The detailed description of RID is provided in the section of Methodology. While an RCA analysis reveals the comparative advantage that a country enjoys in the export of certain commodities in general, it does not necessarily tell us about the specific import requirements of the countries being focused for exports. So, although India may have a comparative advantage in the export of certain commodities, it may not be necessary that Iran would have the requirement for the same commodities. A comparison of the RCA for the commodities in India with the RID of commodities in Iran and also RCA of the commodities in Iran with RID of commodities in India will give a more reliable picture of the export potential of the Indian goods to Iran and Iranian goods in India (Table 3).

The RCA and RID of 16 commodity categories were calculated and presented. Both the indices (RCA and RID) were calculated for the time period of 12 years (2000 to 2012) and the average value is presented for the purpose of analysis which would give an appropriate picture regarding the commodity trade of India and Iran. A comparison of RCA Index of the various products between India and Iran helps us in identifying the group of commodities, which either compete or are complementary in nature.

The Table 3 presents the RCA and the RID value for India and Iran, when the RCA of India is matched with the RID of Iran and vice versa it has been observed that out of the 16 commodities taken up for study 9 commodities reveal the feasibility for trade between both the economies. The commodity categories *1. Agricultural products, 2. Food, 3. Iron and Steel, 4. Chemicals, 5. Pharmaceuticals, 6. Machinery and Transport Equipment and 7. Electronic Data processing and office equipment* present a higher value of RCA for India (>1) and lower RID value for Iran (<1) which infers the possibility for trade between them. Similarly two commodities *1. Fuel and mining products and 2. Fuels* reveal a higher RCA value for Iran (>1) and a lower RID value for India (<1) presenting the potentiality for trade in these commodity category between the two nations (Table 4).

Table 3: RCA and RID Index Comparison: India-Iran (2000–2012)

S. No.	Commodity Category	India (Average 2000–2012)		Iran (Average 2000–2012)	
		RCA	RID	RCA	RID
1.	Agricultural products	1.399	0.716	0.503	1.431
2.	Food	1.422	0.566	0.569	1.492
3.	Fuels and mining products	0.946	2.365	5.165	0.398
4.	Fuels	0.808	2.649	6.452	0.385
5.	Manufactures	0.978	0.685	0.157	0.851
6.	Iron and steel	1.542	0.917	0.403	3.91
7.	Chemicals	1.038	0.943	0.401	0.96
8.	Pharmaceuticals	1.118	0.29	0.041	0.956
9.	Machinery and transport equipment	1.318	0.554	0.032	0.224
10.	Office and telecom equipment	0.129	0.552	0	0.35
11.	Electronic data processing and office equipment	1.097	0.516	0.001	0.327
12.	Telecommunications equipment	0.195	0.86	0.009	0.569
13.	Integrated circuits and electronic components	0.075	0.236	0.001	0.134
14.	Automotive products	0.294	0.128	0.039	0.733
15.	Textiles	4.078	0.561	0.788	0.51
16.	Clothing	3.007	0.023	0.115	0.017

Source: Author's Calculations based on data from wto.org

A total of *nine commodity categories* has been identified which hold the potential for trading between both the nations to enhance bilateral trade relations between the economies. This also address the problem of addressing India's high trade deficit, where India can take up a strategy to boost the exports of the commodity categories in which it enjoys the Revealed Comparative Advantage (where the RCA>1) and which also features Iran's Import Dependence (RID>1). Similarly, Iran can make up a strategy for exports of commodities in which India's Revealed Import Dependency is higher to tap the trade potential among them for their mutual benefit.

Table 4: Commodities Feasible for Trade between India-Iran

	India	Iran
	(Average 2000–2012)	*(Average 2000–2012)*
Commodity Category	RCA > 1	RID > 1
Agricultural products	1.399	1.431
Food	1.422	1.492
Iron and steel	1.542	3.91
Chemicals	1.038	0.965
Pharmaceuticals	1.118	0.956
Machinery and Transport Equipment	1.318	0.224
Electronic data processing and office equipment	1.097	0.327
Commodity Category	RID > 1	RCA > 1
Fuels and mining products	2.365	5.165
Fuels	2.649	6.452

Source: Author's Calculations based on Table.

India has been the major source for Iran's global imports of organic chemicals, cereals, articles of iron or steel and manmade staple fibres, accounting for a significant share in Iran's global imports. However, in the case of other major commodities imported by Iran, such as machinery and instruments, iron and steel, pharmaceuticals, vehicles other than railway, India's share in Iran's global imports is low, and in some cases has even declined over the years. Given India's export capability in these sectors revealed by the RCA index, and huge demand existing in Iran revealed by the RID index, potential exist to further enhance India's trade relations with Iran in line with potential sectors which present export opportunities for India. Similarly Iran has been one of the major sources of imports for India for mineral fuels and oils, due to the latest changes in the international political scenario Iran has fallen to the 7th position in Oil imports for India. In this background if both the nations can develop a strategic plan to intensify their bilateral trade and economic relations it would be a win-n-win situation for the two countries.

CONCLUSION

For India, Iran continues to remain important for various reasons: energy security, making its way to Central Asia and Afghanistan for access to trade and transport connectivity, for countering Pakistani Taliban in Afghanistan and, to some extent, for managing the domestic political dynamics. But US policy in the West Asia has been other wards and India does not want to be a victim of this. However, equally important for India is its strategic partnership with the US and other allies... In this scenario India has to carefully develop a strategic plan to maintain and sustain the current momentum of its trade and economic relation with Iran for their mutual benefit and prosperity.

REFERENCES

[1] Asian Development Bank (1997). "Emerging Asia", ADB Publication.
[2] Arunachalam, S., Mapping life sciences research in India: A profile based on BIOSIS 1992–1994, *Curr. Sci.,* 1999, 76, 1191–1203.18.
[3] Amit Baruah, "LNG deal is off: Iran" at "Iran to develop 3 Persian Gulf Oil Fields" at http://old.mehrnews.com/en/newsdetail.aspx?NewsID=1821283accessed on May 6, 2013.
[4] Brooks, R. and Tao, R. (2003). "China's labour market performance and challenges", IMF Working Paper paper 03/210, Asia and Pacific Department.
[5] Balassa, B. (1965). "Trade liberalization and revealed comparative advantage", Manchester School of Economics and Social Studies, 33, pp. 99–123.
[6] Balaram, P., Scientometrics: A dismal science. *Curr. Sci.,* 2008, 95, 431–432.
[7] Iran for more trade with India in non-oil Sector", at http://zeenews.india.com/business/news/international/iran-for-more-trade... (accessed on May 12, 2013).
[8] "India set to scale up ties with Iran; joint explorations on card", at http://economictimes.indiatimes.com/news/politics-and-nation/india-set-t... accessed on 12/5/2013.
[9] Joint Press Statement on 17th India-Iran Joint Commission Meeting, May 4, 2013 athttp://www.mea.gov.in/outgoing-visit-detail.htm?21652/Joint+Press+Statem...
[10] Meena Singh Roy (2013), "India and Iran Relations: Sustaining the Momentum", Institute of Defense Studies and Analysis, Issue Brief.
[11] Meena Singh Roy, Ajay Lele (2011), "Engaging Iran in the New Strategy Environment: Opportunities and Challenges for India". Strategic Analysis, Vol.35, Issue.1.
[12] Meena Singh Roy, "Iran: India's Gateway to Central Asia", Strategic Analysis, Vol. 36, No. 6, November–December 2012, 957–975
[13] Mohammad Sadegh Avazalipour (2011). "A Comparative Study of Consumption Function in India and Iran", *Int. J. Contemp. Math. Sciences,* Vol. 6.2011, No. 11. 545–556.
[14] Mahmoud Balooch (2011), "Iran and India's Cooperation in Central Asia", China and Eurasia Forum Quarterly, Vol. 7, No. 3, pp. 25–29.
[15] "Transcript of the Media Briefing by Foreign Secretary in Tehran on Prime Minister's meetings in Iran", Government of India, Ministry of External Affairs, August 30, 2012.
[16] Views expressed by the Iranian side during the IDSA-IPIS Bilateral Dialogue at IDSA in Delhi on December 12, 2012.

ANNEXURES

Annexure 1: Trade Intensity Indices of India with Iran

Year	Export Intensity Index (EII)	Import Intensity Index (III)
1995	1.845	8.122
1996	1.921	9.400
1997	1.897	5.860
1998	1.796	4.665
1999	1.769	10.198
2000	2.010	5.670
2001	2.096	2.482
2002	3.033	1.814
2003	4.487	1.414
2004	4.385	1.584
2005	2.754	2.070
2006	3.886	10.185
2007	3.743	15.072
2008	3.308	16.434
2009	2.865	12.331
2010	2.595	8.816
2011	2.443	7.604
2012	2.852	12.602

Source: Author's Calculations based on data from Unctad.org

Annexure 2: Trade Intensity Indices of Iran with India

Year	Export Intensity Index (EII)	Import Intensity Index (III)
1995	4.023	5.028
1996	4.381	4.018
1997	3.859	4.606
1998	4.253	6.153
1999	6.100	3.910
2000	2.151	3.307
2001	1.406	5.290
2002	1.462	5.605
2003	1.011	6.802
2004	1.018	6.146
2005	0.956	4.060
2006	5.419	5.068
2007	5.939	3.750
2008	6.132	4.737
2009	5.579	2.699
2010	4.535	4.230
2011	3.193	3.133
2012	7.940	7.244

Source: Author's Calculations based on data from Unctad.org

The Long Run Relationship between Exports and Imports: The Experience of India and Iran

G. Ramakrishna

INTRODUCTION

Imports and exports are the two important components of the current account of Balance of Payments (BOP) of any country. Of late, there has been an increasing interest among the economists to study the long run relationship between exports and imports as it reflects the efficacy of trade and macro policies of a country. The knowledge of cointegration between these variables is of paramount importance to policy framing as it is vital to formulate trade policies with special reference to sustaining trade balance of a country. Cointegration between exports and imports implies long run equilibrium and trade deficits are only short run phenomena. If the estimated coefficient between exports and imports is equal to one, it implies that the country in question satisfies international budget constraint.

Trade relations between India and Iran have witnessed a significant rise during the last decade, with India's total trade (exports plus imports) with Iran rising from US$ 520 million in 2001 to US$ 10.5 billion n in 2010. This buoyant trend has been supported by both rise in India's exports to and imports from Iran, with India's imports from Iran showing a much higher growth as compared to India's exports to Iran (EXIM Bank of India, 2012).

Since the advent of the floating exchange rates during the early 1970s, and the trade liberalization during 1990s, there has been an extensive debate about the impact of exchange rates and other macro variables on imports and exports. Despite the availability of vast literature on exchange rates, exports and imports, there is little or no evidence available on the co-integration relationship between exports and imports. After the publication of seminal work by Husted (1992) several researchers have tried to verify this relationship. The present paper is an attempt in this direction and tries to empirically verify the long run relationship between exports and imports of Iran and India separately.

The economy of Iran has been experiencing several changes and shocks. It had to face the 1974–75 OPEC oil crises and a consequent decline in its exports, political upheaval associated with the 1979 Islamic Revolution, a prolonged war with Iraq (1980–1988), a volatile international oil market, economic sanctions and the decline in the growth rates. Iran has been experiencing deterioration in its exchange rate coupled with volatility, and lesser economic growth due to structural problems and exogenous factors such as economic sanctions. Starting from the late 1950s to the mid-1970s the country has seen a rise in its imports and a decline in exports. During this period and particularly after 1973, the oil prices have risen resulting in an increase in national income. During this period imports also have risen due to the removal of several restrictions. However, during war period, due to the problem relating petroleum exports foreign exchange has dwindled and also the import capacity. Shortly afterwards, imports have increased as the reconstruction of the economy has started and due to the trade liberalization policies. But during the years, 1993 and 1994, the imports have decreased due to restrictive atmosphere. During 1995–1996, government set the limits on imports with less intensity; furthermore, it increased oil price and foreign exchange incomes, consequently the amount of imports have risen again. In 1997 along with decreasing the global oil price, the value of imports decreased by 6.1%. This trend continued up to the year 1999, but since 2000 the global oil price along with redemption and decrease of the restriction of import policies, imports have continued to increase. In brief, the imports and exports of Iran have been experiencing a rise with fluctuations due to internal and external factors. Iran's trade deficits have also started rising phenomenally during the recent period (see Table 1).

Table 1: Growth Trends in Exports and Imports of India and Iran (1970–2010)

Year	India			Iran		
	Growth in Exports	Growth in Imports	Trade Deficit	Growth in Exports	Growth in Imports	Trade Deficit
1970–2010	11.20	11.19	1.04E+09	4.73	4.52	2.11E+08
1970–1990	10.58	11.82	2.78E+08	9.21	4.16	−7.66E+08
1991–2010	14.85	15.66	3.51E+09	8.75	7.36	4.87E+08

Source: World Development Indicators (WDI), 2012 and Trade map data.

Note: the growth rates are computed using semi log trend growth model. Trade deficits are based on the estimation of a linear trend line.

India has been experiencing persisting trade deficits and the problem has become more pronounced in recent years. Though, exports rose significantly due to export promotion and trade liberalization policies, imports have outweighed exports due to the larger base and due to the imports of crude oil and gold. The persistent decline in the exchange rates and rising oil and gold prices has led to an increase in the trade deficits in India. Prior to 1970s, India's trade deficits rose as a consequence of its inward looking policy and export pessimism. During 1970s and 1980s, India attempted passive liberalization but imports have risen faster due to oil price hikes in 1970s and 1980s. During 1990s exports grew at a faster rate (15.66 percent) and in the post liberalization period, export and import growth has picked up. However, during the entire study period trade deficits have risen.

The empirical work involves estimating the relationship between exports and imports using Engel-Granger method and Johansen's cointegration and vector error correction methods. The remaining paper is structured as follows: The second section deals with review of empirical literature. The third section is on data and econometric models. The fourth section discusses the empirical findings and the final section is on conclusion and policy suggestion.

REVIEW OF LITERATURE

Based on budget constraint, Husted (1992) proposes a theoretical relationship between exports and imports as follows:

$$C_t = Y_t + B_t - I_t(1 + r)B_t$$

Where Ct is the aggregate consumption, Y_t is the aggregate income, It is the aggregate domestic investment, r is the rate of interest and Bt is the budget constraint. Under several restrictions he derives the final equation which brings in the relationship between exports and imports:

$$X_t = a_0 + a_1 Mt + e_t$$

Alternatively Arize (2002) proposed an alternative model,

$$M_t = a_0 + a_1 Xt + e_t$$

In both the models the coefficient (a_1) represents budget constraint and remains stable if exports and imports are cointegrated. Cointegrating relationship between exports and imports implies that countries do not violate their international budget constraint and therefore supports the effectiveness of their macroeconomic policies in attaining the long-run equilibrium. Otherwise, it is unstable and the economy cannot meet its foreign debt liability. Several researchers have tried to analyze the long-run or cointegrating relationship between exports and imports. Using quarterly US trade data for the period 1967–1989, Husted (1992) has shown that exports and imports are cointegrated in the long run and therefore supports the effectiveness of their macroeconomic policies in attaining the long-run equilibrium. In another study, Herzer and Nowak-Lehmann (2006) and Erbaykal and Karaca (2008) have shown the existence of a cointegrated relationship between exports and imports, which suggest that trade deficits are only short-term phenomenon therefore, sustainable in the long-term. Peder (2007) examined the cointegration of imports and exports in India and found the cointegrating relation between these variables. Lehman (2005) found cointegrating relation between exports and imports in Chile in spite of its balance of payments problems. Similar to these studies, Bahmani-Oskooee and Rhee (1997) used quarterly data of Korea and found evidence of cointegration with a positive impact of exports on imports. Similarly, Apergis (2000) found cointegration between exports and imports for Greece. Using Indian data for the period 1949–50 to 2004–05, Upender (2007) has shown that India's nominal exports and imports are cointegrated. Vipin Jain and Janesh Sami (2012) have studied the cointegration between exports and imports in Singapore and provided evidence for the long run equilibrium using ARDL bounds test. Contrarily, using ARDL bounds test, Narayan and Narayan (2005) studying the relationship for 21 least developed countries have concluded that exports and imports are cointegrated only for six out of the 22 countries, and the coefficient of exports is less than one. Arize (2002) used quarterly data for the period 1973–1998 from 50 OCED and developing countries to examine the same question. He found that for 35 of the 50 countries, there was evidence of cointegration between exports and imports; and 31 of the 35 countries had a positive export coefficient. There are other studies, which concentrated on studying the structural breaks using Gregory-Hansen methods (see Konya and Singh 2008). The review of the empirical studies reveals the fact that there are not many country specific studies on the long run relationship between exports and imports and more so on Iran. The present study tries to fill this gap.

DATA AND ECONOMETRIC MODEL

The data for the present study have been collected from World Development Indicators (WDI) and Trade Map, IMF for the period 1970–2010. The data on exports and imports are in dollar terms and have been transformed into their natural logarithms. With such data we can avoid hetroscedasticy problem and the coefficients of the regression models can be interpreted as elasticities. A bivariate cointegration methodology is used to investigate the hypothesized long-run equilibrium relationship between exports and imports of Iran and India. To make cointegration analysis sensible, it is necessary to examine the order of integration. This paper implements Augmented Dickey-Fuller (1981) and Phillips-Perron (1988) procedures for testing the presence of unit roots.

To explore long-run equilibrium relation between the series we use Engel-Granger method and apply VER procedure following Johansen (1991), and Johansen and Juselius (1990) to estimate the cointegrating regression. If the Granger causality test confirms the existence of a cointegrating relationship, the relevant error-correction term (ECT), obtained from the cointegrating regression, must be included in the standard causality test. This helps avoid problems of misspecifications due to omissions of relevant constraints. Due to its ability to combine the long-run relationship with the short-run dynamics, Granger causality test within the Vector Error-Correction Model (VECM) environment is preferable. The existence of cointegration implies that unidirectional or bi-directional Granger causality exists. The usual t-test is applied to the coefficient of the error-correction term, lagged by one period (ECT_{t-1}). A significant t-statistic suggests long-run relationships, and a significant F-statistic for the joint test suggests short-run causality. According to Engel and Granger representation, the two variables Y and X, despite the fact that they are non-stationary in levels, are said to be co integrated, if the residuals from the cointegration regression are integrated of any order less than d. For instance, if $[Y] \sim I\,(1)$ and $[X] \sim I\,(1)$, the residuals from the cointegration regressions of Y on X or X on Y have to be I (0) in order to have co integration between Y and X. Then there will be long run equilibrium relationship between Y and X. In the short run there may be disequilibrium between actual value of Y [or X] and long run equilibrium values. An Error Correction Model helps to examine the presence of equilibrium or disequilibrium in the short run. Further, the estimate of error correction term explains the extent of disequilibrium that can be corrected at each period. How quickly disequilibrium can be corrected depends on the magnitude of the estimate of error correction term. Therefore, the coefficient of the error correction term can also be interpreted as the coefficient of speed of adjustment between short run dynamics and long run equilibrium values.

In order to verify the causality between exports and imports, we follow a two-step procedure as follows: The first step in causality investigation is to verify for the existence of a unit root in the variables. Since many macro-economic series are non-stationary, unit root tests are useful to determine the order of the variables and, therefore, to provide the time-series properties of data. In order to verify the presence of a unit root in variables, the popular ADF test and Philips-Perron (PP) test have been employed.

The second step explores the causal relationship between the series. If the series are stationary, then the standard Granger's causality test should be employed. But, if the series are non-stationary and the linear combination of them is stationary, the ECM approach should be adopted. For this reason, testing for co-integration is a necessary pre-requisite to implement the causality test. We have used Engel-Granger method for verifying the co-integration between exports and imports. However, in the first step, ADF and PP unit root tests have been used to verify the degree of integration between variables. Following Husted (1992) we have estimated the following cointegration equations:

$$X_t = a_0 + a_1 Mt + e_t$$

Where, X_t and M_t are exports and imports respectively.

EMPIRICAL FINDINGS

The unit-root test helps to identify whether a variable is stationary or not. The test also helps in finding the order of integration at which the variables become stationary. These tests are necessary to avoid spurious correlation between variables. Testing for the presence of unit root in the variables is the primary task before attempting cointegration. The augmented Dickey-Fuller and Philips-Perron unit root test values of the variables (both at levels and at their first difference) are presented in the following Table 2.

TEST FOR COINTEGRATION

Initially, we have employed Engel-Granger procedure for testing for cointegration and estimating the error correction model. In the first stage, we have estimated the model is based on our equation:

ln Export $s_t = b_0 + b_1$ ln Imports$_t + e_t$.

Where, $b_1 = d$ lnExports$/d$ lnImports$_t = $ long run [static] percentage effect.

In the second stage, ADF test on residuals has been conducted based on the following equation:

$$\Delta U_t = b_0 + b_{1t} b_2 U_{t-1} + b_3 \Delta U_{t-1} + e_t$$

Table 2: ADF and Philips-Perron (PP) Unit Root Test

	ADF Test Statistics		PP Test Statistics	
Variables	*With Constant*	*With Constant and Trend*	*With Constant*	*With Constant and Trend*
Exports of India (XI)	0.2830	−1.0478	0.2803	1.3372
Imports of India (MI)	−1.26232	−3.0923**	0.5915	−1.208
Exports of Iran (XIR)	−3.0829**	−2.4871	−3.0988**	−2.5823
Imports of Iran (MIR)	−2.5070	−2.5902	−2.4967	−25903
ΔXI	−3.6104*	−4.8150*	−23.6400*	−22.0672*
ΔMI	−4.1219*	−4.1272*	−10.1683*	−11.1346*
ΔXIR	−3.5031*	−3.7031*	−8.2079*	−18.1450*
ΔMIR	−4.8731*	−4.8489*	−14.0983*	−14.5224*

Note: *denotes rejection of the null hypothesis of non-stationarity at 1% ** at 5% significance level.

Where, Δ is the first difference operator. If ADF is significant, then exports and imports are cointegrated and the error correction model may be estimated as follows:

$\Delta \ln \text{Exports}_t = b_0 + b_1 \Delta \ln \text{Imports} + b_2 EC_{t-1} + e_t$.

Where, b_2 = Error Correction Term.

$b_1 = \partial \Delta \ln \text{Exports}_t / \partial \Delta \ln \text{Imports}$ = Percentage effect in short run

$b_2 = \partial \Delta \ln \text{Exports}_t / \partial EC_{t-1}$ = Proportion of disequilibrium in t–1 time period can be corrected t period by changes in Y.

ADF and Philips-Perron tests suggest that both exports and imports are integrated of order one, I (1) at their levels. This implies the non-stationary of the variables and we cannot use the OLS (ordinary least squares) estimation and apply the usual statistical tests to infer about the relationship between savings and investment. When the variables are non-stationary at the level, the relevant method is the cointegration as suggested by Johansen. And to infer the short run causality between variables we should use VECM methodology. The implementation of VECM involves the following steps:

1. Deciding the optimal lag length of the of the variables in VAR Test for the number of cointegrating vectors using the trace statistics [λ_{trace}] and maximum Eigen value [λ_{max} statistics]. The λ_{trace} and λ_{max} statistics are used to determine whether the number of cointegrating vectors.

2. In λ_{trace} if H_0: r = 0, then H_1: r > 0. If the test result rejects the null hypothesis the indication is that there are cointegrating vectors and we proceed by setting r = 1 ...2.. in the null hypothesis until we fail to reject it. In λ_{max} if H_0: r = 0, then H_1: r =1. Rejecting the null hypothesis implies the existence of an exactly one cointegrating vector.

3. If there is cointegration, we run VECM and generate the long run cointegrating parameters which show the long run relation between the variables considered and adjustment coefficients which convey information about the speed of adjustment to long run equilibrium. This is accompanied with VEC diagnostic tests to ensure the adequacy of the model.

4. Conduct weak erogeneity test to identify the dependent and independent variables using the results and construct the long run equation. Then generate Error Correction Term (ECT) from the regression of the long run equation and formulate the Error Correction Model (ECM).

Table 3: Cointegration Between Exports and Imports: India and Iran (1970–2010): Engel-Granger Method

Variable	Cointegration Equation	ADF Statistic	PP Statistic
Exports of India (XI$_t$)	LnX$_t$ = –0.0197+ 1.0051lnM$_t$(0.06027) (73.70909) R^2 = 0.99268 0.6675	–2.8570*	–2.8537*
Exports of Iran (XIRt)	LnX$_t$ = –4.5702+0. 0.8073 lnM$_t$ (1.9392) (8.0773) R^2 = 0.6259 DW = 1.0755	–3.2240*	–3.2160*

Note: Figures in the parentheses are t values and * indicates Significance at five percent level.

The results based on cointegration and error correction models suggest that the exports and imports of India and Iran are cointegrated. The positive and statically significant regression coefficient (Table 3) indicates the long term relationship between these variables. The long run elasticity of exports with respect to imports of India has been estimated to be 1.00 and the elasticity of exports with respect to Iran's imports is estimated to be 0.81. The results based on ECM model (Table 4) suggest that the short run elasticity between exports and imports in India is 0.37 and for Iran it is 0.43.

Table 4: The Results of Error Correction Model

Variable	Coefficient	t-statistic	Probability	
Constant	0.0510	0.7968	0.4306	R^2 = 0.59958
Δ ln Imports of India (ΔlnMI)	0.8758*	5.5657	0.0000	Adjusted R^2 = 0.57795
ECT(–1)	–0.3762*	–2.9590	0.0050	DW = 1.86
Constant	0.0304	0.4107	0.4106	R^2 = 0.1293
Δ ln Imports of Iran				Adjusted R^2 = 0.0822
(ΔlnMIR)	0.5317	1.2212	0.2297	DW = 1.3382
ECT(–1)	–0.4287*	–2.3200	0.0260	

Note: *indicates significance at 1% level.

We have also conducted the multivariate cointegration test suggested by Johansen using different lag lengths. However, the test statistics in terms of λ_{trace} and λ_{Max} could not provide any conclusive evidence. Hence, the present study confines to Engel-Granger method and provides some policy suggestions based on this method.

CONCLUSION AND POLICY SUGGESTIONS

The present paper aimed at studying the long run equilibrium relationship between exports and imports of India and Iran separately in order to verify the Husted (1992) hypothesis. For this purpose, Engel-Granger and Johansen's methods of testing for cointegration have been used. The empirical evidence based on ADF and PP unit root tests illustrate that the aggregate exports and imports of South Africa are stationary at the first difference level. The estimates based on Engel-Granger cointegration and error correction models suggest that the exports and imports of India and Iran are cointegrated implying the existence of long run equilibrium relationship between these variables in these countries during 1970–2010. The results based on error correction model based on Δ ln exports and EC_{t-1} suggestthat there is a short run equilibrium as well, indicating that the changes in exports adjust to the changes in imports in the same year. There is disequilibrium between actual values of imports and equilibrium values of imports in the short run. However, thirty seven percent of disequilibrium between long run and short run periods is adjusted every year in India. While in Iran, forty three percent of disequilibrium is adjusted every year. It implies that the present macro and trade policies have been effective in attaining long run equilibrium between exports and imports in these countries. In view of this finding it may be suggested that these countries should continue with their current trade and macroeconomic policies.

REFERENCES

[1] Ahmad, Z.B., Lau, E. and Fountas, S. (2003). "On the sustainability of current account deficits: evidence from four ASEAN countries. *Journal of Asian Economics*, 14, 465–487.

[2] Arize, A.C. (2002). "Imports and exports in 50 countries: Tests of cointegration and structural breaks", *International Review of Economics and Finance*, 11: 101–115.

[3] Bahmani-Oskooee, M. and Rhee, H.-J. (1997). "Are Exports and Imports of Korea Cointegrated?" *International Economic Journal*, 11, 109–114.

[4] Dickey, D.A., Hasza, D.P. and Fuller, W.A. (1984). "Testing for unit roots in seasonal time series."*Journal of the American Statistical Association*, 79, 355–367.

[5] Erbaykal, E. and Karaca, O. (2008). "Is Turkey's foreign deficit sustainable? Cointegration relationship between exports and imports."*International Research Journal of Finance and Economics*, 14, 177–181.

[6] Edwards, Lawrence and Lawrence, Robert (2006). South African Trade Policy Matters: Trade Performance and Trade Policy, CID Working Paper No. 135, October,

[7] Edwards, Lawrence and Lawrence, Robert (2006). "South African Trade Policy Matters: Trade Performance and Trade Policy, NBER Working Paper No. 12760, December.

[8] Engel, R.F. and Granger, C.W.J. (1986). "Cointegration and Error Correction: Representation, Estimation and Testing", *Econometrica*, 55(2).

[9] Export-Import Bank (2012). "Potential for Enhancing Trade with Iran: A Brief Analysis," Working Paper No. 18, July.

[10] Gregory, A.W. and Hansen, B.E. (1996). Residual-based tests for cointegration in models with regime shifts.*Journal of Econometrics*, Vol. 70.

[11] Herzer, D. and Nowak-Lehmann D. Felicitas (2006). "Is there a Long-run Relationship between Exports, and Imports in Chile?" *Applied Economics* Letters, 13, 981–986,

[12] Husted, S. (1992). "The emerging US current account deficit in the 1980s: a cointegrationanalysis"*Review of Economics and Statistics*, 74, 159–166.

[13] Jain, Vipin and Sami, Janesh (2012). "Understanding Trade balance in Singapore: empirical Evidence from Cointegration Analysis", View Point, 3, 1, 3–9, Jan–June.

[14] Johansen, S. (1991). "Estimation and Hypothesis Testing of Cointegration Vectors in Gaussian Autoregressive Models", *Econometrica*, 59, 1551–80.

[15] Johansen, S. and Juselius, K. (1990). Maximum Likelihood Estimation and Inference on Cointegration—With Application to the Demand for Money, Oxford Bulletin of Economics and Statistics, 52, 169–210.

[16] Konya, L. and Singh, J.P. (2008). "Are Indian Exports and Imports Cointegrated?" *Applied Econometrics and International Development* 8, 177–186.

[17] Mallick, S.K. (1996). "Causality Between Exports And Economic Growth in India: Evidence from Cointegration Based on Error Correction Model", *The Indian Journal of Economics*, Vol. LXXVI, No. 302.

[18] Narayan, Paresh Kumar and Seema Narayan (2005). "Are Exports and Imports Cointegrated? Evidence from 22 Least Developed Countries," *Applied Economics Letters*, 12, 375–378.

[19] Perron, P. (1989). The Great Crash, the Oil Price Shock, and the Unit Root Hypothesis, *Econometrica*, 57, 1361–1401.

[20] Ramakrishna, G. and Ravinder, Rena (2013). "An Empirical analysis of Energy consumption and Economic growth in India: Are they causally Related?" *Oeconomica*, 58(2) 22–40.

[21] Roy, Meena Singh (2013). "India and Iran relations: Sustaining the Momentum," Institute for Defence studies and Analyses (IDSA), New Delhi, 20th May.

[22] Tiwari, A.K. (2011). Are exports and imports cointegrated in India and China? An empirical analysis, *Economics Bulletin*, 31(1): 1–11.

[23] Upender, M. (2007). "Longrun Equilibrium between India's Exports Imports during 1949–50 - 2004–05", *Applied econometrics and International development*, 7(1):187–196.

The Iranian Nuclear Issue and Standoff with Western Power

Dahiphale Vithal

INTRODUCTION

The victory of Hassan Rohani in the Iranian presidential elections put forward possibility to resolve the Iranian Nuclear Issue but it will depend upon how the super powers reacts with internal politics in Iran, as well as Syrian Issue. Rohani has indicated during his election Campaign and in his post election press conference that he will initiate talks with the neighbors as well as the US over the nuclear issue. A possible first step to resolve the Iranian nuclear issue for Iran to sign the IAEA Additional Protocol (AP). The AP is a necessary instrument apart from the comprehensive safeguards Agreement (CSA) to help address the extant unresolved contentions as well as possible future concerns regarding potential Iranian attempts to acquire nuclear weapons grade fissile material. Iran currently insists that it is not bound to implement a 'voluntary' measure like the AP, it is pertinent to note that the last time it agreed to voluntarily follow its provisions when the current president elect Hassan Rouhani was the chief nuclear negotiator. The future of Iran-US dialogue process will depend upon the support of other powers, specially Russia as well as members of the US congress to Obama administration for to get the Iran to sign the AP. If Iran and the west become able to strike a deal over the nuclear issue, India will also benefit from the situation and as a permanent presence on the IAEA Board of Governors, ensure that the IAEA safeguards department behaves impartially towards Iran and concludes its examination in a frank, free and transparent manner within the time frame agreed to by the parties. The objective of the article is to highlights US global dominance. The aim of the US vis-à-vis Iran has been how to undermine the regime and make it subordinate. The US wants to go to any extreme to have an excuse to put the squeeze on Iran in consonance with its wider ambitions which to beyond the issue of that Asian country's nuclear weapons-making prospects. The author tries to search what options are available for India on the ground of Iranian Nuclear Issue and the way forward while in the contemporary phase of globalization, Iran will be increasingly important for India's commercial and political interests.

Iran is one of the world's oldest countries. Its history dates back almost 5000 years.[1] It is situated at a strategic juncture in the Middle East region of south Asia. Its traumatic Journey across the twentieth century, through the discovery of oil, imperial interventions, the rule of the Pahlavis and in 1979, the Islamic revolution and the birth of the Islamic Republic. In the intervening years, Iran has experienced a bitter war with Iraq. The twentieth century demonstrates the transformation of society and more recently the expansion of the state and struggle for power between the old elites, the intelligentsia, and the commercial middle class.[2] A long-long time people of Iran have endured and survived a century of war and revolution. Continues fear, instability, arrogance of the politicians, challenges to its security by neighbors, Iran experienced all throughout the century.

Iran entered the twentieth century with oxen and wooden plough. It exited with the discovery of oil in the soil of Iran as well as Middle East as a source of energy brought profound change in economic condition and the polity. At one angle it is a necessarily boon for Iran but its other side full of negative conscientiousness. Supper powers attracted to Middle East only because of oil discovery in this region. Therefore one should always keep in mind the history and dynamics of political development in Iran for understanding the nature of Iranian Nuclear Issue.

US' DOMINANCE POLICY

Before trying to sketch the picture on Iranian Nuclear Issue, one needs to analysis the US (United States of America) Dominance policy. The US since the end of the cold war has been seeking to establish a permanent global dominance, an informal global empire or what some prefer to call a stable and enduring unipolarity. To achieve this it must achieve dominance over the strategically vital region of west Asia. There are two external factors that have consistently affected Iran's as well as Arab World's economic performance, internal political situation and foreign policy initiatives.[3] First, Iran and its neighbors have been undergoing unprecedented political turmoil characterized by protracted armed conflicts, ethnic tensions, civil wars and political instability. For instance, the Iran-Iraq war of the 1980s. Iraqi invasion of Kuwait (1991), resurgence of Kurdish ethnic nationalism in Iraq and Turkey and the demand for a separate Kurdistan, intensification of ethnic conflicts in Pakistan, the civil war in Tajikistan between pro-communist and pro-Islamic forces, emergence and fell of 'Taliban' in Afghanistan led towards violence and instability, civil war and assassination of Gaddhafi in Libya, Experiment of chemical weapons against civilians in Syria, all these incident provide a free road to western powers for military or political Interventions. To surmount these problems Iran has had to deploy its number of resources to fight war, contain the massive inflow of refugees from Afghanistan and control drug related activities. These incidents are responsible for continuous fear and insecurity in Iran, Naturally, political leaders of Iran decides to have a sufficient armament.

The second factor, Iran has also been forced to counter the serve consequences of the sustained hostility of the US.[4] After dubbing Iran as a rough state the US chose to apply a full trade embargo against Iran in 1995 with the idea of isolating it internationally. The US has been highly critical of Iran's urge to obtain weapons of mass destruction, stockpile offensive weapons and provide assistance to fundamentalist forces throughout the Muslim world. It has also accused successive Iranian regimes of violation of human rights. The US-led western force is operating with 27 vessels and 27,000 troops in the Persian Gulf to protect its interests and those of its allies like Kuwait and Israel. Iran has responded to such diverse external challenges by strengthening its naval power and opening up its ties with the states of central Asia. West is not ready to do Iran so, is serious fact.

The aim of the US since the fall of the Shah in 1979, has been constant, how to undermine the Iran and make it subordinate through regime change, if necessary. For a long time that's why the US has selectively opposed certain governments developing nuclear weapons. It had slightly change after September 11,2001 incident and added a new dimension.[5] Now the US is not satisfy on only letting certain countries to get the bomb but that even their capacity to make the bomb must be denied. Since this capacity is inseparable from the inherently dual-use nature of nuclear civilian energy production this had to mean US intervention to prevent complete control of the entire nuclear fuel cycle by some countries, like Iran. But till there is contradiction, where Indian elites are also not serious concern past to yet, countries like Germany, Japan, etc, who are non-nuclear signatories to the NPT but which have complete control over their respective nuclear fuel cycles and can, if they put their minds to it, make nuclear weapons much more quickly than Iran. Expert estimates suggest that it would take Iran several years, possibly a decade, to make the bomb after it takes such a decision, whereas Japan can make a bomb in a few months.

Above discussion indicates that, US and west became more concerned from the late 1980s—early 1990s that about such dual-use capacities because of fears that North Korea, Libya and Iraq (all signatories to the NPT as non-nuclear states) might be taking advantage of this carrot to create the nuclear weapons option, or even secret exercise it. But it took September 11, 2001 to really implement US strategic thinking vis-à-vis Iran in this regard. Here we are discussing some of the aspects or characteristics of US strategic dominance policy after 9/11 incident, so that US could outline a path to how it might fulfill its longer running strategic goal of undermining Iran.

1. The policy of dominance is built around the ability of the International community, mainly the US-led western alliance, to impose its collective will in order to restore a worse situation which leads to violence, war or violation of human rights.[6]

2. Justifications for the right to intervene militarily by western powers propagated as-defense of democracy and prevention of the excessive curtailment of a people's fight to participate in decision making; prevention of severe violation of human rights of a people by totalitarian regime; protection of minority groups from severe repression; prevention of acute environment degration; and, prevention of possible attempts to use, acquire or develop weapons of mass destaction.[7]

3. Carry out necessary doctrinal changes in the US' own security policies that can give it the flexibility to pre-emptively attack countries that the US considers a threat to its security. Thus preventive war against such countries suspected of having or even wanting weapons of mass distraction (WMD) or of harboring terrorists to be justified by national policy.[8]

4. Suborn and manipulate the International Atomic Energy Agency (IAEA) to push US perspectives.

5. Publicly isolate Iran from the world community at large, as wrongdoer.

6. Before thinking of militarily attacking Iran in any way whether indirectly through Israel or directly by the US, Iran should be weakened and politically-diplomatically isolated by getting the UNSC to impose sanctions. To achieve this US brought EU as well as all important countries like Russia, china together on board for their consent.[9]

These are the some aspects of US dominance policy without to examine the nature of it, we can not evaluate Iran's wrongdoer activity. The IAEA leadership has exhibited a fundamental moral and political dishonesty and lack of courage. Several times including India have been fully prepared to accept the dishonest rabble-rousing and hypocritical posturing of the US and its allies.

THE NATURE OF IRANIAN NUCLEAR ISSUE

The article examines the four issue-points regarding Iran's nuclear issue to sketch the broad picture on the nature of Iranian Nuclear Issue.

What geopolitical conditions in and around Iran have? Is it responsible to lead Iran to have a nuclear capability?

Iran is the eighteenth largest country in the world, with an area of 1,648,195 km$^{2[10]}$ (636372 sq mi) Its area roughly equals that of the united Kingdom, France, Spain, and Germany combined, or some what more than the US state of Alaska. Its borders are with Azerbaijan (611 km) and Armenia (35 km) to the north-west; the Caspian Sea to the north; Turkmenistan (992 km) to the east; Turkey (499 km) and Iraq (1458 km) to the west; and finally the water of the Persian Gulf and the Gulf of Oman to the south. Iran is not the product of imperial map-making as any most of the other countries. It established its own identity and emerged as a regional power-certainly in the Persian Gulf, If not in the entire Middle East. It plays a key role in the organization of petroleum Exporting countries (OPEC), is the world's third largest producer of oil and has the globe's third or perhaps even second largest proven reserves of gas and oil".[11] High oil revenues, it has brought citizens a respectable slandered of living; low infant mortality, reasonable longevity, high literacy, sound infra-structure, modern transportation, large salaried middle class and educated working class, in many ways, the country is no longer part of the Third world therefore one can not says 'Iran' as a 'failed state'.

But the contemporary geopolitical situation around Iran is not favorable her interests. In context of the region, the major stakeholders which directly effect Iran are the Gulf Cooperation Council (GCC) countries, Turkey, Israel, Egypt and of course, Syria. Although newly elected president Hassan Rohani expressed his desire to establish a friendly relations with GCC countries and neighbors but it depends on how Rohani has tackles nuclear issue with US and its allies. The Gulf countries relationship had came under considerable strain during Ahmedinejad, especially in the last couple of years since the onset of the Arab Spring. Ahmedinejad rigorously pursued the nuclear agenda and he never gave any convincing response to the GCC countries anxiety over the Iranian nuclear programme, on the contrary Rohani has, in the past, headed the nuclear negotiating team, creates a space for possible solution.

Iran's ambition is not hiding to spread its influence and dominate the GCC countries for her national interests. GCC countries are more worried of Iranian connection with the Shia population in other countries and especially with the Hezbollah is notable. Political developments in the west Asia region such as the Syrian crisis, Yemen conflict, insecurity in Iraq, Egypt, the emergence of Islamist political forces such as Muslim Brother-hood and ennahda are some of the challenges that Rohani will have to face immediately.[12] Iran's relationship with Saudi Arabia, to a large extent, defines Iranian motives in the region. Both on their part, expressed hope that Saudi-Iran relationship will strengthen during the Rohani presidency. If it happened, then it would be a game changer in the region. But has less possibilities as Iran supported the protesters on the streets against the rulers and Saudi Arabia asked Iran not to intervene in the Arab affairs. Turkey is along with Saudi Arabia and has even permitted Stationing of NATO patriot missile batteries on Syrian- Turkish border. Israel's prime Minister Benjamin Netanyahu has warned that international pressure on Iran must not be loosened on nuclear issue.[13] Above all geopolitical condition itself shows that Iran is bitterly found in such situation where there is profound fear, insecurity, worries, economic instability, possibly opens option of to be a nuclear power in the region to overcome all problems. Although it is at emotional level but it is a fact and not to denial.

What type of dialogue process is going on between Iran and the West? Is there some non–negotiable positions?

The second question is very important to know the nature of Iranian Nuclear Issue. According to west the basic cause of tension between Iran and the west is of course Iran's hidden nuclear program. It sees Iran's nuclear program as a persistent danger and catalyst for other states to acquire nuclear weapons options of their own. If Iran succeeds to breakout of the NPT and quickly acquire nuclear weapons, it will demonstrate to the world (and every other nation that might want nuclear weapons) how any state can use the NPT to get the bomb making capabilities it wants.[14] US and it allies do not want to do so. After the Syrian crisis the situation become very serious. Israel warned west powers to take certain steps against Iran, other-wise it will free to target where nuclear activities are going on in Iran. On this background Dialogue process have its own significance.

The victory of Hassan Rouhani as the new President enhanced prospects for dialogue. But still Iran's engagement with the International Atomic Energy Agency (IAEA) and the P5+1 (UN Security Council permanent members and Germany) is currently at a stalemate. There have been 10 rounds of talks since January 2012 between the IAEA and Iran, including a visit by IAEA DG Yukiya Amano to Tehran in may 2012. There has however been no progress in agreeing for a 'structured framework' to address issues like Parchin—a military facility where Iran is alleged to have conducted high-explosives testing activities—which IAEA wants to inspect but Iran is refusing to give access. The Iran-P5+1 talks are also stuck, despite five rounds since they were restarted in April 2012 in Istanbul. The most recent of these talks were held in Almaty in April 2013. The IAEA in May 2013 reported that Iran had in its possession 8960 kgs of uranium enriched to 5 percent U-235 and 324 kgs enriched to 20 percent U-235. All of this material is under IAEA safeguards.[15]

The US meanwhile has continued with its policy of imposing even tougher economic sanctions on Iran. As already stated, Israel has continued to insist that it will not allow a nuclear Iran and will strive to prevent that possibility. The GCC countries have been stating that they will pursue similar capabilities if Iran does go nuclear. It means situation is very complicate and serious. Report prepared by S. Samuel C. Rajiv and Daneesh Sethna for IDSA examined three issue areas that politicized nature of the interactions between Iran and the IAEA. First; dispute over access to military sites life Par chin where nuclear- related activities could have taken place. Second; leaks of confidential information provided to the IAEA by Iran, such subjects life 'Plutonium research project'. Iran has also been urging the IAEA to share information about the member-states/sources which indicated 'possible military dimensions' (PMD) of its nuclear activities. Third; as for the third issue area, the authors noted that the role of the ISIS (western non-governmental organizations) and its nuclear activism highlighted the political jesting that accompanied safeguards implementtation in Iran, especially on such aspects as posting of IAEA DG reports on its website on the day they are presented to the Board of Governors, which Iran takes exception to. The ISIS however contends that it is doing a 'public service' by disseminating the reports which are not 'safeguards confidential'. According to authors these are the major issue areas that are crabbing dialogue process between IAEA and Iran.[16]

Indeed, there are certain non-negotiable issues that are barrier in the way of dialogue:

- Iran is come to the point numerous other officially non-nuclear countries, e.g., Brazil. South Africa, have more advanced uranium enrichment programmes than Iran. None of them have been subject to the kind of pressure the US and its allies are imposing on Iran. Nor has the IAEA seen fit to behave in the same way with regard to these other countries nor in those cases made any reports in the kind of carefully worded language that in the case of Iran can create "uncertainties" that can then be used by the US for its purposes.
- Talks without pre-conditions—which the Iranians insist is necessary for the success of conversation 'among equals' to take place.[17]
- Suspension of uranium enrichment activities.

- Which the P5+1 insist is essential as mandated by the various UNSC/ IAEA resolutions. However, the Iranian government has declared that it has the right under all its legal obligations to have full control over its nuclear fuel cycle, By Iran's approach this is its 'inalienable right' and having spent so much political capital for so long on insisting on the right—it is not conceivable that Iran's leadership would risk being seen as 'capitulating to western pressure' and the formal domestic political backlash and forced to stop its enrichment activities.[18]
- Lifting of sanctions—which Iran insists is certainty of verifiable steps by Iran to restore confidence in the 'exclusively peaceful nature' of its nuclear programme. It is equally pertinent to note that given that these sanctions once lifted will be very difficult to be imposed again. Obama Administration as well as western powers are unwilling to consider this step.[19]
- Another fact is that all of the countries of the Arab League and also Iran have long declared themselves in favors of the immediate establishment of a Middle East Zone Free of Nuclear Weapons. The only country in the region that refuses to accept this proposal is Israel, which insists that this must wait for a final peace settlement in west Asia of the kind that Israel would accept. In this shameful filibustering Israel is, of course, supported fully by the US.[20]
- The IAEA has had to make similar time consuming investigations to clear other non-nuclear NPT signatories like Japan and Canada and took five and six years respectively to carry this out. There are number of EU Countries for which the IAEA is still in no position to arrive at such a broader conclusion. However, it is only Iran that is being pressured in the way that it is. It is only in the case of Iran that the IAEA is accepting being quick activity by the US.
- These are the some questionable or non-negotiable positions which break off the dialogue process.

Is really Iran able to make Nuclear weapons? What are the options available for Iran for being a nuclear power?

The authoritative reports on the status of Iran's nuclear programme are published time to time by the safeguards Department. There have been 41 reports so far till May 2013.[21] Since Iran restarted its enrichment activities in August 2005, the May 2013 report to the IAEA BOG indicates that Iran has in its possession 8960 kgs of UF_6 enriched up to 5 percent U-235 and 324 kgs. Enriched up to 20 percent U-235. The amount of 20 percent

U-235 was 44 kgs more than the figure mentioned in the February 2013 report. Out of the 324 kgs, 142 was being processed into uranium fuel pellets, effectively leaving only 182 kgs UF_6 enriched to 20 percent U-235 in Iran's possession.[22] It means, could potentially take Iran 3–4 months to acquire sufficient quantities of the fissile material sufficient for one device. Even if it acquires sufficient quantities of weapons grade uranium, it needs to be borne in mind that Iran has to further machine this material into a weapon design-along with the concomitant requirements like conventional explosives for triggering an implosion device if it pursues that design-which could conservatively take it anywhere between 6 months to 1 year.

It clearly shows that, it is not easy for Iran to acquire desired goal. Then what are the possible options available for Iran to pursue its alleged goal of acquiring a nuclear weapons capability. It could do so potentially by following ways.

1. Within the confines of the NPT or outside of it. If Iran quits the NPT of course, it will immediately raise 'red flags' among members of the international community as to its intentions and motives. There have been some instances of Iranian lawmakers in the past threatening to do so in the face of rising international pressure. But, if it indeed takes steps to enrich uranium to weapons grade by continuing to be a member of the NPT, it will not be difficult for the IAEA inspectors to potentially notice the activity and inform the IAEA BOG.

2. The other option for Iran is to develop the capability covertly, while continuing to be a member of the NPT. Unlike India, Pakistan and some extent North Korea—where IAEA had no safeguards inspections—Iran continues to be under safeguards.

3. The only covert option left for Iran to build sufficient quantities of weapons-grade fissile material by continuing to be a NPT-member state is in undeclared facilities. It could use its uranium resources and the expertise gained by the running of the declared enrichment facilities at Natanz and Fordow to build more efficient infrastructure. But IAEA had acknowledgement from past experience of Iran's pattern of concealment as well as undeclared nuclear activities, therefore it would be difficult.

4. Another possible option available for Iran is of course to 'buy' a weapon—from North Korea for instance—and test it to demonstrate it weapons capability. Such an option of course will leave it open to an almost definite Israeli/US military strike, to not only set back its nuclear facilities but also target its economic assets like oil and gas producing infrastructure.

All above options are demonstrates that, it will very tough task for Iran to pursue the Nuclear capability. Therefore an acceptable solution is needed for both parties. There is only hope of ray is remained for acceptable solution is the Additional protocol (AP).

Is the Additional Protocol (AP) an acceptable solution? Can this be reconciled?

The AP is a necessary instrument apart from the Comprehensive Safeguards Agreement (CSA) to help address the extant unresolved contentions as well as possible future concerns regarding potential Iranian attempts to acquire nuclear weapons grade fissile material. But, Iran currently insists that it is not bound to implement a 'voluntary' measure like the AP. It is pertinent to note that Iran accepted and went along with the AP in past, while 26 of 71 states with significant nuclear activities do not have such Additional protocols in force. Last time Iran agreed to voluntarily follow AP provisions in December 2003 when the current president Hassan Rouhani was the chief nuclear negotiator.

The main issue is the inability of the IAEA to convincingly certify that no non-peaceful activities are taking place inside Iran ('completeness'), along with ensuring that no diversion of fissile material ('correctness') is taking place.[23] The IAEA has been able to verify both 'correctness' and 'completeness' even in countries where significant nuclear activities are going on like Canada or South Korea, both have the CSA in place as well as the Additional protocol. Actually the model of AP was approved by the BOG on May 15, 1997.[24] The AP according to the IAEA Fact sheet is a 'legal document' whose 'principal aim is to enable the IAEA inspectorate to provide assurance about both declared and possible undeclared activities.[25] The future of the Iranian Nuclear Issue is depends upon how Obama administration can get Iran to sign the AP for friendly solution.

THE ROLE OF THE INDIA

The Indian government and its supporting elites have been continuously under pressure. US putting pressure on the Indian government to support in the IAEA. Question is that is it in its interest to support the US? According to US, India is the key for it to get Russia and China on board. The big two Russia and China are going in supporting direction or at least not obstructing the US plans vis-à-vis Iran. Actually Iran government is in dilemma, on one side it claims that it is not doing so under US pressure, but fact is different, actually US is getting what it wants from Indian Government. India is aware of no serious opposition to significant powers for her interests. It is more than delighted if an Indian government and its supporting elites can convince themselves that the best way for India to grow strong and the best way for a multipolar world to emerge is through support for the unipolar ambitions and plans of the US. Indian left is unwilling to do so, but have limited voice. Cost is India pay off the Iran-India gas pipeline project.

On the particular ground what options have left before India:

- Oppose the unfairness of US and its purposes behind, the whole Iranian-IAEA nuclear imbroglio and get praise from other peaceful countries.
- Support US and its allies and enhance strategic partnership.
- Oppose any every country going in for nuclear energy. This must be done not only for reasons related to alternative and superior forms of energy production but because as long as civilian nuclear energy programmes are around one is creating the potential for nuclear weapons programmes to also emerge.
- Demand complete transparency for all nuclear energy programmes everywhere and not just for Iran or selectively for same countries. That is to say, demand the formulation of an international or multilateral treaty for full transparency in all aspects of the civilian nuclear fuel cycle for all countries having such programmes, including all nuclear weapons states.
- It will dishonest of Indian government to have own nuclear power and put pressure on Iran not to be a nuclear power. India justified acquisition of nuclear weapons in the name of security, indeed citing China as a threat. But India never ever faced the kind or level of security thereat and pressure that Iran is facing today from US and Israel.
- A potential way India could play a more active and direct part in the resolution of the issue is through its presence on the IAEA BOG. If really Iran can sign the AP, India, as one of the founder members of the IAEA and having a permanent presence on the Board of Governors, could exercise a certain degree of influence within that organization to ensure that the IAEA safeguards department behaves impartially towards Iran and concludes its examination in frank, free and transparent manner within the time frame agreed to by the parties.

REFERENCES

[1] Dr. Zayar, "The Iranian Revolution Past, present Future", copyright @Iran chamber society.

[2] Ervand Abrahamian (2008) 'A Hisotry of Modern IRAN, Cambridge University press, Cambridge.

[3] Rajen Harshe (1997). 'India-Iran Relations under Globalisation', *Economic and Political weekly*, Vol. No. 33/34, Aug. 16–29, 1997.

[4] Harshe, Rajen (1997). 'India-Iran Relations under Globalisation', *Economic and Political weekly*, Vol. No. 33/34, Aug. 16–29, 1997.

[5] Vanaik, Achin (2006). "The Iran Issue", *Economic Political Weekly*, Vol. 41, No. 6 (Feb. 11–17, 2006).

[6] Gurmeet Kanwal (2013). 'Debating the Doctor Military Intervention', IDSA COMMENT, www.

[7] Kanwal, Gurmeet (2013). 'Debating the Doctor Military Intervention', IDSA COMMENT, www.

[8] Vanaik, Achin (2006). 'The Iran Issue', Economic Political Weekly, Vol. 41, No. 6 (Feb. 11–17, 2006).

[9] Vanaik, Achin (2006). 'The Iran Issue', Economic Political Weekly, Vol. 41, No. 6 (Feb. 11–17, 2006).

[10] CIA World Factbook. "Iran" Retrieved 7 August.

[11] Abrahamian, Ervand (2008). 'A Hisotry of Modern IRAN, Cambridge University press, Cambridge.

[12] Roy, Meena Singh; Agarwal, Rajeev; Pradhan, Prasanta Kumar and Alam Rizvi, M. Mahtab (2013). 'under Hassan Rohani: Imperatives for the Region and India', IDSA ISSUE BRIEF, www.idsa.in

[13] "Iran election: Israel issues warning after Rouhani win", BBC News, June 16, 2013.

[14] Henry sokolski, Patrick clawson (Edited) Report 'Checking Iran's Nuclear Ambitions' 2004.

[15] Balachandran, G. and C. Rajiv, S. Samuel (2013). Iranian Nuclear Imbroglio: The way Forward IDSA ISSUE BRIEF, www.idsa.in.

[16] C. Rajiv, S. Samuel (2013). 'Iran, IAEA and the challenges of ' politicized Safeguards', Implementation' report prepared for IDSA, spetember 20, 2013.

[17] Balachandran, G. and C. Rajiv, S. Samuel (2013). Iranian Nuclear Imbroglio: The way Forward IDSA ISSUE BRIEF, www.idsa.in.

[18] Balachandran, G. and S C Rajiv: (2013), Iranian Nuclear Imbroglio: The way Forward IDSA ISSUE BRIEF, www.idsa.in.

[19] G Balachandran and C. Rajiv, S. Samuel (2013). Iranian Nuclear Imbroglio: The way Forward IDSA ISSUE BRIEF, www.idsa.in.

[20] Vanaik, Achin (2006). 'The Iran Issue', Economic Political Weekly, Vol. 41, No. 6 (Feb. 11–17, 2006).

[21] Balachandran, G. and C. Rajiv, S. Samuel (2013). Iranian Nuclear Imbroglio: The way Forward IDSA ISSUE BRIEF, www.idsa.in.

[22] Balachandran, G. and C. Rajiv, S. Samuel (2013), Iranian Nuclear Imbroglio: The way Forward IDSA ISSUE BRIEF, www.idsa.in.

[23] C. Rajiv, S. Samuel (2013). 'Iran, IAEA and the challenges of 'politicized Safeguards' Implementation' report prepared for IDSA, spetember 20, 2013.

[24] The document is available at http://www.iaea.org publications/Documents/Infcircs/1997/infcirc540.pdf

[25] See 'IAEA safeguards overview: comprehensive safeguard Agreements and Additional Protocols, at http://www.iaea.org

Culture and Civilization

Storytellers across Digital Regionscapes: Affective Mapping as a Platform for Iran-India Dialogue

Upamanyu Sengupta

The practice of mapping involves a documentation of spaces in a process that provides not merely visual cues but also politicizes space. In doing so, maps transfer and translate political actions into a cartographic/visual medium. No cartographic practice is ever a disinterested depiction of space. The various interests involved- economic, political and epistemic-continually shape it and leave their traces in the formation of a map. This is particularly true of the contemporary scenario where, as Dipesh Chakrabarty rightly notes, the long sustained divide between the natural and the man-made and by extension, the geopolitical and the geological appears increasingly blurred- thanks largely to our own activities (Chakrabarty http://www.eurozine.com/articles/2009-10-30-chakrabarty-en.html). This means that the dominant modes of historiography without doubt dictate as always the cartographic processes and in a sustained effort to achieve their ends, practice a methodology of stringent discrimination. A classic example of this process of meticulous streamlining is to be found in the introduction of triangulation as a fool-proof method of topoanalysis in British India. The obsession regarding the degree of accuracy with which angles served to indicate distance between points blinded the methodology to other spatial nuances (Edney 43). As a result, such methodologies often tend to overlook the way spaces are often locally constructed, networked, and narrated into existence. This also betrays the privileging of one kind of political articulation over others. Websites of affective mapping practices such as *They Draw and Travel*, on the other hand, create alternate possibilities of narration and spatialization. In the context of India-Iran relationships, this paper seeks to explore and understand the degree to which such practices may facilitate multiple strands of international relations.

One of the major facilitators of such interactions among practitioners of affective mapping is obviously the digital medium. It has rendered possible creation of hitherto unimaginable archives of such spatial depictions through websites like *They Draw and Travel*. The thrust of the present study, though reliant on the secure cover of the digital medium, lies elsewhere. This project would probe at a greater detail the enabling possibilities affective maps posit in reconceiving bilateral relations between polities. To that end, the discussion would be largely centered around the maps themselves.

The practice of affective mapping is founded on a framework of cartography that does not require of the mapmaker to provide precise delineations of topographic features but allow him to arrange his spatial bearings in a somewhat customized cartographic orientation. While introducing the idea, Christopher Spencer and Jill Dixon in their essay "Mapping the development of feelings about the city: A longitudinal study of new residents" affective maps note- '(human beings) process some forms of sensory input from the milieu, arranging and converting it so that they can operate as if they were using a map' (Spencer and Dixon 373). There is no emphasis, in this case, on syncing the representations on the map with the layout of the 'actual' places as such. This has two possible implications. To a large extent, such practices call into question the taken for granted-ness of spatial representation. Our daily encounters- especially in the larger urban areas- with a spatial imagination that follows a set of standard cartographic procedures are temporarily unhinged and held in suspension. Plans ranging from improvement of public transport to layout of new localities follow and reinforce the established cartographic representation as provided by the civic authorities and public works of a city and cannot deviate from it. Our own understanding of our surrounding spaces is therefore governed, to a large extent, by these standard maps we look up every now and then to commute for example and thereby to situate ourselves. This is not to say that a stroll in our neighborhood would always necessarily be imagined in terms of that representation. A cartographic imagination of the same, however, tends to locate itself within the larger paradigm of the city's layout and transit which, in turn, depends on standard cartographic procedures. Affective maps, seemingly bereft of any such large scale commitments, can choose to ignore the finer details of standard procedures of representation and set forth their own, alternate perception of a lived place.

At another level, affective maps do have an obvious advantage over the more technical kind of representations. As has been already indicated, these standard maps reach us only at two removes from reality- that is to say, we do not encounter these maps as they are but are constantly controlled and governed as per the paradigms set by them in institutions such as public transport and public bodies. Affective maps, on the other hand, help us literally carve a niche for ourselves where we can relate more easily and in a sense, more immediately with our lived experiences of everyday spaces. I would argue that this advantage posits affective maps as a potential site for political exchanges on a very different level.

What stands out as a distinguishing mark of affective maps however, is their simultaneous straddling of many divergent modes of representation. Despite the fact that all of these maps are usually very subjective in nature-depicting one's personal impressions and so on- they do not fail to connect at some level with the others who may see the map. That is because the maps constantly draw from established norms of cartography. In the map of Tehran here, for example, the depiction of a particular road network in the city is just like it would appear in any other standard road map- thin pipeline like layout crisscrossing a part of the map. The map for Mumbai titled "My Bandra" again, faithfully puts into place a practice of color-coding whereby each kind of building is assigned a specific color code. The local hangouts such as the cafes, shopping streets etc are color coded as purple across the map. Affective maps then, draw from established carto-graphic procedures, expropriate them, to their own ends and by tweaking these, reveal, the many possibilities of depiction inherent in an otherwise streamlined, rigorous, strictly academic discipline. In doing so, they also to an extent dismantle the claims to empirical precision in cartography and bring forth its status as yet another mode of imagination and depiction.

This unique communicability of affective maps thus draws from a paradigm of simultaneous subjectivity and comprehensibility. On the one hand, the mapmakers create a spatial image of what strikes a chord in them- with street corners, niches and points of a city they relate with the most. The affective maps then, are also means of narrating one's own life story as experienced in the multiple spatial experiences that define our bearings. This is a storytelling of a very different kind which does not tread any of the conventional trajectories such as recitation or writing. Affective maps resort to a non-logocentric mode of articulation by engaging extra-linguistic modes of expression- in colors and in images- for an activity now regarded largely linguistic: storytelling. Interestingly, such non-linguistic modes of depiction of stories are not at all alien to our cultures- in India and in Iran. Both countries have long traditions of scroll painters such as *patachitrakars* in eastern India and *pardeh-dars* in Iran dating back to several centuries.

An added advantage of the spatial depiction of stories as they appear in affective maps lies in the non-linearity of their narration. The stories are scattered across a topographic field as spatial cues without a formal arrange-ment as a narrative as such. This makes possible many simultaneous readings outside a given framework. This flexibility is what accounts for the greater communicability and perhaps, appeal, of these maps. In poring over these maps, one often encounters an alien, unknown place which can nevertheless be read, understood and interpreted within one's familiar conceptual horizons. Bereft of the usual narrative constraints, affective maps therefore not only tweak the ontological limits of mapping but also of standard literary practices and tap the communicability of stories.

The notion of unique communicability of stories also underlies Adriana Cavarero's discussion of the contribution of narratives in delineating our idea of a self in *Relating Narratives: Storytelling and Selfhood*:

> *…that is, existing consists in disclosing oneself in a scene of plurality where everyone, by appearing to one another, is shown to be unique. They appear to each other reciprocally-first of all in their corporeal materiality and as creatures endowed with sensory organs. Put another way, the language of the existent assumes the bodily condition of 'this and not another' in all of its perceptible concreteness. (Cavarero 20-1)*

According to Cavarero, it is this relational uniqueness that sets stories bring forth in the process of narration. In telling a life story, the person reveals his or her unique identity- an attribute that defies any effort of conceptual categorization. The trajectory of the life story is in some ways uniquely his own. While it does intersect and coincide with several other strands, the story retains its own unique way of unfolding in the course of a life. These points of intersection and coincidences however, figure as crucial. It is here that the story, unique to one's life, becomes relatable not only as something that can be narrated and told or depicted but in a more fundamental sense of relating to another person. A story is a process of reaching out beyond one's immediate horizons and enabling the other to do the same. To the extent that they facilitate a flexible spatial comprehension, the affective maps also feature as strongly relatable.

Both the maps of Mumbai and that of Tehran show these features. None of these maps are likely to elicit a constrained step by step, systematic way of understanding the spatial experience they intend to convey. Instead, the map appears as a whole- a wholeness that cannot be analytically splintered into its constituent parts. This impossibility of fractional analysis of certain kinds of narratives is again something that Cavarero emphasizes on (Cavarero 113). It is not possible, for example, to home into any definite starting point for the Bandra map. There are multiple cues of spatial functions such as inhabiting, shopping, going to work, worshipping, scattered across the map. It is perfectly possible to initiate one's journey across the map from any of these points. The same holds true for the

Tehran map. The statue of Ferdous drawn in the bottom centre of the map is equally eye grabbing as the monument on the top left annotated as Azadi Square and the entrance to Tehran. In the process of narrating the story of their own spatial experiences, the mapmakers simultaneously leave room for others to venture around and take in the place of their own accord. I would suggest that this lack of a designated trajectory of spatial experience serves to enable the reliability of affective maps and empowers them as tools for political interaction.

In relating with these stories and the places they spatially narrate, one essentially relates to a region. These stories do not seek to narrate the layout of an entire city as may be required of official maps but depict specific portions within vast conurbations. The maps put forth very ordinary, commonplace narratives woven around localized settings within a city. While this is evident in the map "My Bandra", it also holds true for the map of Tehran. Though the map seems to depict monuments and important landmarks across the city, it is all very subjective. There exists only a bare minimum fidelity to geographical fact-roughly in terms of the location of the monuments in the map. The depiction of road network is not entirely perfect with respect to the monuments. Only certain roads are highlighted and the route layout is complemented by the presence of a coffee shop at one end of the map. This selective depiction of the urban space is thus effectively a representation of regionscapes across the city. The image that comes forth is not that of the entire city with its finer details but one that concentrates more on specific spatial attributes within the conurbation.

The overwhelming prevalence of regionscapes in affective maps has profound implications—especially to the extent that these regionscapes appear as depictions of individual stories. The aspect of unique communic-ability that Cavarero identifies as the sine qua non of stories also holds true for the depiction of the 'regional' in its portrayal of a spatiality that is not really constrained by the requirements of a cartographic or narrative fixity. While devoid of an overarching structure, this cartographic arrangement does not however, lack any coherence and is perpetually open to several simultaneous readings. In fact, it is this flexibility that serves to encourage a multiplicity of participation in understanding a place and relating one's own position within it to the others. In the following sections, I would try and delineate how this unique communicability imbibed in the region as well as in the stories serves to posit an alternate political and diplomatic platform. While Cavarero in her work has already hinted at the political dimension of stories, an analysis of their ramification as spatial narratives of regions remains to be analysed. My paper proposes to do just that.

MANIPULABLE SPATIALITY

The region, as depicted in practices of affective cartography, comes forth as an extremely malleable and ductile spatiality. Rooted in a very subjective manner of representation on the one hand, the region and the stories that appear in the wake of its depiction nevertheless facilitate interpersonal communication at a very localized level. The depiction of Bandra, for example, is replete with references such as a friend's house, a favorite hangout, the few green spaces dotted across the neighbourhood. The map of Tehran, though more expansive in scope, also focuses on certain localized depictions of the environments around each of the monuments and roads. References such as cafes, for instance, add a strong personal undertone and betray the bearings of a heavily customized map. This customizability, one may argue, is not restricted only at the level of the mapper but extends to include the ones who read the map as well. In the process of encountering the map, what confronts an observer is not an abstract, disinterested system of cartographic symbols and notations but hints and clues of very relatable everyday spatial experiences. In the process, the interpreter of the maps also introduces new layers of spatial meaning into the map. The effort to understand another person's spatial experience and the stories embedded therein is negotiated across a very relatable terrain of spatiality—at the same time intimate and strongly communicative. As a result, the regional in a affective map is irrevocably a site of multiple overlaps that continually inform its dynamics and negates any notion of centrality of the urbanscape. No particular depiction is privileged and depictions of favorite hangouts and monuments of national importance can coexist sans any mismatch. Paul Claval, the prominent French geographer of the region notes: 'In urbanized areas there is always a multiplicity of communities, each one built on a specific feeling of belonging. For each of these groups, the problem is to create or maintain symbolic centres and meeting places in order to keep identities alive' (Claval 23). The political specter of the urbanscape is thus nuanced to a significant degree by the region. In defying any notion of centrality, the regional core renders the city perpetually manipulable and posits it as a space that can constantly reframe and reinvent itself.

THE PROTEAN SPACE

Affective maps render the urbanscape fluid in several counts. One of the most obvious among these would be the dilution of established boundaries within the city and in its outer limits. This is not to suggest that the boundaries fade away altogether as boundaries themselves are a very crucial component of the regional consciousness. What affective maps and their unique reliability trigger however, is the sustained realignment of these boundaries. The boundaries no longer appear fixed and inviolable but are constantly called into question by spatial narratives that seek to realign and redefine the spatial paradigm as per their own requirements. This realignment of boundaries is according to me the inception of regional assertion within the urbanscape. In the map for Bandra, for example, the perimeter of Bandra does not really match with the 'Google Maps' version of Bandra. The Bandra we have is effectively the mapper's own Bandra where even within the confines of the area portrayed, the spatial limits of each segment of place are altered and realigned. This aspect of the Bandra map can be put into direct conversation with the map of Tehran. There too, the limits of each region within the city are extremely fluid and the boundary consciousness is purely arbitrary- to be gauged and interpreted by the viewer of the map. Within the context of diplomatic exchange between the two countries, it might be worthwhile to examine the possibilities of alternative spatial consciousness such representations bear. Positing narratives relevant to such consciousness, these, I would suggest, serve as relevant nodes of interaction at a micro and informal level. This in turn creates possibilities of stepping aside from the established realms of diplomacy and opening up a greater focus on the region as a platform for exchange of ideas.

AN ALTERED LANDSCAPE

The altered conception of the urbanscape, it may be argued, makes possible very different ways of relating to a particular place. The most decisive shift with this regard probably occurs in the manner in which one perceives the interrelations of the proxemic and distemic spaces. I have borrowed the terms as well as their conceptual connotations from Barrie B Greenbie's deployment of the same in her work *Spaces: Dimensions of the Human Landscape*. According to Greenbie, the proxemic space constitutes the more personal kind of space for an individual and more often a community which may not render itself usable or passable in the same terms as that of the immediate members of the community. A well grounded neighborhood in a city is a good example of a proxemic space (Greenbie 101). Distemic spaces, on the other hand are more open in a sense and do not belong to any particular community (Greenbie 102). The single largest contribution of affective maps is possibly an alteration of the dynamic between this proxemic and the distemic. The distemic is often equated with the public property where individual or micro-communal aspirations can stake no claim. Affective maps such as those of Mumbai and Tehran expose the constant expropriation of the distemic by the proxemic. This recognition of the presence of the proxemic also underscores the necessity of accommodating the proxemic—the city and the region within the city as players in processes of diplomatic negotiation. The local, communalized, and personal sphere cannot possibly be cauterized off the 'public' space of negotiation—a divide that is rampant in most diplomatic relations where the technicalities of political exchange dominate and often erase other possible avenues of interaction. The region, as depicted in both these maps, lies at the precipice of the transition from proxemic and distemic and vice versa and therefore presents the most opportune scope of expanding negotiation beyond certain established constraints.

THE TRIVIAL

This brief study of affective maps points strongly to the need of recognizing the local, the insignificant, the uncertain- in short, the trifling, as a major potential deployment for diplomatic processes between Iran and India. Practices of affective mapping bring forth the informal channels of potential exchange into focus and facilitate a reconsideration of the conventional parameters of interaction. There is a need to explore and understand the political dynamic inherent in the trifling and the not to scientific depiction that seeks to portray something other than what is readily available and taken for granted. Understanding the trifling as a major player in the political process would help resolve complications at a more localized level and can be addressed with greater person-to person interaction. This approach seeks to first and foremost decenter the idea of interaction from the accepted domains of politics and bureaucracy. In my opinion, the stories and the way they narrate regions in affective maps holds a prominent cue in that direction.

SOURCES

Primary

[1] Dmonte, Rinka. "My Bandra, India". Painting. *They Draw and Travel*. 26 May 2011. Web. 13 August 2013.

[2] Moghadasi, Armineh. "Tehran, Iran". Painting. *They Draw and Travel*. 07 November 2011. Web. 13 August 2013.

Secondary

[3] Cavarero, Adriana. *Relating Narratives: Storytelling and Selfhood*. Trans. Paul A. Kottman. London: Routledge. 2000. Electronic.

[4] Chakrabarty, Dipesh. "The Climate of History: Four Theses" Eurozine Mag., 30 October 2009. Web. 17 January 2011.

[5] Claval, Paul *Region in Geography, Regional Geography: Past and Present—A Review of Ideas, Approaches and Goals.* New Delhi: Critical Quest. 2012.

[6] Greenbie, Barrie B. *Spaces: Dimensions of the Human Landscape.* New Haven: Yale University Press. 1982.

[7] Spencer, Christopher and Dixon,Jill. "Mapping the Development of Feelings about the City: A Longitudinal Study of New Residents' Affective Maps". *Transactions of the Institutes of British Geographers* Vol. 8, No. 3, 1983, pp. 373–383. Jstor, Web. 17, March 2012.

[8] Edney, Matthew H. *Mapping an Empire: The Geographical Construction of British India 1765–1843.* London: The University of Chicago Press. 1997.

Strengthening India-Iran Relations: Commercial Contacts and Cultural Commonalities

M. Vishnu Prakash

"Among the many people and races who have come in contact with Indians and influenced India's life and culture, the oldest and most persistent have been the Iranians".

—*Jawaharlal Nehru*

India has good relationship with the Iran from the antiquity. The bond between world's oldest civilizations continued through silk route. They have warm, extensive and uninterrupted relations. In a recent official five-day visit, the Iranian Parliament Speaker Ali Larijani is in India upon an invitation from the Indian counterpart said that "Tehran welcomes expansion of ties with New Delhi in all areas, including the fields of culture, economy and regional and international politics and described Iran-India relations in cultural and political areas as remarkable".[1]

Throughout the history the relations between India and Iran were good except under some startling incidents. However the recent pressures exerted by third parties in the bilateral relations irked both the nations and will be normalized in due course as they are unfailing friends in their rapport. Time and again proved that this historic connection will get fortify and yield fruits to both sides of the nation.

COMMERCIAL CONTACTS

The trade existed between the coast of southern Iran and India through the Persian Gulf and the Arabian Sea. Some Indus seals have been excavated at Kish, Susa and Ur in Iran. The Harappan people are believed to have imported silver, copper, turquoise and lapis lazuli from Persia and Afghanistan.[2] Trade expanded mainly because Achaemenians introduced coinage, which facilitated exchange. India exported spices, black pepper and imported gold and silver coins from Iran. The grape, introduced from Persia with the almond and walnut, was cultivated in the western Himalayas.[3]

Commerce between the mouth of the Indus and the Persian Gulf was unbroken down to the Buddhist times. There is evidence of trade between the Phoenicians of the Levant and western India as early as 975 B.C. Trade between the Indus Valley and the Euphrates seems to be very ancient.[4] The Achaemenians brought rice from India to be planted in the Near East. It is also believed that cane sugar was first used by man in Polynesia from where it spread to India. In 510 BC the Emperor Darius found in India "the reed which gives honey without bees", which he then brought to Persia.[5]

Horses were another Persian export in great demand in India. Largely for reasons of climate, high-quality, indigenous horses could not be bred locally, a deficiency which left the Indian military establishment dependent upon external supplies. Other Persian commodities like animal products, especially wool, leather, tobacco, nuts, fruit and fruit products, pearls, and the medicinal resin asafetida. Gold and silver were also important exports from Persia to India. Whereas Persia generally enjoyed a positive balance of trade with neighboring Russia and Ottoman Turkey, it was not the case with India.

Until the Industrial Revolution changed the nature of European textile production in the 19th century, textiles were the most important Indian commodity imported into Persian markets, especially those made of cotton, such as calico and muslin of various qualities, as well as linen. Persia imported a considerable variety of spices from India and Indonesia, both for domestic use and for transport to further markets, the most important of which were pepper, cinnamon, ginger, cardamom, cloves, nutmeg, mace, and turmeric.

Indian merchants were among the most active groups mediating Indo-Persian commerce in this period, but they were not the only participants in this trade. In Persia, minority groups such as the Parsis and New Julfa Armenians continued to play an active role in Indo-Persian trans-regional trade through their own commercial networks. Additionally, from the middle of the 18th century, British merchants enjoyed trading privileges in Persia and began to take an increasingly active role in the mediation of Indo-Persian trade. The post-Indian independence too had very cordial relations with Iran.

In reaction to the anti-Iran vote cast by New Delhi at the International Atomic Energy Agency (IAEA) governing board meeting in September, 2005 the Iranian Ambassador in Vienna conveyed to Dr. Sheelkant Sharma, India's Permanent Representative in Vienna, a message from Ali Larijani, Iran's top nuclear negotiator, that Teheran was no longer willing to go ahead with the $21-billion deal.[6] Though India reduced oil imports from Iran, it is trying to expand trade in other commodities like tea, pharmaceuticals, automobile, electronics, spare parts and agricultural products.[7]

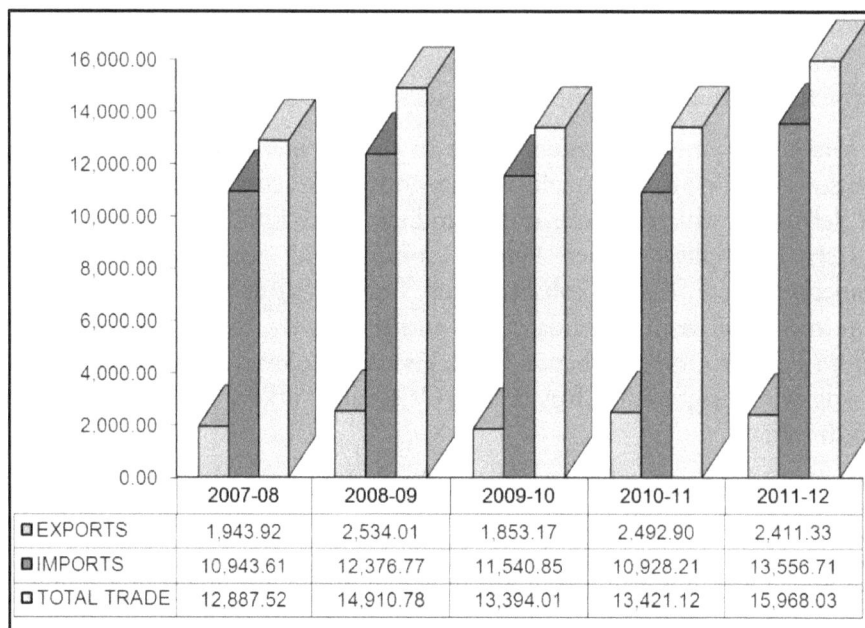

	2007-08	2008-09	2009-10	2010-11	2011-12
☐ EXPORTS	1,943.92	2,534.01	1,853.17	2,492.90	2,411.33
☐ IMPORTS	10,943.61	12,376.77	11,540.85	10,928.21	13,556.71
☐ TOTAL TRADE	12,887.52	14,910.78	13,394.01	13,421.12	15,968.03

Fig. 1: Trade between India and Iran (US$ Mi)

Source: Ministry of Commerce and Industry, Government of India.

The two-way trade between India and Iran has shown good growth in recent years. In fact, it has grown more than 25 percent during the last five years from US$ 12887.52 million in 2007–08 to US$ 15968.03 million in 2011–12. India's export to Iran has grown more than 25% from about US$ 1943.92 million in 2007–08 to US$ 2411.33 million in 2011–12. Iran's exports to India during these years have registered an increase of almost 30% from US$ 10943.61 million in 2007–08 reaching US$ 13556.71 million in 2011–12. The trade balance continues to be in Iran's favor, although India's imports are also increasing as well.

India and Iran are making robust efforts to renew and brace the bilateral economic and trade relations. The relationship between the two countries has evolved into a significant partnership in the economic and commercial sphere. At the same time, Indians have emerged as important investors in the Iran, and India as an important export destination for the Iran manufactured goods. In an important development India, Iran and Russia have signed an important agreement in 2000 on a "North-South Corridor" for transit of goods from India through Iran to Russia and the region andhas come into force since 16 May 2002.[8] The Chah Bahar is the continuation of that concord.

The Indian cooperation in the development of Chah Bahar port complex, the construction and development of Chah Bahar-Fahraj-Bam railway link, the Chah Bahar-Delaram route and the Marine Oil Tanking terminal at an agreed location, as also the Iranian interests to invest and participate in infrastructure projects in India are likely to further boost non-oil trade and investment in infrastructure projects between India and Iran.

Fig. 2

Source: The Hindu, May 5, 2013.

To instill fresh impetus in the ties, particularly in strategic areas, the 17th Session of the India-Iran Joint Commission was held in Tehran on May 4, 2013. The session was co-chaired by H.E. Dr. Ali Akbar Salehi, Foreign Minister of Islamic Republic of Iran and by H.E. Mr. Salman Khurshid, External Affairs Minister of India. The two sides discussed bilateral and regional issues of mutual interest. They discussed Indian participation in Chah Bahar Port project which will provide connectivity with Afghanistan and will give an impetus to Afghanistan's economic development. The two sides also reiterated the importance of greater connectivity between Russia, Central and South Asia through the International North South Transport Corridor (INSTC). The two sides discussed some core ideas and among them some are:

1. Regional connectivity
2. Enhancing bilateral trade and economic cooperation

3. Cooperation on regional security issues
4. Enhancing cultural and people-to-people contact.[9]

The two sides reiterated importance of enhancing cooperation in expanding trade and banking relations. The two sides agreed to study the prospects of joint investment in both countries. The two sides, while noting their capabilities in the industrial sector, agreed to diversify their cooperation in this regard. Mr. Salman Khurshid inaugurated the Indian Cultural Centre in Tehran on May 3, 2013.

At the bilateral level the growing strategic convergence between the two countries, has to be underpinned with a stronger economic relationship including greater trade and investment flows and exhort the entrepreneurs in both the countries to harness each other strengths for mutual benefit and promote the process of economic rapprochement actively, including through expert studies on trade and investment facilitation, holding of exhibitions and seminars, promotion of business travel, and joint ventures to boost the business confidence of the entrepreneurs.

Mr. Ajai Sahai, Director General of the Federation of the Indian Exports Organization said that "India has taken many initiatives to expand its sales to the Islamic Republic of Iran". Sahai's remarks came a week after US Secretary of State John Kerry announced a 180-day exemption from Washington's sanctions on Iran for nine countries, including India. Mr. Sahai noted that India is willing to increase the volume of its exports to Iran to about 6 US$ billion in the current year.[10]

The Consul General of Iran, Mr. Hassan Noorian, speaking at a meeting said "Iran is looking for more business with India in non-oil sectors to boost the bilateral trade and there is great potential for cooperation in various non-oil fields like pharma, IT, electronics, automobile spare parts and food processing". He pointed out that both the countries had agreed to focus on trade in non-oil sectors and planned to increase the bilateral trade to US$ 25 billion in four years.[11]

The bilateral trade relations between India and Iran has witnessed a robust trend, with total trade between the two having stood at US$ 10.5 billion in 2010. At the same time, bilateral trade balance has been in Iran's favor. Machinery and instruments is the largest item in Iran's import, amounting to US$ 11.6 billion in 2010, India's share in Iran's imports was marginal at 1.2%, which highlights the potential to further enhance these exports to Iran.

According to the Associated Chambers of Commerce and Industry in Delhi the Islamic Republic offered massive potential for export of Indian products and commodities annually worth over $10 billion. Association Secretary-General D.S. Rawat said that "The potential of trade and economic relations between India and Iran can touch $30 billion by 2015 from the current level of $13.7 billion".[12]

Iron and steel, electrical and electronic equipments, medical apparatus, pharmaceutical products, and oilseed are other areas where India can enhance its imports to Iran as a good partner. Industry Associations and Chambers of Commerce and Industries should focus on the potential items and sectors identified to further trade between the two countries. Various trade promoting activities such as organizing Business—Government and Business—Business delegation visits relating to identified potential sectors has to encourage. Organizing fairs and exhibitions in Iran to showcase competencies of Indian corporate and to capture market opportunities and tie ups with select industry in Iran in potential sectors would serve to boost India's trade linkages with Iran.

CULTURAL COMMONALITIES

There seems little doubt that the Indus Valley civilization had contacts with the contemporaneous civilizations of Persia and Mesopotamia. There is a striking similarity between some of the designs and seals. It is believed that Indians and Persians belonged to one single family before the beginning of the Indo-Aryan civilization and lived together with a common language for many centuries in pasturelands of Oxus valley in Central Asia. In the second millennium B.C. there was close agreement between the language and mythology, religious traditions and social institutions of Indians and Iranians on the one hand and those of the Greeks, Romans, Celts, Germans and Slavs on the other. For a considerable period after their separation from their western kinsmen, the Indians and Iranians are believed to have lived together.[13]

Achaemenian art and architecture had a significant influence on India. Before the Ashokan period of history, there is no evidence of epigraphy in India. It has been suggested that the idea of issuing decrees by Ashoka was borrowed from the Achaemenian emperors, especially from Darius. The pillars, with their animal capitals, are influenced by Achaemenian pillars. The use of this means of propagating official messages and the individual style of the inscriptions both suggest Persian and Hellenistic influence and India under the Mauryas was certainly more continually in touch with the civilizations to the west than ever before. At Kandahar, Ashoka left instructions in both Greek and Aramaic.[14]

Vedic and Persian religions mingled in Gandhara, where stood the Indian city called Taxila by the Greek. By the age of Darius, the most refined of its cult had evolved into what was later known as Zoroastrianism—a dualist religion accounting for the problem of evil in terms of struggle of a good with an evil god. To this day, there are close similarities in the Persian festival of Nowruz also celebrated by Parsis in India and Holi as both are centered towards fire.[15]

The Parsis are so called because they hail from Pars in south-west Iran. The holy text of the Zoroastrians is the Avesta, composed in a language belonging to the early Iranian group of languages and resembling the language of the Vedas. Zoroastrianism flourished during the Acharminian dynasty of Cyrus, Darius, Xerexes and others.

The Indian province of Darius was the richest in his empire and the most populous. Herodotus tells us of the wealth and density of the Indian population and of the tribute paid to Darius: 'The population of the Indians is by far the greatest of all the people that we know; and they paid tribute proportionately larger than all the rest. Herodotus also mentions the Indian contingent in the Persian armies consisting of infantry, cavalry, and chariots. Later, elephants are mentioned.[16]

India is mentioned in the Avesta and there is some description of north India in it. In the Rig Veda there are references to Persia—the Persians who were called Parshavas and later Parasikas, from which the modern word Parsi is derived. The Parthians were referred to as Parthavas.[17] The name of India has come from Iran through a long relay—Iranic to Greek to Latin to English and finally to India with its dominance of English. India is a Greek word written 'India in the Greek alphabet and pronounced Hindia. It comes from Hindos 'the river Indus' from the old Persian Hindu, the Persian pronunciation of the Sanskrit Sindhu. In Avesta and old Persian an initial 's' was pronounced 'h'.[18]

The ancient Persian also used the name 'Arya' and the word survive in the word 'Iran'. Iranians are one of three peoples of the world who have called their countries 'Land of Nobility' or 'The Noble Land'. 'Iran' is the Avesta word – 'airya'—'noble' with the toponymic suffix—an, denoting a geographical area. The name of Ireland is Eire in Irish language and *'aire'* means 'noble' in Irish.[19]

Gatha, the hymns of Prophet Zoroaster, included in a part of the Avesta, the holy book of the Zoroastrians, suggests a close link with the ancient

Indian hymns, the Rig Veda of circa 1700 B.C. This is the period prior to the migration of Nomadic tribes into Iran and India.[20] The hymn of Gayatri resembles the Gatha of the ancient Iranians. The vedic ritual of Agni and the Avestic ritual of Atar were similar. The Hindu Gods and Goddesses like Indra and Bhadrika resemble Ahura Mazda and Mithra.[21] All followers of Zoroastrianism have to wear the Sadra and Kusti, a narrow band round the waist, similar to the upavita of the brahmanas. The band is wound thrice round the waist symbolizing the three cardinal tenets of the faith: good thoughts, deeds and words.

After Islam took over Persia, Zoroastrianism all but disappeared from Persia. The followers of the religion fled Persia and took refuge in Western India enriching the cultural and social life of India. They are today known as Parsis. The Parsis began arriving in India from circa 636 A.D. Their first permanent settlements were at Sanjan, 100 miles north of Bombay. They are believed to have built a big fire temple at Sanjan in circa 790 A.D. with the fire which they had brought from Iran with them.

Even today, Parsis maintain a cultural relationship with Iran, travelling to the cities of Tehran, Yazd (a centre of Zoroastrian culture) and Kerman (Zoroastrian Fire Temple) in Iran for pilgrimage. There have been several prominent Indians—political leaders, industrialists, Government officials— from this community. These include Dadbhai Nowroji, Field Marshall Manekshaw, the great scientist Dr. Homi Bhabha, the former Chairman of Atomic Energy Commission of India, Homi Nusserwanji Sethna, Pherozeshah Mehta, pioneer of Indian freedom movement, and the leading business groups of Tata, Godrej, Birla and Wadia among others. Despite being a small community, they have contributed enormously to India.

During the reign of Sassanian king Noshirvan (531–576 AD), scientists and other scholars were exchanged between Persia and India. During this period, the game of chess (Chatur-ang) is believed to have been introduced in Persia from India. Later, when Persia was conquered by the Arabs, the game quickly spread all over the Middle East and then to Europe. The original game was played on 64 squares (Asta-pada) with a king piece and pieces of four other types, corresponding to the corps of the ancient Indian army—an elephant, a horse, a chariot or ship and four footmen.[22]

During Khosrau I's reign in the 6th Century, many books were brought from India and translated into Pahlavi, the language of the Sassanian Empire. Some of these later found their way into the literature of the Islamic world. A notable example of this was the translation of the Indian *'Panchatantra'* by one of Khosrau's ministers, Burzoe; this translation, known as the *'Kelileh va Demneh'*, later made its way into Arabia and Europe. The details of Burzoe's legendary journey to India and his daring acquirement of Panchatantra is written in full in Ferdowsi's *'Shahnameh'*. [23]

The century following the Arab conquest of Sind was one in which the Hindu culture influenced the Arab culture. The scientific study of astronomy in Islam was commenced under the influence of an Indian work *'Siddhanta'*, which was brought to Baghdad. In circa 800 A.D. Aryabhatta's treatise *'Aryabhatiyam'* was translated into Arabic under the title *'Zij-al-Arjabhar'*. Brahmagupta's two works, the *'Brahmasphuta-Siddhanta'* and the *'Khandakhadyaka'*, were taken to Baghdad and translated into Arabic. The knowledge of Hindu numerals and the decimal place-value system reached the Arabs along with the Indian mathematical-astronomical works rendered into Arabic in the 8th and 9th century AD.

The language of the records of the early period of the Delhi Sultanate is Arabic. Majority of epigraphical records is in Persian in view of the fact that Persian had been the state or official language right from the beginning of the Muslim rule up to 1857 AD, spanning six centuries and a half. Persian played an important role in the educational and cultural life of the various regions of the sub-continent in varying degrees depending upon local factors. [24]

According 11th century poet Ferdowsi in *'Shahnameh*, the 5th century AD Sassanian king Behram Gur requested Indian king Shangol to select 12,000 gypsies—expert Indian musicians—and introduced them into Persia from India. These gypsies are believed to be the ancestors of the Persian gypsies. They propagated Indian music and dancing in Persia and travelled to all parts of the world from there. [25]

The earliest evidence of Persian influence on Indian astronomy is of the second half of the fourteenth century. Mahendra Suri, a court astronomer of Firuz Shah Tughlaq, composed a treatise entitled *'Yantraraja'*. But it was Sawai Jaya Singh II who showed the greatest interest in Arabic/Persian astronomy. The Iranians had strident arguments regarding the relative virtues of their Arab and non-Arab cultural traditions. These arguments culminated in the Sh'ubia movement. They owned the non-Arab traditions and put their knowledge to translate Sanskrit works on mathematics, astronomy, medicine and other sciences into Arabic. They used their learning of Sanskrit grammar to systematize Arabic grammar.

The Mughal emperor Humayun played a pivotal role in re-establishing Mughal authority over North India, however tentatively, as well as facilitating what was one of the most significant migrations in early modern history, that of litterateurs, soldiers, Sufis, poets, painters, horsemen and other talented individuals from Iran and Central Asia into India, giving rise to the particular Indo-Persian synthesis of culture that gave Mughal India its identity and continues to inspire us today.

The late Sukumar Ray provides us with a letter written by Shah Tahmasp in his own hand to Humayun, whom he refers to as "the asylum of brother-hood," while the latter was in Kandahar: "I hope that my brother will not forget me and always there will be exchange of envoys between us so that we may be aware of the affairs of each other and without formality may also write about the mutual desires of our heart. Nothing more to add. Let your kingdom be perpetual."[26]

Indian universities are a popular destination for Iranian students for higher studies. Several high ranking Iranian officials and professionals have studied in India. There are a large number of Iranian students studying in universities at Hyderabad, Mumbai, Pune, Bangalore and Delhi. There is a large Iranian community settled in India, including students who stayed back after completing their studies. On the occasion of Iran's National Teacher's Day, Dr. Ali Azam Khosravi, Research Counsellor at the Embassy of Iran in New Delhi, hoped that Indian teachers continued academic relationship with the Iranian students, even after the completion of their Ph.D. degree, will further strengthen academic ties between the two friendly nations, Iran and India.[27]

India should meet the demands of the Iran in education as it has good institutions and especially some areas like studies on Gandhism, which is needed for the present society and the IITs are best in providing a top class technical education. The India-Iran Friendship Association was established by the embassy of India to promote India-Iran relations by holding cultural activities and events. Dr. Abdul Sami currently heads India-Iran Friendship Association. The India-Iran Friendship Association is giving free Hindi classes for Iranian nationals at the Indian embassy in Tehran. The classes are organized in partnership with the embassy of India in Tehran and the Indian Council for Cultural Relations.[28]

The former President of Islamic Republic of Iran, Mr. Khatami has rightly said "Had the present world not seen Gandhi, it would not have believed that politics could possibly blend with ethics and morality, resistance and struggle with love... He taught us that real victory was not victory over the opponent but victory along with the opponent. Gandhi does not belong only to India. He is the Gandhi of world of mysticism of both the Iranians and the Moslems. The real meaning of what I have called the Dialogue between Civilizations can easily be seen in the life and thoughts of Gandhi. Today, the world is more than ever in need of the voice of Gandhi". [29]

India and Iran have exchanged cultural delegations regularly and there exists a Cultural Exchange Program between the two countries. Bharat Ratna Bismillah Khan gave concerts in Tehran in 1992. A hall at the prestigious Bahman Cultural Centre in Tehran is named after Ustad Bismillah Khan. Iran has three Cultural Centres in India-New Delhi, Mumbai and Hyderabad.

The emphasis should be to promote more exchanges between leading cultural institutes, libraries, media persons and films, sports organizations and participation of teams from the two sides in each other sports tournaments. Translations in each other languages of literary works from the two countries should also be included. Legendary Persian poets Hafez, Sa'di, Ferdowsi, Rumi and Omar Khayyam continue to be widely read in India. Works by Mahatma Gandhi, Nehru, Tagore, Indira Gandhi, V.S. Naipaul, R.K. Narayanan and other Indian writers have been translated into Persian.

The Vice President of Islamic Republic of Iran Mr. Esfandiar Rahim Mashaei called on India's Tourism and Culture Minister Smt. Ambika Soni to increase cooperation in tourism and cultural sectors between India and Iran. Smt. Soni said the element of spiritualism in the lives of the people of the two countries make them different from others and bring them closer to each other because of this commonality and both the countries can offer affordable tour packages to the citizens of India and Iran to increase tourist traffic. [30]

To streamline the relationship between the people of India and Iran, Mr.Hassan Nourian, Consul-General of the Islamic Republic of Iran in Hyderabad said that the Government of Islamic Republic of Iran has eased visa rules for Indian tourists, businessmen and pilgrims. [31] He also said that the twice-a-week flight, to be operated by his country's Aseman Airlines, would make it easy for tourists wanting to visit the second biggest Iranian city. [32]

Indian cinema has a large audience in Iran. Early Iranian cinema had close links with India. The Iranian films have garnered international fame in the past three decades, and the Hyderabad Film Club opened three-day festival of Iranian films in Hyderabad on 17th August, 2013, organized in collaboration with Iranian Cultural House, New Delhi. [33] Exchanges should also include joint participation of children and teenagers in activities like yoga, paintings, and other creative works. The Cultural Exchange Program is expected to further strengthen friendship and cultural bonds between the two countries.

CONCLUSION

India has welcomed the far-sighted initiative of the former President, Islamic Republic of Iran, Khatami in calling the year 2001 as the year of *"Dialogue Among Civilizations"*.[34] This should be the motto of the world's two oldest civilizations in maintaining and intensifying relations. Mysticism, philosophy, mathematics and medical science are some of the areas where India and Iran have been working and can work further to fortify bilateral ties.

The desire to toughen the ties on the basis of the values that the two people of the two great nations shared and to build upon the common fount of knowledge and wisdom which will help India and Iran in overcoming whatever differences that will come their way in future in a peaceful way. The mutuality of economic and commercial interests have cemented this rediscovered amity, and cooperation in other fields like cultural exchanges, science and technology has diversified and added vigor and color to bilateral relations.

Earlier the President of the Tehran Chamber of Commerce, Industry and Mines Yahya Al Es'hagh has rightly said that "The fact is that the economies of India and Iran should work together. Others like or do not like, we should work together and everybody should think for their interests".[35]

By pledging to grow deeper interactions in the fields of cultural exchanges, and areas like communication, railways and IT sector, as also by initiating mutual interaction on areas like vocational training for labor, urban water management and hydrological studies, biotechnology, pharmaceuticals and food technology, India and Iran should reinforce bilateral relations between them.

REFERENCES

[1] http://en.trend.az/regions/iran/2123252.html.

[2] The Wonder that was India' by A L Basham, 1967, p. 19.

[3] Ibid, p. 196.

[4] 'Eastern Religions and Western Thoughts' by S. Radhakrishnan, Oxford University Press, p. 121.

[5] http://www.sucrose.com/lhist.html

[6] http://hindu.com/2005/09/28/stories/2005092813940100.htm

[7]   http://www.idsa.in/issuebrief/India-IranRelations_msroy_200513

[8]   http://www.brookings.edu/research/articles/2002/07/03russia-spector

[9]   http://www.mea.gov.in/pressreleases.htm?dtl/21652/Joint+Press+Statement+on+17
       th+IndiaIran+Joint+Commission+Meeting

[10] http://www.islamicinvitationturkey.com/2013/06/16/india-keen-to-broaden-trade-
       ties-with-iran

[11] http://zeenews.india.com/business/news/%20international/iran-for-more-trade-with-
       india-in-non-oil-sectors_75977.html

[12] http://www.telegraph.co.uk/news/worldnews/middleeast/iran/9115192/India-begins-
       use-of-Chabahar-port-in-Iran-despite-international-pressure.html

[13] 'Eastern Religions and Western Thoughts' by S Radhakrishnan, Oxford University
       Press, 1992, p. 118–119.

[14] 'The Penguin History of the World' by J.M. Roberts, 1987, p. 399.

[15] Ibid., p. 169.

[16] The Discovery of India' by Jawaharlal Nehru, Oxford University Press 1992, p. 147.

[17] Ibid., p. 147.

[18] 'The Wonder that was India' by A.L. Basham, 1967, p. 1.

[19] 'India and Iran: A Dialogue' paper by Prof. Lokesh Chandra.

[20] 'Persian Myths' by Vesta Sarkhosh Curtis, British Museum Press 1996, p. 8.

[21] 'Iran and India: Age old Friendship' by Abdul Amir Jorfi, India Quarterly, Oct.–Dec.
       1994, p. 68.

[22] 'The Wonder that was India' by A.L. Basham, 1967, p. 210.

[23] David, Nicolle, Sassanian Armies: the Iranian Empire early 3rd to mid-7th centuries
       A.D., Montvert, 1996, p. 11.

[24] http://asi.nic.in/asi_epigraphical_arabicpersian.asp

[25] 'Iran and India: Age old Friendship' by Abdul Amir Jorfi, India Quarterly, Oct.–Dec.
       1994, p. 71.

[26] http://english.irib.ir/subcontinent/culture/history/item/87385-
       humayun%E2%80%99s-role-in-cementing-india-iran-relations

[27] http://www3.chb.irna.ir/en/News/80640551/Politic/Iran,_India_academic_relations
       _grow_every_day__Iran

[28] http://www.heraldboy.com/india-iran-friendship-association-plana-free-hindi-classes-
       in-tehran/1278

[29] From the translation of the speech of the Iranian President Khatami on January 27,
       2003, circulated by IRNA.

[30] http://www.namnewsnetwork.org/v3/read.php?id=NDcxNzg=

[31] http://www.thehindubusinessline.com/news/iran-urges-india-to-allow-visaonarrival-
       facility/article4393439.ece

[32] http://articles.timesofindia.indiatimes.com/2013-05-11/india/39185823_1_hassan-
       nourian-direct-flight-south-india

[33] http://www3.kermanshah.irna.ir/en/News/80776469/Art_&_Culture/Iranian_Film_
       Festival_kicks_off_in_India

[34] http://www.unesco.org/dialogue/en/khatami.htm

[35] http://www.tehrantimes.com/economy-and-business/97713-india-studying-preferen
       tial-trade-pact-with-iran.

Sociological Investigation of Cultural Historical Relations of Iran and India

Azar Eskandari Charati

INTRODUCTION

In order to have a discussion regarding cultural relations, there is a need to have a brief mention on knowledge of sociological investigation, which is sociology and culture in this writing. One of the approaches of sociologists in defining culture is descriptive definition. In this approach, "culture or civilization is a woven generality including knowledge, religion, art, law, ethics, custom and any ability and habit the human gains from the society". However, in the historical approach, "culture means a correlative set of actions and believes which are inherited by society that composes the texture of our life (Ashoori, p. 380).

In this definition, two components are more observed; one is actions and the other is believes, thus sociology of audience makes the social-political reality for managing the cultural-artistic world perceptible and gives the elements for understanding the education and artistic taste of the active person. Relations, interactions and cultural common points of Iran and India go back to over 3000 years ago and the Aryans immigration. The proof of that is the common legendaries of the ancient time. The relations of Iran and Indian subcontinent before Islam have been based on common race, language and custom. Iran and Indian subcontinent with the Dari Persian language created the same relation they had with Pahlavi, Avestan and Sanskrit languages before Islam and by prevalence of different languages that today 22 languages officially has been recognized in different states of this country and 1400 official accent has turned this society to a large democracy and have provided a bed for propagation of different religions. For people of Iran and the history and literature of Iran no land is more famous and known than India. No historical-literature and geographic book is found in Persian that has not talked about India, in a way that the most important and ancient legendary book of Iranians, Shahnameh has mentioned the name of India, Sindh and Macran for over a hundred times. Perhaps, one of the best descriptions from the cultural closeness of two nations and their common interest in each other is provided by "Subramania Swamy", the post minister of India and the head of Janata movement. After visiting Iran, several years ago he writes:

"India and Iran have centuries of cultural and civilization relation and have many cultural common points. In the past, Iran has influenced India via Persian language, art and architecture. However, the critical aspect I encountered during my visit of Iran is related to the great interest of Iranians in India, ordinary people usually feel good of India and this goes back to clean cultural and civilization connections of the two countries and has nothing to do with the overseas policy of Iran" (Soami, 1831, p. 15).

Commencement of political relations began in 1947, wherein a Iranian delegation participated in the Asian Conference held in New Delhi and announced its interest to the newly independent country of India. And signed in 1950, the treaty of friendship between Iran and India. While emphasizing on the principle of peace and friendship, this treaty has predicted peaceful methods for removing disturbances between the two countries. Also, the two countries agreed to establish several consulates in each other's countries and to have respective contracts in the fields of commerce, custody, shipping, airways, culture, etc.

THE PRECEDENT OF CULTURAL RELATIONS OF IRAN AND INDIA

The antiquity of cultural, language and immigration relations of Iranians and Indians is so famous that there is no need for explanations, for about 2500 to 3000 years ago, a large wave of immigrants started from north-east Iran to Sand which is called 'Aryans' immigration. There have always been exchanges and immigrations between Iran and India since then and in the Achaemenid scripts India is mentioned and the territory of Great Darius has been continued beyond Sand civilization. Since Sasanid, a cuneiform (ancient system of writing) inscription is there in Saint Thomas church, that Dr. Aliasghar Hekmat has shown its picture on page 11 of the book on Persian Symbols on Indian Stones (Hekmat, 1959, p. 91).

The famous sentence of Jawaharlal Nehru "the relations between two countries of Iran and India is an old story of the history of the universe, it seems even older than that. Now we should rewrite this old story by the pen of enthusiast, stability and pencil of coalition on the page of universe and renew this old wine...

(Persian poem by Hafiz) بیا تا گل بر افشانیم و می در ساغر اندازیم فلک را سخت بشکافیم
وطرح نو در اندازیم.

A REVIEW OF THE HISTORY OF RELATIONS OF IRAN AND INDIA

In the explorations conducted in 1930 at Kashan Silk Hill by archeologists, it is discovered that Kashan old town has been the intersection of ancient civilization of Iran and India. Few archeologists think that the old relation between Iran and India in fact goes back to the time before Medians and Sumerians (before invasion of Aryans). From the ancient time in the past, Iran and India have had integrated historical and cultural relations with each other and in the speeches of Jawaharlal Nehru the Late Minister of India and Alameh Shebeli Namani it is said that: "in the history of the whole world, two nations of Iran and India have been so close to each other that no more example can be found like them".

These old relations existed before the entrance of Aryans to the Iranian plateau. By investigation of archeologists and the stuff gained from excavations in the Indian lands and the stuff remained near Tigris and Euphrates rivers are indicative of the fact that stable relations have existed between Indians and Iranians in the far past. A group of archeologists believe that the stuff gained is indicative of a unique family from the two civilizations of Iran and India.

However, even after Aryans entered into the lands of Indian subcontinent, due to relations of Aryans with each other, they had good interactions. As a result of the same race and origin of these two civilizations, is there compatibility and similarity of Avestan Language in Iran and Veda Language in India. From these evidences, we can conclude that from a very long time, the Iranians and Indians were living with each other. And by emerge of Sasanid dynasty good relations existed between Iranian Royals and Indian Maharajahs that the historians call it as "The Golden Age of Iran". The Indian lands were known by the kings from Punjab and Kashmir, in North India, was ruled by them.

THE AGES OF CULTURAL PROSPERITY AND CULTURAL EXCHANGES

If we consider culture as a complicated issue which includes studies, beliefs, arts, techniques, ethics, rules, custom, habits, behaviors and regulations that a person learns as a society member and has duties and responsibilities against that for the society (Salimi, 1998, p 11), then Iran and India with the ancient background from the ancient times until Goorkanian and Safavian, have had cultural exchanges in different ways.

The common roots and mutual contacts for cultural exchanges have been established between the two nations. With the creation of the powerful emperor of Goorkanian, the relations of Iran and India entered a new step. The rulers of the two countries were very close to each other and were cooperating and this relation penetrated deep into the life of people. In fact, the ages of Goorkanian kingdom in the Indian land is the age of cultural transformation, revitalization of literature and philosophy of old India and the age of prosperity and development of Persian language, literature and culture. The most important faces for cultural penetration can be observed in development of Persian language and literature in India and the Hindu-Iranian art such as painting and architecture.

Persian Language and Literature

Persian language and literature is the most important symbol for effectiveness of the two cultures. Before empowerment of Goorkanian, the Persian language was prevalent due to relationshipbetween the two nations and many Persian terms were extracted in Indian language. Indian languages such as Urdu-Hindi, Bengali, Sindi, Kashmiri, Pashto-Hindi, Daccan, Gujarati, Marathi, Bihari, Tamil, Kannada and Malayalm have taken advantages of Persian language (Yektaee, 1974, p 164). Some of the well known names in Indian-Iranian Persian languages and literature are; Mirzameno, Hartoseni, Krishnavasi and Chandarbahan Berahman (Hekmat, 1958, p 91). Another important factor in immigration of Iranian scientists and poets to India was due to the presence of great Iranian ministers in Goorkani emperor, were "Nawab Biramkhan son of Seifkhan and father of Abdolrahim Khan Khanan, Mirza Hassanollah son of Khajeh Abolhassan, Nawab Zafarkhan Ahsan and Haj Mohammad Ghodsi" (Shahbi, 1937, p. 80).

The Goorkani kings of India were interested in Persian poetry and literature and were promoting it. When Babarshah attacked Delhi from Kabul and conquered North India, Persian poets such as Atashi Ghandehari came to India with him (Ibid, Hekmat, p. 11). Also Khandmir, the great Iranian Historian joined the Babar's kingdom (Ghiaseddin Homam Khandmir, 1983, p. 9). Therefore, not only Persian language was considered by the Indian Muslims, but the Hindus learnt it too and soon communicated with it.

Dr. Tarachand, "the Premier Consul of India in Iran" has considered two elements regarding relations of Iran and India civilizations; one is Islamic mysticism of Iranian people and the other is the Persian language and he says:

"Cultural relation between two civilizations of Iran and India empowered by emergence of Islam and penetration of this religion in Indian subcontinent (Tarachand, 1958) and for Islam found India via Iran lands most Islamic trainers, teachers and missionaries were Iranians. Shoulder by shoulder of Islam, Persian language expanded in Indian land and even Persian language was considered as the official language of Muslims. Mystic poets were the critical factor in development of Persian language and literature. From one side the Sufi Sheikhs were effective in thinking of Indian people and on the other hand they fascinated by the custom and thought of Indian people and as a result their thoughts was mixed as milk and sugar. At the end, we can say that among relations of the two nations of Iran and India there are many reasons, but what the Persian language and literature and especially the Persian poem and Persian poets did is observed in the eye of one by one of culture friends and from Ferdosi to Saadi the members of the two civilizations of Iran and India and the world are honored for that. As a result of cultural relation between Hindus and Persian language, a deep transformation has occurred in Indian culture specifically in the field of poetry, terminology, biography, journalism, study of India and translation of texts" (Roohollah Amini, 1986, p. 11).

Painting

During the time of Goorkani kingdom in India the influence of Iranian painting art was more obvious and the footprint of Iranian immigrants is clearly apparent. Wall drawing and miniature painting which was flourishing in Safavi era in Iran was brought to India by the students of Kamaleddin Behzad. When Humayun was in Iran, he learnt miniature painting and while returning to his country, he took a number of students of Behzad including Abdolsamad Shirazi and Mirseyed Ali Tarizi with himself (Farhang Ershad, 1986, p. 275).

Mughal painting in India was transmitted from Iran and was refined by the methods of Teymoorian which was primarily of Safavian school. This painting had no relation to the past and neither with the Indian painting methods which was forgotten long ago and later was assumed as a sample based on Iranian paintings. The colors used were from Iran and its perspective was thoroughly Iranian (Farhang Ershad, Ibid, p. 276).

The influence of Iranian painting school was not a transient and sectional issue, because several Indian artists were trained by Iranian painters and were working in the Teymoorian kingdom, among them were Beshnovas, Dolat and Dasvanet. In the book of Akbari Bylaw, name of a number of Indian painters is recorded who have been students of Abdolsamad and Mirseyed Ali (Farhang Ershad, Ibid, p. 257).

Architecture

The art of architecture in India was evolved by taking advantage of Islamic Iranian Architecture. The influence of Iranian architects on creation of this art is observed as well. Humayun Shah accepted Iranian architecture, and his tomb was made by an Iranian architect called Mirza Mirak Ghias and Iranian symbols were used in it. Iranian architecture reached its peak at the time of successors of Humayun. The most ancient of Hindu-Iranian architecture is the tomb of Etemadudllah in Agra, Royal Mosque of Lahore, (at the time of Jahangir), Tajmahal in Agra (the tomb of Mumtaz Mahal the spouse of Shah Jahan) thus they took them from local architects based on their taste and by mixing of both the styles, the Hindu-Iranian style was created. The architectural immigrants returning to Iran from India and the Indian artists who probably immigrated to Iran left some footprints in the Iranian architectural culture. For instance, Sabat (the roofs seen on some Iranian alleys) by the local name of Sovat, is a sample of architecture belonging to India applied in Iran. The crescent forms and arch buildings, simple walls and narrow smooth columns with vast piles and astonishing arches are signs of Iranian architectural style. In many buildings a mixture of Iranian-Hindu architecture is observed.

CONCLUSION

With this sociological investigation, we observed that the two civilizations of Iran and India, with a rich and ancient cultural history have friendly and good relations with each other. Since ancient past, they have had stable relationship with each other and with the people of these two civilizations (Iran and India) they have ancient precedence in race and culture and they have the same origins (Aryan tribes). In fact, the common points of two civilizations can be realized through language, custom and other behavioral and ethical specifications of the people of those lands and on the other hand, the effects remained from Iranian culture on the culture of Indians in the recent millennium is undeniable. Accordingly great men such as The Great Minister of India, Jawaharlal Nehru, in the book "Discovery of India" writes: "among many nations and races who had relations with India none of them had continuous and lasting influence in life and culture of India like Iranians, Iranians were effective in cultural and political relations between the two governments, in return Indian merchants played critical role in economical relations, however following emergence of social and political evolutions in India and emergence of critical changes in common geographic boundaries between the two countries of Iran and India and after Goorkanian dynasty and at the time of colonization, the Persian language which had become the common language between Iran and India was forgot and the common culture which was the result of thousand years of cultural exchanges was neglected and the relations of two nations were reduced. However today by efforts of cultural representatives Iranian Cultural Relations Organization of settled in New Delhi and Mumbai of India we are observing prosperity of the old relations of these two civilize countries with the common history that is reflecting day by day in the fields of culture, policy, etc and now at the beginning of third millennium, cultural studies in the global extension between the two countries have found dual importance and we will observe expansion in relations of the two historical civilizations. Also, by considering development of communication and emergence of Information revolution that among its resultant is explosion of information, the culture has found a daily increasing and comprehensive role. At the end, we hope to observe progress and development of relations between two lands of Iran and India in different fields especially cultural fields."

SOURCES

[1] Ahmad, A. (1987). *The history of Islamic thought in India* (N. Lotfi and M.J. Yahaghi, trans). (1st ed.). Tehran: Keyhan Publishing, 191–192.

[2] Ahmad, A. (1976). *Safawid Poets and India*. Tehran: Iran 14. 32–117.

[3] Ashoorian, D. (2001). *Definition and concept of culture* (3rd ed). Tehran: Agah publishing, 47.

[4] Bin Hammam khand Mir, Gh. (1983). *Habibolseir history.* Tehran: Khayyam Book. Introduction, 9.

[5] Eaton, R.M. (1993). The Rise of Islam and the Bengal Frontier.Berkeley. 1204–176 Guidance cultural (1986). *Historical migration to India* (1st ed.). Tehran: Institute of Cultural Studies, 275–276 Guidance cultural (1986). *Historical migration to India* (1st ed.). Tehran: Institute of Cultural Studies, 276 Guidance cultural (1986).

[6] *Historical migration to India* (1st ed.). Tehran:Institute of Cultural Studies.

[7] Golombek, L. (1981). *From Tamerlane to the Taj Mahal*. Daneshvari, A.(Ed). Essays in Islamic Art and Architecture in Honor of Katharina Otto-Dorn.Malibu. 43–50.

[8] Hekmat, A.A. (1957). *Indian Territory*. Tehra: Tehran University Press, 11.

[9] Halabi, A.A. (1991). *Understanding Sufism and Iranian mysticism* (3rd ed). Tehran: Zavar Press.

[10] Hekmat, A.A. (1957). *Indian Territory*. Tehra: Tehran University Press, 91.

[11] Rohol Amin, M. (1986). *Field of culture* (1st ed.). Tehran: Attar, 18.

[12] Shariati, A. (1992). *Islamic Iranian identity recognition* (3rd ed). Collection, No. 27, 142.

[13] Shahabi, A.A. (1937). *Iran- India relations literature*. Tehran: Printing and Central Bookstore.

[14] Salimi, M. (1998). *Cultural relations between Iran and India* (1st ed.).

[15] Salimi, M. previous, 108.

[16] Tehran: Institute of Foreign Affairs Press. Introduction, 11.

[17] Subtelny, M.E. (2002). Le Monde est un jardin: Aspects de l'histoire culturelle de l'Iran medieval. Paris: Studia Iranica, Cahier 28.

[18] Stewart, D.J. (1966). *The First* Shaykh al-Islam *of the Safavid Capital Qazvin,* JAOS 116/3. 387–4.

[19] Tsukinowa, T. (1982). *The Influence of Seljuq Architecture on the Earliest Mosques of the Delhi Sultanate Period in India*. Acta Asiatica, 43, 54–60.

[20] Tarachnd (1957). *Customs, spirituality, and God* (M.R. Jalali Naini, trans.). Tehran: Taban publishing.

[21] Tsukinowa, T. (1982). *The Influence of Seljuq Architecture on the Earliest Mosques of the Delhi Sultanate Period in India*. Acta Asiatica. 43, 54–6.

[22] Yektaei, M. (1978). *The influence of Islamic culture and civilization in India and Pakistan*. Tehran: Iqbal, 164.

Acronyms

ACU	:	Asian Clearing Union
AEOI	:	Atomic Energy Organisation of Iran
BIPPA	:	Bilateral Investment Promotion and Protection Agreement
BOP	:	Balance of Payments
CAGR	:	Compound Annual Growth Rate
CARs	:	Central Asian Republics
CENTO	:	Central Treaty Organisation
CIRE	:	Centre for International Research and Education
CIS	:	Commonwealth of Independent States
CISADA	:	Comprehensive Iran Sanctions, Accountability and Divestment Act
CPPRI	:	Central Pulp and Paper Research Institute of India
CSA	:	Comprehensive Safeguards Agreement
CTBT	:	Comprehensive Test Ban Treaty
DTAA	:	Double Taxation Avoidance Agreement
ECT	:	Error Correction Term
EIA	:	Energy Information Administration
EII	:	Export-Intensity Index
EU	:	European Union
FFEP	:	Fordow Fuel Enrichment Plant
FICCI	:	Federation of Indian Chambers of Commerce and Industry
GCC	:	Gulf Cooperation Council
GUASNR	:	Gorgan University of Agricultural Science and Natural Resources
HEU	:	Highly Enriched Uranium
HOA	:	Heads of Agreement
IAEA	:	International Atomic Energy Agency
ICCR	:	Indian Council for Cultural Relations
ICWA	:	Indian Council of World Affairs
IDSA	:	Institute of Defence Studies and Analyses
III	:	Import-Intensity Index
ILSA	:	Iran and Libya Sanctions Act
IMIDRO	:	Iranian Mines and Mining Industries Development and Renovation Organisation
INC	:	Indian National Congress
INSC	:	International North South Corridor

INSTC	:	International North-South Transport Corridor
IOR-ARC	:	Indian Ocean Rim Association for Regional Cooperation
IPIS	:	Institute of Political and International Studies
IR	:	International Relations
IRISL	:	Islamic Republic of Iran Shipping Lines
ISA	:	Iran Sanctions Act
ISIPO	:	Iranian Small Industries and Industrial Parks Organisation
ITDC	:	Indian Tourism and Development Corporation
ITEC	:	Indian Technical Education Cooperation
J and K	:	Jammu and Kashmir
JBC	:	Joint Business Council
JCM	:	Joint Commission Meeting
JWG	:	Joint Working Group
MRPCL	:	Mangalore Refinery and Petrochemicals Ltd.
MRPL	:	Mangalore Refinery and Petrochemicals
NCRI	:	National Council of Resistance of Iran
NDAA	:	National Defence Authorization Act
NIOC	:	National Oil and Gas Company
NPT	:	Nuclear Non-Proliferation Treaty
NPT	:	Nuclear Non-Proliferation Treaty
NSIC	:	National Small Industries Corporation
OPEC	:	Organization of Petroleum Exporting Countries
OVL	:	ONGC Videsh Ltd
PLO	:	Palestine Liberation Organization
PP	:	Philips-Perron
PSLV	:	Polar Satellite Launch Vehicle
PSUs	:	Public Sector Undertakings
RBI	:	Reserve Bank of India
RCA	:	Revealed Comparative Advantage
RCSTT	:	Regional Centre for Science and Transfer of Technology
RID	:	Revealed Import Dependency Index or Trade Dependency Index
SNEP	:	Subterranean Nuclear Explosions Project
TNRC	:	Tehran Nuclear Research Center
TSL	:	Targeted Subsidies Law
UMIOR	:	University Mobility in the Indian Ocean Region
USA	:	United States of America
VECM	:	Vector Error-Correction Model
WANA	:	West Asia North Africa
WDI	:	World Development Indicators
WMD	:	Weapons of Mass Distraction

www.ingramcontent.com/pod-product-compliance
Lightning Source LLC
Chambersburg PA
CBHW080608270326
41928CB00016B/2965